Military Space-A Air Basic Training™
and Reader Trip Reports

by
L. Ann Crawford
Vice-President, Military Marketing Services, Inc.
and Publisher, Military Living Publications
and
William "Roy" Crawford, Sr., Ph.D.
President, Military Marketing Services, Inc.
and Military Living Publications

Vice President - Marketing - R.J. Crawford

Editors - Donna L. Russell and Kathie J. Russell
Assistant Editors - R. Nicole Clark,
Elizabeth M. Ksiazek, and Margaret M. Volpe
Cover Design - Susan P. Druzak

Chief of Staff - Timothy G. Brown, TSgt, USAF (Ret)

Office Staff:
John Camp, Beth Casteel, Nigel Fellers, Maureen Fleegal,
Irene Kearney, Lourdes Medina, Sandy Moore,
Tin Ngo, Karme Raggio, Joel Thomas, MSgt, USA (Ret),
Ricardo Thomas, Larry Williamson.

Military Living Publications
P.O. Box 2347
Falls Church, Virginia 22042-0347
TEL (703) 237-0203 - FAX (703) 237-2233
E-mail: milliving@aol.com
Home Page: http://www.militaryliving.com

Y0-BND-823

NOTICE

The information in this book has been compiled and edited either from the activity/facility listed, its superior headquarters or from other sources that may or may not be noted. All listed facilities, their locations, hours of operation and telephone numbers could change. Flight schedules, including destinations, routings, frequency of flights and aircraft used, are always subject to change. Space-A passenger eligibility could change; however, we have published the most up-to-date information available. The "how to travel Space-A" supporting information in the appendices is subject to change, but the latest changes to these appendices were included at press time. This book should be used as a guide to Space-A travel with all of the above in mind. **Please forward any additions or corrections to the publisher.**

This guide is published by **Military Living Publications,** a private firm in no way connected with the US Federal or other governments. The guide is copyrighted by L. Ann and William Roy Crawford, Sr. Opinions expressed by the publisher and writers herein are not to be considered an official expression by any government agency or official.

The information and statements contained in this book have been compiled from sources believed to be reliable and to represent the best current opinion on the subject. No warranty, guarantee or representation is made by **Military Living Publications** as to the absolute correctness or sufficiency of any representation contained in this or other publications, and we can assume no responsibility.

Copyright 1997
L. Ann and William Roy Crawford Sr.
September 1997

MILITARY LIVING PUBLICATIONS
MILITARY MARKETING SERVICES, INC.

All rights reserved under International and Pan-American copyright conventions. No part of this book may be reproduced in any form without permission in writing from the publisher, except by a reviewer who wishes to quote briefly from listings in connection with a review written for inclusion in a magazine or newspaper, with source credit to **Military Living's Military Space-A Air Basic Training™ and Reader Trip Reports**. A copy of the review when published should be sent to Military Living Publications, P.O. Box 2347, Falls Church, VA 22042-0347.

Library of Congress Cataloging-in-Publication Data

Crawford, Ann Caddell.
   Military Space-A air basic training and reader trip reports / by L. Ann Crawford and William "Roy" Crawford, Sr. ; editor, Donna L. Russell.
       p.   cm.
   Includes index.
   ISBN 0-914862-66-9
   1. United States -- Armed Forces -- Transportation. 2. Air Travel. 3. Military dependents -- Transportation.   I. Crawford, William Roy, 1932- . II. Russell, Donna L. III. Title.
UC333.C72523   1997
355.3'4 -- dc21   97-29517
                                                                                                        CIP

ISBN 0-914862-66-9

CONTENTS

Introduction vii
Background 1
What is Space-A Air Travel? 1
Space-A Air Travel Study and Training 2

SECTION I: AN IMAGINARY OVERSEAS SPACE - A AIR TRIP WITH THE FAMILY

TRIP PLANNING 3
Typical Space-A Air Trip 3
Planning Your Space-A Trip 3
Backup Plans 4
PRE-FLIGHT 6
Registration/Sign-in at Terminal(Station/Aerial Port) 6
Documents 7
Application for Space-A Air Travel 7
Registration for Return Travel 10
Travel Dates 10
Travel Ready 10
Space-A Flight Call/Selection Process 11
FLIGHT PROCESSING 12
Space-A Processing Fee 13
Payment of Fees and Document Review 13
Baggage Processing 13
Dress 14
In-flight Meals 15
Boarding Pass/Ticket/Receipt 15
Bumping 16
Parking 16
Passenger Security Screening 17
Boarding/Gates 17
IN-FLIGHT 18
Seating 18
Clothing 18
Rest Rooms 18
Climate Control 18
Noise 19
Safety 19
Electronic Devices 19
Smoking 19
Refreshments 19
POST FLIGHT 19
Arrival of Aircraft/Clearance 19
Deplaning 20
Immigration 20
Customs 20

CONTENTS, *continued*

Registration for Return Space-A Air Opportunities 21
RETURN FLIGHT TO CONUS 21
Side Trips 21
Circuitous Routing..22
Return Flight 24
Arrival and Clearing 25
POST SPACE-A TRIP REPORT 25
Lessons Learned 26

SECTION II: AN IMAGINARY SPACE-A AIR TRIP BY CONUS MEDICAL EVACUATION (MEDEVAC) FLIGHT

BACKGROUND..27
Medical Evacuation (MEDEVAC) Flights 27
The MEDEVAC System 27
CONUS MEDEVAC Flight Equipment 27
What is Different About Space-A on MEDEVAC Flights? 27
PLANNING YOUR CONUS MEDEVAC FLIGHT 28
Registration and Departure 29
Routing and Remaining Overnight (Lodging)...29
The Scheduled MEDEVAC System 30
Lessons Learned 30

SECTION III: NATIONAL GUARD AND RESERVE PERSONNEL ELIGIBLE FOR SPACE-A TRAVEL

National Guard and Reserve Personnel 31
Active Duty Status Reserve Component Members 31
Retired Reservists (Gray Area)..31
Documentation Required for Guard and Reserve Component.................. 31
Guard and Reserve Travel - Geography and Dependents 32
The Scope of National Guard and Reserve Space-A Travel 32
**AN IMAGINARY SPACE-A AIR TRIP BY NATIONAL
GUARD AND RESERVE PERSONNEL** 32
TRIP PLANNING..32
An Imaginary Space-A Air Trip by Guard and Reserve Personnel 32
Routing..32
Application for Space-A Travel...33
THE OUTBOUND TRIP 34
Overnight 34
Meeting 34

iv

CONTENTS, continued

Vacation..34
RETURN FLIGHT..34
Reflections...35
Lessons Learned..35

SECTION IV: AN IMAGINARY SPACE-A AIR TRIP TO AUSTRALIA AND NEW ZEALAND

Trip Planning...36
Pre-Flight...39
Flight Processing...40
In-Flight...40
Post-Flight...41
Our Visit to Australia...41
Our Visit to New Zealand..42
Return Flight to Conus..43
Lessons Learned..43

SECTION V: AN IMAGINARY SPACE-A AIR TRIP TO SOUTH AMERICA (CHILE AND ARGENTINA)

Trip Planning...44
Pre-Flight...47
In-Flight...47
Post-Flight...48
Our Visit to Chile and Argentina...48
Return Flight to CONUS...50
Lessons Learned..50

SECTION VI: READER TRIP REPORTS

Hops and Dreams..51
Patience and Flexibility Pay Off..53
Chaplain and Wife Enjoy Camaraderie...55
Cybertalk on Space-A..56
Delightful Trip to Germany by Space-A...59
Sharon and Joe Felts Find Free Army Lodging at Frankfurt................60
Places to Stay..61
Lessons Learned From Navy Ensign...62
Space-A to Europe from the West Coast..63
First Space-A Trip...64
They Were Flexible!..65
Combine Low Cost Flights to Europe and Space-A.............................69
A Far East Journey by Space-A...70
Space-A to Israel...71

v

CONTENTS, *continued*

Space-A Tips 72
Europe by Space-A 73
Space-A to Alaska 74
Lemons to Lemonade 75
Some Places to Stay in the USA 77
Bride Loves Space-A 78
Another Space-A First Timer! 81
Space-A to the Orient 82
Space-A to Hawaii 84

APPENDICES

Appendix A: Space-A Passenger Regulations 85
Appendix B: Procedures for Remote Space-A Travel Sign-up
and One-Time Sign-up 108
Appendix C: Space-A Air Travel Remote Sign-up 111
Appendix D: Space Available Travel Request (AMC Form 140) 113
Appendix E: International Civil Aviation Organization(ICAO)
Location Identifiers and Federal Aviation Administration (FAA)
Location Identifiers (LI) Conversion Tables 114
Appendix F: Julian Date Calendars and Military (24-Hour) Clock 127
Appendix G: Standard Time Conversion Table 133
Appendix H: Authentication of Reserve Status for Travel Eligibility
(DD Form 1853) 137
Appendix I: Boarding Pass/Ticket Receipt (AMC Form 148/2) 138
Appendix J: Baggage Identification (DD Form 1839,
AMC Form 20-ID, and USAF Form 94) 139
Appendix K: Air Passenger Comments (AMC Form 253) 140
Appendix L: International Certificates of Vaccination and
Personal Health History (PHS Form 731) 141
Appendix M: A Brief Description of Aircraft on Which
Most Space-A Travel Occurs 143
Appendix N: Space-A Questions and Answers 153
Appendix O: Space-A Travel Tips 167
Appendix P: Before You Go---Travel Aids and Travel Publications 174
Appendix Q: Passports 178
Appendix R: Passport Agencies 182
Appendix S: Visa Information 183
Appendix T Customs and Duty: 189
Appendix U: Air Mobility Command (AMC) In-Flight Food Service 197
Appendix V: Major Worldwide Space-A Routes 200
Appendix W: Passenger Bill of Rights 204
Appendix X: State, Possession, & Country Abbreviations 205
Appendix Y: General Abbreviations Used in this Book 207
AFTERWORD 208

INTRODUCTION

If you have never flown Space-A or if you have not flown Space-A recently, *Military Space-A Air Basic Training*™ *and Reader Trip Reports* has important information to help make your next trip successful. The new Space-A rules are entirely different from previous years.

The privilege of flying Space-A on US military aircraft has saved literally millions of military and their family members a great deal of money. More importantly, however, is that this unique privilege has enabled military and their families to take morale-boosting trips that they could not have afforded otherwise.

Have you and your family joined in on the fun? *Military Space-A Air Basic Training*™ *and Reader Trip Reports* will give you the information you need to get started *"traveling on less per day...the military way!"*

In surveys, military ID card holders (active, guard/reserve and retired) have responded that Space-A air travel is one of the privileges that they value most because it gives the military member and his/her family an immediate cash-saving benefit in addition to the unmeasurable value of being a part of the military family.

Space-A air travel is also important to retirees giving them a continued sense of camaraderie and recognition for their service to their country.

HOW SPACE-A AIR TRAVEL HAS CHANGED IN RECENT YEARS

The Space-A travel fee has been eliminated thanks to General Colin Powell USA, (Ret) and General Ronald R. Fogleman, Chief of Staff, USAF, and his staff. General Fogleman, while commander of AMC, did everything possible to help uniformed service personnel have a simpler and easier Space-A system. His staff diligently worked on new initiatives which are now a huge success. Subsequent AMC commanders have continued to improve Space-A air opportunities.

Space-A regulations have changed dramatically in the last few years for the better; many of the bureaucratic procedures have been eliminated. Here are just a few of the changes which you will learn about in *Military Space-A Air Basic Training*™ *and Reader Trip Reports:*

In the early years of Space-A travel, potential passengers had to show up at every flight call or be removed from the list. Later, passengers did not have to show up for every flight, but they had to revalidate their records every 15 days (in person) to indicate they still wanted to fly Space-A.

Sponsors from one place in the country had to make their way to a military air passenger terminal (sometimes across the entire USA) to sign up for a flight from a given location. Sometimes, the passenger would go back to his/her home base and wait while their names made their way up the list and then travel back to the air terminal again hoping they would get a flight. Often, the cost involved in this procedure obliterated any savings on the actual flight. All of that has now changed so that a greatly improved system of sign-up is now in place.

Those wishing to fly Space-A no longer have to appear at the departure terminal to sign up; they can now do this by fax, E-mail or letter. The new fax numbers and some E-mail, as available, are included in this book. This remote sign-up capability "levels the Space-A playing field" so that Space-A passengers are treated more fairly in having an opportunity to fly.

For those who still prefer to sign up for a military Space-A trip in person, a self-service sign-up procedure, which is easy to access, is still available in most cases.

A one-time sign-up procedure allows Space-A passengers to keep their original date of being added to the Space-A passenger roster at the originating terminal. If one mission terminates, the Space-A passenger may sign up for a new flight using the original date. Details on this one-time sign-up are in this book.

All of the previous Military Airlift Command (MAC) and the major portions of the Strategic Air Command (SAC) have merged into a highly efficient Air Mobility Command (AMC). Especially good news for Space-A passengers is the AMC now has a wide variety of aircraft including tankers. While the former MAC was very user-friendly to Space-A passengers, SAC was not as well organized to serve them. Now, AMC has applied Space-A regulations on a uniform basis. Many tanker locations have moved to other Air Force bases (many in the heartland of the country) bringing Space-A air travel to new places not previously served by such aircraft. Tankers remain a favorite with Space-A passengers because of the opportunity to observe actual refueling of other aircraft. There is a special and unique excitement to tanker missions.

Attitudes have improved toward Space-A passengers. While many terminal staff members and aircraft crews have been helpful in the past, it appears that there is a new emphasis on courtesy and helpfulness from the very "top" to the "bottom."

Luggage allowances have been increased to 140 pounds per passenger with two bags not weighing more than 70 pounds each. Even so, remember there are no porters in the middle of an airfield where passengers often debark! Smart Space-A travelers travel as light as possible! Golf clubs or other sporting gear can travel as checked baggage.

Another reason to travel light is that by doing so, if an opportunity arises for you to get Space-A on an "executive jet propeller" aircraft, the luggage allowed is only 30 pounds.

On AMC flights returning from overseas, Space-A passengers who are eligible family members may now fly with their sponsor to the final destination of a military flight within the United States; they no longer have to deplane at the first stop. Conversely, family members may take flights with their sponsor which make an interim stop within the

United States on a mission which continues overseas. Also, active duty families which are Command Sponsored Overseas may now fly to CONUS and in overseas theaters without their sponsors.

In-flight meals have been changed to a healthy heart variety and breakfast menus have been added. The meals are very reasonable in cost, and we have heard many good comments about them from Space-A passengers.

The wearing of the military uniform by active duty except USMC personnel on USMC aircraft when traveling on a Space-A basis has been eliminated. All service members and their accompanying family members must be in clean clothes. No open-toed sandals or T-shirts with slogans or vulgar language are allowed.

Eligible passengers who are handicapped will now find AMC to be a lot more helpful than in previous years.

Passengers will find many improved terminals due to extensive ongoing renovation projects. Many terminals are now brighter and much more comfortable. "No smoking" rules now apply to all DoD and DoT aircraft missions.

Now that AMC has made all of these improvements, those who have a desire to fly Space-A should learn the rules and customs of flying Space-A in order to be knowledgeable about how this wonderful system operates. This book, *Military Space-A Air Basic Training*™ *and Reader Trip Reports*, will give you the information you need to have successful Space-A air travel flights on US military aircraft.

Once you have familiarized yourself with the basic information, you may want to delve into our other publications to truly become a *"Space-A Expert."* Military Living currently has three other publications to help you do just that. Our worldwide, all ranks military travel newsletter, Military Living's *R&R Space-A Report*®, will keep you informed on the latest rules, improvements, locations of new opportunities and more. The reader trip reports in the *R&R Space-A Report*® (worldwide military travel newsletter) are invaluable and form the nucleus of a powerful reader clearing house of information.

Military Living also publishes an advanced book on Space-A air travel which gives locations of Space-A opportunities and schedules: *Military Space-A Air Opportunities Around The World*™. In addition, Military Living has its popular map, *Military Space-A Air Opportunities Around The World Air Route Map*™. Check at your military exchange to purchase these helpful publications. Not only will you save money by doing so, exchange profits are recycled back into the military community for their recreation programs. If not available, you may, of course, order them directly from Military Living. Phone orders are accepted with Visa, MasterCard, American Express or Discover. Please call **703-237-0203** for information. An order form also appears in the back of the book.

On behalf of military families all over the world, Military Living would like to thank the Air Mobility Command (AMC) for all they have done to improve the life of military ID card holders. Thanks guys and gals for letting uniformed services personnel and their families tag along on your missions.

You'll never really know how many hearts have been healed by a visit home, how many elderly parents and other family members have given thanks that their loved one could come home for a visit by Space-A, especially emergency leave travel, how many marriages may have been saved when military members serving apart have had reunions by AMC and other service organizations' Space-A flights or even how military families have become better educated by being able to travel to far-off lands and view countries first-hand. Families flying together form unique bonds and have a favorable impression of military life.

AMC's service to those who have also served is a part of military life which makes the bad days be evened out by the good days. **We know how important AMC personnel are because our readers have told us.** AMC would like to hear from you directly. You may pick up special form #253, Air Passenger Comments, at any AMC air passenger terminal or write to: **HQ AMC DOJP, 402 Scott Drive, Unit 3A1, Scott AFB, IL 62225-5302.** Thanks again! Happy Travels!

Ann, Roy Sr & RJ Crawford

NOTICE

Contrary to rumor, unaccompanied family members living in the US or another location CANNOT fly Space-A to join or visit their sponsors in another location. If this rule changes, we will publish the info in Military Living's R&R Space-A Report®. See our Appendix N for info on EML travel for those living overseas on an accompanied tour.

ILLUSTRATION AND PHOTO CREDITS

All Military Living cartoons by Bob Scoggin, deceased, with the exception of the customs cartoon on page 196, which is an Armed Forces Press Service Cartoon.

All aircraft photos courtesy of the Department of Defense.

Photos showing Space-A passengers are courtesy of those individuals, with the exception of the photo on the inside back cover of a woman and baby. That photo shows Ivey Andrews, 1, sleeps on Melinda Barfield's lap on the floor of a C-17 while flying Space-A from Yokota Air Base, Japan to Charleston Air Force Base, South Carolina. Digital image by SSgt Michael C. Leonard, AMC Headquarters

DOLLAR RENT A CAR

For Worldwide Reservations, Call Your Professional Travel Agent or Dollar Rent A Car

Military Living's Travel Club
ID Number
ML3009

Important Dollar Rent A Car Telephone Numbers

1-800-800-4000	Worldwide Reservations
1-800-800-6000	EuroDollar® Reservations
1-800-235-9393	Emergency Roadside Service
1-800-800-5252	Customer Center

www.dollarcar.com

★★★★★★★★★★★★★★★★★★★★★★★★★★★★★★★★

A National Patriotic Organization of American Military Officers
of All Uniformed Services
Active, Reserve, Retired, Former and their Descendants

The Military Order of the World Wars

77 Years of Selfless Service to the Nation
Serving America's Future Through Support of JROTC, ROTC and Youth Leadership Conferences
We Stand To Stimulate Love of Country and Flag • Maintain Law and Order
• Promote Patriotic Education • Defend the Honor and Supremacy of the National Government
• Foster Fraternal Relations Between the Services
Members include: Pershing, MacArthur, Marshall, Truman, Westmoreland, Mundy, Sullivan and

"Take Time To Serve Your Country"

Name_____ Rank/Status_____
Address_____ City_____ State____ Zip_____
Service Branch_____ Telephone (___)_____

__Regular Annual $30   __*Regular Perpetual $250 (Four Installments of $62.50)
__Heredatary Annual $30   __*Hereditary Perpetual $250 (Four Installments of $62.50)
__Former Member $30   __*Hereditary Perpetual (Under 21) $125 (Four Installments of $31.25)

Membership includes subscription to *Officer Review*.
* Perpetual memberships are a one time cost.

Detach and remit to: MOWW, 435 North Lee Street, Alexandria, VA 22314
Phone (703) 683-4911 • Fax (703) 683-4501
E-Mail: MOWWHQ@aol.com • Homepage: moww.org

NAUS

NAUS is Different

The National Association for Uniformed Services is the

ONLY

Military/Veterans Association to Represent

★ ALL Grades ★ ALL Ranks ★ ALL Services
★ ALL Components

Officer and Enlisted! Active, Reserve, National Guard, Retired, Other Veterans - Families and Survivors!

Aggressive, non-partisan lobbying for military/veterans concerns is what we do best!

Join today and receive a one-year complimentary trial membership!

Call 1-800-842-3451

Or Write to: NATIONAL ASSOCIATION FOR UNIFORMED SERVICES • 5535 Hempstead Way • Springfield, VA 22151
• Fax: (703)354-4380 • E-mail:naus@ix.netcom.com
• http://www.naus.org

*Be sure to mention the special complimentary trial membership offer in Military Living's Military Space-A Air Basic Training

Military Space-A Air Basic Training - 1
BACKGROUND

The air cargo and passenger capabilities of all the Military Services were greatly expanded during WWII. They have been maintained since that time to support our worldwide peacekeeping military forces, diplomatic missions, unilateral, multinational and international obligations and commitments. A uniform policy for the administration of this much sought-after air travel benefit was established by the newly created Department of Defense (DoD) in 1947, and communicated through Department of Defense Directive (DoDD): Chapters 1 (portions) and 6, DoDD 4515.13-R, Air Transportation Eligibility, November 1994, as amended.

PAX CAFETERIA

"I know it's a privilege, but I like to think that I'm providing jobs for more than fifty thousand Americans."

This directive ensures that Space-A air travel priorities and procedures are equitably administered for all of **the seven Uniformed Services (US Army, US Navy, US Marine Corps, US Coast Guard, US Public Health Service, US Air Force and the National Oceanic and Atmospheric Administration).**

WHAT IS SPACE-A AIR TRAVEL?

Space-A: The term Space-A is used in the military community to mean many things. Space-A is used to describe the use of or access to facilities and transportation of the military services, after all known required and authorized use and access has been satisfied. The term Space-A is primarily used to describe the availability of air passenger travel to Uniformed Services members (active, Reservist and retired), their dependents and eligible DoD and other civilian employees when they are stationed overseas. **(See Eligible Passengers, DoDD 4515.13-R, Paragraphs 2-B, 6-C and Table 6-1: Eligible Space-A travelers, priorities, and approved geographical travel segments.)**

2 - Military Space-A Air Basic Training

Space-A is also used to describe travel on military trains (discontinued in Germany in 1991), buses, temporary military lodging or use of military recreational facilities which are available after all required official duty and other authorized uses have been satisfied.

The DoD has described Space-A air travel as a "by-product" of the DoD's primary mission, which is the movement of space-required military cargo and passengers. This means that space not required for the movement of official cargo and passengers can be used for the worldwide travel of Uniformed Services members and their dependents on flights with overseas destinations.

SPACE-A AIR TRAVEL STUDY AND TRAINING

SPACE-A AIR BASIC TRAINING: All Uniformed Service members undergo elementary or basic training. If you hope to save thousands of dollars on air fares, you too will need some basic training or at least a refresher course because policies, procedures and techniques of Space-A air travel are constantly changing. If you have never availed yourself of the highly sought-after benefit of Space-A air travel or if you have several Space-A trips under your belt, you can learn a great deal from this book. This book can save you a great deal of money in your air travels.

This *Military Space-A Air Basic Training™ and Reader Trip Reports* book will be kept simple. We are using a "step-by-step" approach which will cover, by example, all of the essential elements of Space-A air travel. We will also repeat key points to reinforce your training. This basic training will give you all the information that you will need to plan and successfully complete a typical Space-A air trip. We recommend that you, as the sponsor, study the *Military Space-A Air Basic Training™ and Reader Trip Reports* book and each dependent family member traveling with you study along in order to sweep away some of the mystery and unknown. The information in this book will instill confidence in military members and their families while traveling Space-A.

R&R Space-A Report®

A six-time yearly by-subscription all-ranks travel publication specializing in bringing our readers the latest news on Space-A air travel; temporary military lodging; military RV camping & rec areas and military discounts in the civilian travel sector. Reader trip reports give you first-hand info. Sometimes, just one tip can save you hundreds of dollars on your military travel! Please see our coupon in the back of this book for prices. If coupon is missing, call us for more information.

SECTION I

AN IMAGINARY OVERSEAS SPACE-A AIR TRIP WITH THE FAMILY

TRIP PLANNING

TYPICAL SPACE-A AIR TRIP: For the purpose of *Military Space-A Air Basic Training*™ *and Reader Trip Reports*, this typical Space-A air trip is made by **a sponsor (active or retired), his/her dependent spouse, and two dependent children up to 21 years of age (or 23 years of age if a full-time college student with a valid military dependent ID card (DD Form - 1173).** NOTE: The sponsor may take some or all of his/her eligible family members (dependents).

Some readers may prefer the term **"family members"** to **"dependents"** (we will discuss the documents required for Space-A travel later), but "dependents" is a necessary legal term in regard to the Space-A air travel regulation which must be met for Space-A air travel. (The DoD office of General Counsel has ruled that the use of "dependent" may be avoided, except to the extent necessary to satisfy explicit statutory requirements regarding entitlement to benefits and/or privileges.)

The typical trip begins on the East Coast of the Continental United States (CONUS) and continues to Western Europe and returns to CONUS; or it begins on the West Coast of CONUS and continues to the Western Pacific and returns to CONUS. A full description of worldwide major scheduled Space-A air routes is in Appendix V.

There are other typical variations, such as trips to the Middle East, Africa, Central and South America, the South Pacific (Australia/New Zealand), Alaska and Hawaii. We cannot cover all possible alternatives in the limited space of this book. We have covered all of the major Space-A air routes. **The most popular Space-A air trip is from East Coast CONUS to Western Europe and return.** We have selected this trip but with slight adjustments. You can adapt this scenario to your own travel needs.

Hang on - here we go on a Space-A air adventure from the East Coast CONUS to Western Europe and return.

PLANNING YOUR SPACE-A TRIP: Your most important task to ensure success of your voyage is **PRE-TRIP PLANNING.** Most Space-A travelers have selected a destination or destinations for a variety of reasons which are clear, logical and rational for the travelers. Based on our scenario, we are going to Western Europe. Let's get more specific: What is our prime and most desired destination in Western Europe? We want to make the central Rhein River area of Germany our base of operation.

First we should consult Military Living's *Military Space-A Air Opportunities Air Route Map* (**Military Living's SPA Map**), which, along with its many other essential information features, is a prime route planning guide. It is indispensable to both the basic and advanced Space-A air traveler. This guide shows you, in graphic multi-color design,

4 - Military Space-A Air Basic Training

the scheduled air routes around the world. For convenience, this world map is centered on the continents of North and South America. From this air route map we can see that the best destinations in the German Rhein River area are **Ramstein AB (RMS/ETAR), Germany, and Rhein-Main AB (FRF/EDAF), Germany.** These three and four character letters/symbols are the Federal Aviation Administration (FAA) Location Identifiers (LI) and the International Civil Aviation Organization (ICAO) location identifiers, which are fully explained in Appendix E. The popular FAA three character location identifiers are being replaced or supplemented more frequently by the ICAO four letter identifier for international stations (airports) in order to improve the positive identification of all stations worldwide. We will list these identifiers after each location/destination when it is first mentioned in order to reinforce the identifiers in your mind. You will find that these identifiers are indispensable to your understanding of basic Space-A air travel.

We also note that we can depart from a variety of East Coast stations (north to south): McGuire AFB (WRI/KWRI), NJ, Philadelphia IAP (PHL/KPHL), PA, Dover AFB (DOV/KDOV), DE, Andrews AFB (ADW/KADW), MD, Dulles IAP (IAD/KIAD), VA, Norfolk NAS (NGU/KNGU), VA and Charleston AFB/IAP (CHS/KCHS), SC.

The key question at this point in our trip planning is from which CONUS East Coast locations can we depart in order to reach our desired destination in Germany? The Location Identifiers and Cross-Reference Index, **upfront after the contents in *Military Living's Military Space-A Air Opportunities Around the World*** book, also gives departure locations (other than the East Coast) for reaching the central German Rhein River area. As you can see from *Military Living's Military Space-A Air Opportunities Air Route Map* and *Military Space-A Air Opportunities Around the World* book, there are more opportunities in terms of the number of flights to our destination **from Dover AFB, DE, or from McGuire AFB, NJ,** than the other departure locations. Do not rule out these other departure locations because they all have potential for flights to our selected destination. In fact, as you will see later, armed with a Space-A tip from **Military Living Publications,** we are going to register or apply for Space-A travel from at least five of the above listed departure locations/stations in order to increase our chances of selection for a Space-A flight. The Dover AFB, DE, departure location is feasible for us since we live in the Mid-Atlantic states area (Falls Church, VA, only seven miles from Washington, DC). *Please note: The Location Identifiers and Cross-Reference Index, (**upfront after the contents in the Military Space-A Air Opportunities Around the World** book) gives other departure locations for reaching the central German Rhein River area.

BACKUP PLANS: If making this trip is very important to you, you will want to have backup plans to insure that you reach your goal or destination and return within your desired time frame. You cannot rely on DoD for this assurance. As the DoD Space-A directive says: *"DoD cannot guarantee seats to Space-A passengers and is not obligated to continue travel or return Space-A passengers to the original point of travel"* (DoD 4515.13R, Chapter 6, Par A-9).

Military Space-A Air Basic Training - 5

"How much is economy, round trip, double occupancy fare?"

If you must return by a specific date, you may want to purchase backup commercial tickets. The commercial tickets will assure that you will be able to return within your desired time frame. If you do not use the tickets, there is a cancellation fee of $50-$150 (at the time we went to press) for each leg of the trip. For example, if you purchase tickets to fly from Washington, DC, or Philadelphia, PA, to Germany and return and you do not use the tickets, a cancellation fee would be charged. The terms and conditions of commercial air travel tickets change frequently as marketplace supply and demand, among other factors, change. Even with this cancellation fee, the savings of flying Space-A is far more than the cost of flying round trip commercially.

Unlike military Space-A travel, dependents/family members using commercial airlines may fly without their sponsor accompanying them. Another advantage of making commercial backup plans is that you do have a **reserved** seat on a flight heading for a definite location. If you have left your car at a particular base or airport, or if you need to return to CONUS by a certain date, you can rest easy. Commercial backup assures you that you can return to your point of departure in a timely fashion. Also, should you fall in love with a place and want to stay an extra day, week, month or even up to a year of the date of purchase of the tickets, you can do so with commercial backup tickets. You will need to call the airline involved and see if a seat is available on the day you wish to travel.

Military air fares may be available (situation changes with market conditions) from most major cities throughout the United States to Germany. The tickets are usually good for one year from the date of purchase. Be sure and ask about this, travel "blackout" days or days that you cannot travel with your particular restricted ticket and other restrictions when buying a ticket. Rules are subject to change and may vary from airline to airline.

In ***Military Living's R&R Space-A Report*** ®, we often have one or more travel agency sponsors who are knowledgeable in locating a military fare in their computers, and who will work with you in the event you need a backup ticket. Some agents do not want to work with anyone attempting to fly Space-A part or all of the way. Armed Services Vacations, a sponsor of **Military Living Publications**, has agreed to work with our military readers to help them utilize a combination of military Space-A and commercial travel. For information on backup tickets, please call Godfrey Crowe, Colonel USA (Ret) at (703) 836-1100 or toll free 1-800-833-4382. Godfrey may also be reached by mail at Armed Services Vacations, A Division of MacNair Travel Management, 1703 Duke Street, Alexandria, VA 22314. We hope that you will reward our sponsor with any other travel business you may have, as there is not a substantial profit in issuing backup tickets which may well be cancelled!

6 - Military Space-A Air Basic Training

In addition, if in attempting to return home by Space-A you find yourself in a tight spot overseas, you can check with the base travel office provided by various contractors who have ticket facilities on many US military installations overseas. Some of our readers have reported that they were able to buy discounted one-way tickets from other commercial ticket agents located in or near the military air passenger terminals. We have heard that the closer you get to departure time the cheaper the remaining tickets become!

This backup travel arrangement does not use your Space-A air travel benefit, but it may save you untold money if you cannot for some reason use your Space-A privilege to meet your travel needs.

If you know of any other travel agents who would be interested in serving our military readership in this manner, please have them call Ann or R.J. Crawford at (703) 237-0203. We have 17 different publications which have advertising opportunities.

PRE-FLIGHT

REGISTRATION/SIGN-IN AT TERMINAL (STATION/AERIAL PORT): As the sponsor or lead traveler of a group, you must register at the Space-A passenger departure or service center at each station from which you seek to depart on your Space-A trip. Registration can be made via fax, E-mail, mail/courier or in person. Registration times may be limited at some terminals/stations due to manpower limitations and demonstrated need. Please check *Military Living's Military Space-A Air Opportunities Around the World* book and reconfirm registration times with the terminals from which you plan to register for Space-A air travel. NOTE: In most cases faxes and E-mail may be transmitted 24 hours daily. If a fax or E-mail means is not available to you, try your local service center, i.e. Kinko's. (Save the proof of fax and carry it with you.)

Sponsor or Lead Traveler Registration. The sponsor or lead traveler of a group may register for dependents and other persons who are traveling with them by sending a fax, E-mail, letter/courier application or by presenting all required documents when registering in person. If registering for Space-A travel via fax, E-mail, letter or military/commercial courier, the sponsor must provide the following: **Active Duty** - application and service leave or pass form, a statement that boarder clearance documents are current and a list of five countries (or four countries plus all/any country), overseas destinations or CONUS. See AMC SPACE-A TRAVEL REQUEST, Form 140, Feb. 95, Appendix D (We also have

"I'm signed up for England, Italy, and Iceland, but I'm not going anywhere. Since retiring I just enjoy getting on a roster knowing that I don't have to go."

this form as a pull-out in the back of the book). We recommend that you take all documents of each traveler in your party when registering in person including each traveler's Uniformed Services ID card. There may be some inconvenience, but play it safe. Take the ID cards because one terminal may sign up your dependents without you showing their cards, but the other terminals may not!

DOCUMENTS

For our trip we need the following: DD Form 2 (green) US Armed Forces Identification Card (active), Form 2 NOAA (green) Uniform Services Identification and Privilege Card (active), PHS Form 1866-3 (green) United States Public Health Service Identification Card (active) for the active duty sponsor or DD Form 2 (gray or blue) Armed Forces Identification Card (retired) for the retired sponsor; Uniformed Services Identification & Privilege Card, DD Form 1173 for all dependents accompanying active duty & retired Uniformed Services members; passports for accompanying dependents and retired sponsors (active duty for some destinations); and immunization records (recommended but not normally required). NOTE: Reservist (DD Form 2 (red)) cannot fly to foreign countries but only to CONUS and US Possessions overseas. Reservists may fly to foreign countries when they are retired at age 60 and receiving retired pay.

Visas must be obtained when required by the **DoD Foreign Clearance Guides. See Appendix B, Personnel Entrance Requirements,** in *Military Living's Space-A Air Opportunities Around The World* book or check with the Space-A desk at any DoD international departure location/station or Military Personnel Offices which issue international travel orders. Please note that these personnel entrance requirements to foreign countries may be different (usually more restrictive) if entering the foreign country from a US military owned or contract aircraft. Visas are not required for Western European countries but most Eastern European countries require them. See **Appendix S: Visa Information.**

Also, if you are active duty, you must have valid leave or pass orders in writing and **be in a leave or pass status throughout the registration, waiting and travel periods.** The DoDD no longer requires that active duty personnel travel in the class A or B uniform of their service. At press time, the uniform is not required for active duty personnel except USMC traveling on USMC aircraft.

APPLICATION FOR SPACE-A AIR TRAVEL

As an active or retired member of one of the seven Uniformed Services (US Army, US Navy, US Marine Corps, US Coast Guard, US Public Health Service, US Air Force, and National Oceanic and Atmospheric Administration), you can be the sponsor or lead traveler of a group as shown in our imaginary trip. You may apply for Space-A travel via fax, E-mail, letter/courier or in person to the Dover AFB, DE 19902-5501, Space-A desk/counter at Bldg 500, Passenger Terminal (new in 1997), 24 hours daily; telephone: Commercial (C) 302-677-2854/4088, Fax: C-302-677-2953, Defense Switched Network (DSN) 312-445-2854/4088, Recording: C-302-677-4091, D-312-445-4091. From the

8 - Military Space-A Air Basic Training

main gate on 13th Street turn right onto Atlantic Avenue and continue. The Passenger Terminal is on the left adjacent to the Air Traffic Control (ATC) Building (Bldg 500). **Directions to almost 300 other terminals are listed in** *Military Living's Military Space-A Air Opportunities Around the World* **book.**

Present your documentation and request an application for Space-A air travel. **You will be given a SPACE-AVAILABLE TRAVEL REQUEST, also known as the SPACE-A PASSENGER BOOKING CARD, Air Mobility Command (AMC) Form 140, Feb 95,** to complete. Please see a copy in **Appendix D.** You will be allowed to specify a maximum of five countries as destinations. The fifth designation may be "ALL" to take advantage of airlift opportunities to other countries that may fit your plans. All destinations within a country are included in this definition, i.e., Germany, would include all destinations/stations in Germany. You will be assigned a category for your travel (based on the Space -A DoDD). In our example, active duty (ordinary leave and pass) is Category III, retired is Category VI. Complete Categories, Travelers Status and Situation, approved geographic travel segments and important restrictions/limitations are presented in table format in **Appendix A: Space-A Passenger Regulations**.

The DoD directive states, **"The numerical order of Space-Available categories indicates the precedence of movement between categories, e.g., travelers in Category III move before travelers in Category IV. The order in which travelers are listed in a particular category within table 6-1, Appendix A, does not indicate priority of movement in that category. In each category, transportation is furnished on a "first-in, first-out basis"** to all passengers in that category. This policy is implemented by establishing, at each station, a Space-A roster of categories of travelers arranged higher priority (category) for movement to lower (category) for movement by their registration/sign-in times. There is a Space-A roster for each category, or in effect, a total of six Space-A rosters (kept as one combined roster on the station computer). **These times are recorded in Julian date and time format which is explained in Appendix F**. This system allows registered Space-A persons to compete for seats within categories based on their date and time of registration.

"Hi. How's the waiting list to New Zealand?"

The Space-A desk clerk will verify the information contained in your application, examine your identification and travel documents for validity, and if you are an active duty sponsor, your leave or pass orders will be stamped on the back with the terminal name and the Julian date and time at which you applied for Space-A air travel. **This category of traveler (active duty on ordinary leave) must have a validated copy of the leave or pass document when he/she is processed for the Space-A trip. If the application for Space-A is made by fax or mail/courier, the leave or pass must be transmitted with the fax and will be effective no later than the date of the fax or receipt of the mail or courier Space-A Travel Request.**

Your application for Space-A travel will be entered into a computer-based waiting list by category, Julian date and time, and destination. Our application is entered for **Colonel (0-6) Francis O. Hardknuckle, USA (Ret)** and family for four seats, Category VI for the following maximum five countries which we have specified: Germany, Italy, Spain, United Kingdom and "ALL."

If you are active duty, your application is entered for four seats, Category III and for the same five countries. Whether or not you report for Space-A calls, your application will remain current in the computer for a maximum of 60 days or until the end of your leave or pass, whichever comes first. If you are retired, your application will remain current in the computer for a maximum of 60 days whether or not you report for Space-A calls.

You will compete for seats within your category based on the Julian date and time of your registration. **Reservations for Space-A air travel will not be accepted as there is no guaranteed space for passengers in any category.** If applying in person, as evidence of our application, we will be given a Space-A Travel Information slip (developed locally, see Appendix) which will contain, among other things, the five locations we have

"I have one seat left on this flight."

selected, our Category, Julian date and time (accepted), leave expiration date (active duty only), sponsor's name, rank/grade, number of seats required and the names of each dependent traveler. **The three dependents accompanying Colonel Hardknuckle are Elizabeth Ann Hardknuckle, spouse; Linda Sue Hardknuckle, daughter, age 22, full-time graduate student; and Loren A. Hardknuckle, daughter, age 20, full-time college student. We will need this information anytime we inquire about our application for Space-A air travel.**

As we indicated earlier, in order to maximize our chances for obtaining Space-A air travel to our destination, we are also going to apply for Space-A air travel at several other convenient Space-A departure locations. Why take this action? **Space-A seats are always**

10 - Military Space-A Air Basic Training

a function of the number of perspective passengers waiting for a specific destination, the number of aircraft missions, the carrying capacity (available seats) on each mission and the time at which all of these variables converge. **Sound complicated? Yes, but with so many unknown variables, your chances are improved if you apply for air travel in the Space-A system at five terminals/stations rather than one.**

Through careful study of this text, you can better understand and use the Military Space-A air travel system. We suggest that you also apply for Space-A air travel at Andrews AFB (ADW/KADW), MD, Philadelphia IAP (PHL/KPHL), PA, and McGuire AFB (WRI/KWRI), NJ. NOTE: Application at Philadelphia or McGuire provides automatic application at both. You can send faxes, E-mail or letters to these locations, apply in person, or there are several micro-bus transportation companies that service all of these stations for about $30-$35 for each leg of the journey. Please see *Military Living's Military Space-A Air Opportunities Around the World* book for complete information on ground transportation at each terminal/station. For the strong at heart, you could also apply at Norfolk NAS (NGU/KNGU), VA, to further improve your chances of obtaining a Space-A air trip to Western Europe.

REGISTRATION FOR RETURN TRAVEL: We are very optimistic that we will get our Space-A trip to Europe. In order to obtain an advance/early position on the Germany Space-A rosters for return travel, we fax our Space-A Travel Request, AMC Form 140, Feb 95 to both Ramstein AB (RMS/ETAR), GE, (C-011-49-6371-47-2364) and Rhein-Main AB (FRF/EDAF), GE, (C-011-49-69-699-6309).

TRAVEL DATES: In our planning we should establish approximate desired dates for departure. In addition to when active duty sponsors can obtain ordinary leave, we can establish an approximate departure date by examining several other pieces of information. First, check the Space-A backlog for the desired destinations at the departure terminals through the recording numbers or by telephoning the terminal personnel **(for these numbers consult your copy of** *Military Living's Military Space-A Air Opportunities Around the World* **book or** *Military Living's Military Space-A Air Opportunities Air Route Map***)**. The Dover AFB (DOV/KDOV), DE, passenger information numbers are C-302-677-2854/4088, D-312-445-2854/4088, Fax: C-302-677-2953, D-312-445-2953, Rec: C-302-677-4091, D-312-445-4091 (updated 2000 daily). Also check the number and frequency of flights by consulting the above documents. You must decide how much of your leave time you want to use while waiting for your Space-A flight; if retired, your time is also valuable.

TRAVEL READY

Note carefully! If you are in or near the passenger terminal and you report for each scheduled and non-scheduled flight departure, your chances of obtaining a Space-A flight to your desired destination are greatly improved. You have the right to stand-by for any flight that you believe you may have a reasonable opportunity on which to travel. In fact, you may stand-by for any flight regardless of your chances or circumstances.

Military Space-A Air Basic Training - 11

Many prospective Space-A travelers call the various terminals through the recording number, if available, or speak with the passenger terminal personnel to determine their numerical position on the waiting list for their registered destination. They also check their travel category and traveler's status and situation on the waiting list as well as the waiting list of higher category personnel. They do not go to the terminal to wait for a flight until their names are near the top of the Space-A waiting list and there are one or more flights scheduled in the immediate future. **This is a useful technique, but don't forget that there are flights of opportunity. If you are not in the passenger terminal and "travel ready" (discussed later), you won't fly.**

The passenger terminal will not call you or notify you of a flight. In fact, they are prohibited from doing so by regulations. As a personal note, Ann, our author/publisher, and Roy, Sr. were in the Travis AFB (SUU/KSUU), CA, passenger terminal recently. There were 600 plus Space-A applications for Hickam AFB (HIK/PHIK), HI, and after repeated announcements in the terminal there were only nine passengers who reported for the Space-A call and took the C-5A/B/C flight with 73 available Space-A seats to Hawaii. This Space-A air opportunity is repeated many times every day around the world. To wait or not to wait in the terminal, or nearby, to keep your finger on the pulse of activity should be your informed choice.

SPACE-A FLIGHT CALL/SELECTION PROCESS: If you make the decision to wait in the terminal, or at any time you report to the terminal for the purpose of standing-by for a prospective flight, you should be **travel ready**. Travel ready simply means that you are ready and prepared to travel with very short notice. You have all of your required documentation, baggage, funds, and you are ready to report for a Space-A flight call/selection process and subsequent boarding. We have heard from many of our *R&R Space-A Report®* readers that they have missed a flight opportunity because they did not have enough time to return a rental car, move their baggage to the terminal or other essential chores. You must be **travel ready** in order to maximize your chances for flying as you have planned.

Whether you have been waiting in the terminal for a long time, or you have reported for a flight call based on information that a flight is scheduled for departure to your desired destination, the processing procedure is the same. Many Space-A passengers enter their selected departure terminal and are processed and boarded for their desired destination within an hour, if and only if, they are **travel ready!**

Space-A seats are normally identified as early as two to three hours or as late as 30 minutes prior to departure. The standard notice time (Space-A call) for International/Overseas Space-A flights is two hours. Due to security requirements the notice time can be as much as three hours for some international/overseas flights. This is the same standard for international flights on commercial airlines. In fact, many commercial international flights now require up to three hours for processing. Always check with the passenger service center for the **Space-A show time** for the flight on which you expect to travel. Show time is the time that the Space-A Call/Selection begins and subsequent flight processing and boarding.

12 - Military Space-A Air Basic Training

"I think I'm getting a terminal illness."

Show time is important for the Space-A traveler because it not only means the time at which selection of registered Space-A prospective passengers begins, but **you must now be present to answer when your (sponsor's) name (family/travel group) is called in your travel category (I-VI).**

You will hear the announcement familiar to the seasoned Space-A traveler. **The Space-A flight call: "Anyone desiring Space-A air transportation to a series of stations (e.g., Ramstein AB (RMS/ETAR), GE) please assemble at the Space-A desk" or other location in the terminal. This is a roll call of prospective Space-A travelers.** The Space-A terminal flight processing team will be armed with the latest printout of the station Space-A roster. (In fact, there is a Space-A roster for all categories by date/time of sign-up for ease in processing.) They will first call all the names of Category I: Emergency Leave Unfunded Travel, and process these travelers first. Next they will proceed to call travelers in each travel category (from highest priority to lowest priority) by earliest Julian date and time until they have filled all of the available seats for this flight.

The flight processing team knows the number of seats available and will select a sign-up Julian date and time near the middle of the register. They will ask if anyone has that date and time, or an earlier date and time, then work forward or move back to the top of the list as appropriate. **It is important to remember that the number of seats your party requires is a factor in your selection.** There must be sufficient seats for your party or the processors will move on and select someone with a later sign-up date who requires fewer seats. As you can see, single and couple travelers may have a better chance of selection for Space-A air travel.

FLIGHT PROCESSING

Let us assume that your party has been selected for Space-A air travel, and you are told to proceed immediately to flight processing (this may particularly be the case when the flight is non-scheduled). You must be **travel ready** when you report for the Space-A call. It is not uncommon to proceed immediately to flight processing after the end of the Space-A call. Also, you can be told to report back for flight processing at a later time. In our case, we are told to report immediately to the Space-A desk for processing.

SPACE-A PROCESSING FEE: You may have heard that Space-A is "free." This is true. The Space-A $10 processing fee was eliminated in early 1993 by the then Chairman of the Joint Chiefs of Staff, General Colin Powell, USA (Ret).

Please note that all passengers departing CONUS, Alaska and Hawaii on contract commercial aircraft must pay a $6 head tax that goes toward airport improvements. Also, all Space-A passengers departing on contract commercial missions from overseas to the United States must pay a $5 immigration inspection fee, a $5 customs inspection fee, a $2 agriculture inspection fee or a total fee of $12. Please note that all commercial airline passengers pay these taxes and fees in the price of their airline tickets.

"You don't have to thank them for calling your name!"

PAYMENT OF FEES AND DOCUMENT REVIEW: You must pay these fees in United States dollars or via your personal check. No credit/debit cards, travelers checks or other payment instruments are accepted. These charges may be collected at the beginning or at other times in the flight processing.

The next action is an identification and travel documents check. The processing team will ensure that you have the following documents: appropriate ID cards for all travelers and that they are current; passports (signed) with required visas for active/retired service members and all dependents and that they are current and valid; leave or pass orders for active duty personnel which were effective at the time of initial registration by the terminal and will be in force until at least the end of the flight for which you have been selected.

We have not been asked to show our **International Certificates of Vaccination and our Personal Health History**, both as approved by the World Health Organization, Form: PHS-731 or similar (see Appendix L) for each passenger, but we have them as recommended for use as needed. At some point, **the processing team will want to observe each passenger directly and verify their identity against their travel documents.**

BAGGAGE PROCESSING: You will of course need to pack prudently, sparingly, lightly and appropriately for your planned activities and for the climate of Western Europe during the season in which you will be traveling. Northern Europe has approximately the same climate as US New England except a bit cooler with more moisture. Each person is authorized two pieces of checked baggage, and each piece must not exceed 62 linear inches (length + height + width = 62 inches) and not more than 70 pounds for a total of

14 - Military Space-A Air Basic Training

140 pounds for both pieces (DoD 4515.13-R, Chapter 1, paragraph D, 2a through f). Family members and travel groups may pool their baggage allowances. **A Baggage Identification Tag (DD Form 1839 or AMC Form 20) is available for use on your hand-carried bags/items. Baggage claim tag USAF Form 94 (or similar) will be attached to each bag checked and you will receive a stub copy.** Sample copies are at **Appendix J.**

Space-A passengers may check oversized baggage (golf clubs, snow skis, folding bicycles, etc.) if it is the only piece to be checked (per person) and meets the weight requirement of 140 pounds total. Hand-carried baggage cannot exceed 45 linear inches (length + height + width = 45 inches) and must fit under the seat or in the overhead compartment if available. **Space-A passengers cannot pay for baggage in excess of the allowed weight limit.**

A few precautions: you cannot pack or carry weapons of any type (including cutting instruments), ammunition or explosive devices, chemicals or aerosol cans, or matches or other incendiary devices. NOTE: There are amnesty containers at the entrance to most terminals or boarding areas where you may discard any prohibited items anonymously and without penalty. Also, you must remove the batteries from all electronic equipment in your checked baggage. You may keep the batteries in your checked baggage. **At boarding time, you may be required to undergo an inspection of your hand-carried baggage or all of your baggage in some cases.**

"Will those passengers holding boarding passes on mission four zero two assemble in the base chapel for last rites."

DRESS: Although the wearing of uniforms by active duty and Reservists is no longer required (except USMC personnel on USMC aircraft), every Space-A passenger must be appropriately dressed. For your comfort and safety you will want to dress with layers of clothes that can be added or removed as needed. Prohibited clothing items are open-toed sandals and shoes (on military aircraft), T-shirts and tanktops as outer garments, shorts and revealing clothing. Strictly prohibited as an outer garment are clothing with profane language and any attire depicting the desecration of the US Flag. If in doubt, call your air terminal for specific information. You must use good conservative taste in your dress.

Military Space-A Air Basic Training - 15

IN-FLIGHT MEALS: Since the Spring of 1988, AMC has developed and implemented a series of healthy heart menus for their flights. These meals are prepared in their own in-flight kitchens. Snack menus cost $1.75 and include sandwich, salad or vegetable, fruit, milk or soft drink. Breakfast menus cost $1.75 and include cereal or bagel, fruit, danish and milk or juice. Sandwich menus cost $2.75 and include sandwich, fruit, vegetable or salad, snack or dessert, milk, juice or soft drink. Expect in-flight meal prices to change each 1 October. Also, prices are not standard worldwide. We reserve the sandwich and breakfast menus since we will be most likely departing in the early evening (1900 hours local time) and arriving approximately 0800 hours local time the next day in Germany. If you reserve one or more meals, they will be entered on your **AMC BOARDING PASS/TICKET/RECEIPT, AMC FORM 148/2 (see Appendix I)** or similar form, and your payment will be collected (cash or personal check). **You may bring your own snacks aboard; however, you should check with the Air Passenger Terminal representative regarding any restrictions that may be in place due to Department of Agriculture regulations. Whole fruit is a good snack choice if there are no restrictions. No alcoholic beverages for consumption on military aircraft are allowed.** Meals are free only on AMC commercial contract flights. **Wine and beer are for sale only on AMC commercial contract flights.** Specialized meals are made available for duty passengers only. You can request special food, and passenger service personnel will help if they can. **If you need special food, we suggest that you bring your own in order to maintain flexibility.** (See remarks above regarding snacks.)

"I sure hope he orders an in-flight meal!"

BOARDING PASS/TICKET RECEIPT: At this point, we have successfully passed the flight call/selection process. All of our travel documents have been reviewed and accepted for travel, we have registered for in-flight meals and paid the charge, we have checked our baggage and received our claim checks, we have not selected a smoking section, since smoking on all military aircraft flights (including both military and contract civilian flights) has been eliminated and lastly, we have been issued our Boarding Pass/Ticket Receipt which assigns our seats, verifies and documents the above items **and shows our one-time sign-up Julian date.**

Now we wait for our flight number and destination to be called for boarding. They are listed on our Boarding Pass and the Terminal Departure board as follows:

MISSION	EQUIPMENT	DEPARTURE
SWF-IFR3B	C-005A/B/C	162/97/1830L (2330G)

ROUTING		ARRIVAL
KSWF-KDOV-ETAR-ETAR-KDOV-KSWF		163/97/0730 (0630G)

16 - Military Space-A Air Basic Training

Due to space limitations, we will not decipher the mission numbers in this elementary text. The equipment is a C-005A/B/C, which is described in **Appendix M**. The departure date of 162 is Wednesday, 11 June 1997, 1830 local time which is also 2330. in Greenwich Mean Time (GMT) (Greenwich, United Kingdom). See **Appendices F and G** for a detailed explanation of GMT. The routing is Stewart ANGB (SWF/KSWF), NY joining the flight at Dover AFB (DOV/KDOV), DE, from which we are departing, to Ramstein AB (RMS/ETAR), GE, where the mission turns around, returns to Dover AFB, DE, and terminates at Stewart ANGB, NY. See **Appendix E** for explanation of location identifiers. Our arrival is 12 June 1997 at 0730 local time at Ramstein AB, GE, which is also 0630 GMT.

BUMPING: All Space-A travelers share a common fear that they will be "bumped." The bumping action means that after being manifested (accepted) at a departure location for transportation on a flight or at any station en route to your final destination, you are removed from the flight in order to have the mission essential accommodations for space required cargo and passengers.

"I've heard of getting bumped before, but this is ridiculous."

NOTE: You cannot be bumped by another Space-A passenger except Category I, Emergency Leave Unfunded Travel personnel and then only with the direction of local authority. The good news is that if you are bumped, you are placed on the Space-A list at the location where you are bumped **with the sign-up time, date and category that you received at your originating station**. (This information is included on the manifest.) As a practical matter, bumping occurs infrequently because passenger service personnel take every action possible (reorganize cargo or move cargo to other flights), within appropriate regulations, to preclude bumping one or more Space-A passengers.

PARKING: Since we will be about three weeks on our trip, we will want to park our car in the long-term parking lots at Dover AFB, DE. Long-term parking is in lots 1, 2, and 3, which are marked. Please ask the Space-A desk for directions or a map and procedures. The location is a short distance away (very near the passenger terminal) and the parking fee is approximately $5. There is an honor system for payment: lock the vehicle and keep the keys. Security police will patrol the parking lot often thereby providing security for your vehicle. This is another example of how wonderful it is to be a member of the Military Family. NOTE: Do not leave your car parked in the short-term lot. It will be impounded, and you will pay a towing fee and a fine to get your car back.

Military Space-A Air Basic Training - 17

PASSENGER SECURITY SCREENING: Boarding has been announced as 1730 hours local time on Wednesday. We will be flying directly/non-stop from Dover AFB, DE, to Ramstein AB, GE, on a **C005A/B/C Galaxy.** Our scheduled departure time will be 1830 hours local time, and we are scheduled to arrive at Ramstein AB, GE, at 0730 hours local time on Thursday morning. Similar to commercial airlines, **passengers are screened through electronic gates. Body searches may also be required.** All carry-on baggage, briefcases, purses, packages, etc., are screened before you are allowed to enter the secure boarding area. This security is for everyone's protection.

BOARDING/GATES: Space-A boarding processes are similar to commercial airlines. There is only one passenger class, and with the exception of some sensible and conventional practices, all passengers are boarded alike. Families with infants and small children are boarded first, passengers requiring assistance are boarded next, then Distinguished Visitor/Very Important Persons (DV/VIP) passengers (Colonel USA, USMC, USAF; Captain USN, USCG, NOAA; Director USPHS) in pay grade O6+ and Senior Enlisted Personnel (Pay grade E-9) of the Military Services are boarded. **Colonel (O6) Francis O. Hardknuckle, USA (Ret), is the ranking officer on today's flight, so our party will be boarded next.** Our boarding is followed by a general boarding of the remaining passengers. **(NOTE: Some terminals may not follow the DV/VIP ranking officer boarding and deplaning procedures.)**

"Hi. What have you got from Edwards to Travis next month?"

Gates: There may be a few conventional and some not-so-conventional obstacles to overcome. Today we are flying a **C-005A/B/C Galaxy aircraft.** We leave the boarding gate and enter a **"blue"** Air Force bus for a short ride to the aircraft parked on the ramp near the terminal. Today, courtesy truck stairs are not available. These stairs, when available, will allow easy access to the second deck passenger compartment of the C-005A/B/C Galaxy aircraft. We are instructed to walk through the forward cargo door of the aircraft and up a cargo ramp to a point near the rear of the cargo compartment. **There we will climb (not walk) up an almost vertical (approximately 18 feet), metal ladder with hand rails on both sides to the C-005A/B/C passenger flight deck.** Female passengers should preferably wear slacks (more about travel dress later).

18 - Military Space-A Air Basic Training

The passenger processing team and the aircraft crew will provide you with assistance. Elderly people, mothers with infants in arms and people with physical handicaps will have difficulty in climbing the passenger ladder. Space-A regulations require, however, that you must be capable of boarding and exiting the aircraft with limited assistance unless you are a <u>retired</u> **100% Disabled American Veteran (DAV) (requiring an assistant) and traveling with an assistant entitled to Space-A air travel within his or her own right. (Carefully note that 100% DAVs have the Space-A privilege if and only if they are retired and are in possession of a grey or blue ID card, DD Form 2.) Other less handicapped persons will be assisted in boarding and deplaning by the AMC staff.**

If you have a nonapparent handicap such as a hearing impairment, asthma, heart pacemaker, etc., please advise the passenger processing team at time of check-in. Frequently, the C-005A/B/C and similar aircraft will have mobile stairways (stair truck) for direct access to the passenger deck, but as indicated earlier, no stairs are available for today's flight departure. **This is probably the most challenging boarding encounter that you will find in your Space-A travel experiences.**

IN-FLIGHT

SEATING: The seats in these aircraft are conventional commercial airline seats; however, we immediately note that the seats face to the rear of the aircraft. This configuration is for safety purposes. The only difference you will notice from commercial airline seating, which faces forward, is a different sensation during takeoff and landing of the aircraft. Pillows, blankets, and other comfort items are available. **We hope you have brought along your own reading or other amusement materials (games) as there are no reading materials, in-flight movies or music on military aircraft.**

CLOTHING: Your clothing should be loose fitting and in layers. Wear comfortable walking shoes. Women should preferably wear slacks and a blouse or sweater. Take along a light jacket or coat depending upon the climate. Remember that western Europe is always a bit cooler with more moisture than the corresponding latitudes in North America. The layers of clothes will come in handy if you return, as a passenger not a patient, on a Medical Evacuation (MEDEVAC) flight where the temperatures are kept quite warm for the comfort of the patients.

REST ROOMS: The rest rooms on the C-005A/B/C are adequate in number and are similar to commercial airlines. They are **unisex** and you are expected to keep them clean after your use.

CLIMATE CONTROL: As mentioned, the climate in the cabin is similar to that of commercial airlines. The temperature can vary and you have been given blankets to make your travel comfortable. If it gets too cold or warm, you may ask the cabin personnel to adjust the temperature. Whether or not your wishes are complied with may depend on the capabilities of the aircraft, the crew and other passengers' needs.

Military Space-A Air Basic Training - 19

NOISE: This is not a noisy aircraft in the passenger cabin. You may experience some higher than normal levels of noise during takeoff, landing and special maneuvers and turns. At other times you should be most comfortable. There is no need for ear plugs on this flight (this is not true of some other flights, such as those aboard the C-130E aircraft). If you travel often on noisy aircraft, you should obtain form fitting ear plugs at your medical facility ear clinic. These plugs will improve your comfort and conserve your hearing. The crew may have wax, self-forming ear plugs. Ask for a set if you would be more comfortable.

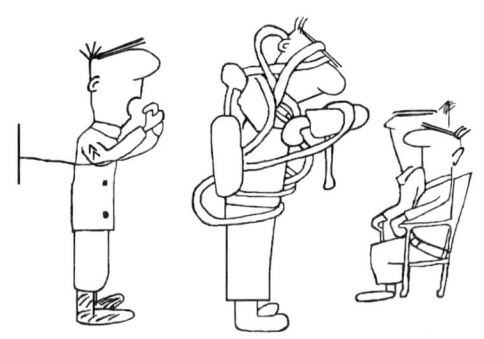

SAFETY: You will be required to use your safety belts as instructed by the aircraft commander or cabin crew. Only walk about the aircraft when allowed to do so. Never tamper with controls, doors or equipment within the aircraft. Listen very carefully to the in-flight safety lecture given by the cabin crew members prior to takeoff. Pay particular attention to the location of exits and identify the exit which is most convenient to your seating. Become familiar with the location of your emergency oxygen supply and life preserver since most of this flight will be over water.

"Airman Smith will demonstrate how to use the life preserver quick release. Fortunately we do not anticipate an in-flight emergency."

ELECTRONIC DEVICES: The playing and usage of radios, recorders, TVs, computers, etc., which may interfere with aircraft navigation, radar and radio systems is prohibited. As noted earlier, these items in your checked baggage must have the batteries removed.

SMOKING: Smoking is not allowed on United States military aircraft or military contract flights.

REFRESHMENTS: There is always fresh water, coffee and tea available in the galley. The meals we ordered will be served at the appropriate times given flight conditions. Our dinner sandwich meal will be served about an hour-and-a-half after departure and our breakfast meal will be served approximately one hour before our arrival.

Our flight departed as scheduled and all travel en route has been flawless. Further, we are told that we will be arriving at Ramstein AB, GE, as scheduled at 0730 Thursday morning. Wow! All this flying for "free."

POST-FLIGHT

ARRIVAL OF AIRCRAFT/CLEARANCE: We are notified that our flight will arrive on time. We are given immigration and customs forms to be completed for each passport and/or ID card holder. The flight attendants spray fumigation/insect repellent throughout the cabin as required by international health rule. After landing, our manifest and declaration of the health of the crew and passengers will be handed over to German immigration authorities or the United States authorities acting on their behalf. This is necessary to obtain clearance for the crew and passengers of our aircraft to disembark. Once clearance has been obtained, deplaning will begin as instructed.

"Air Mobility Command announces the immediate arrival of mission one six two. Passengers will be in the terminal in two seconds."

DEPLANING: Prior to deplaning, we will be given instructions regarding post-flight processing such as immigration, baggage claim and Customs. We're fortunate today in that we'll be deplaning through passenger level doors onto a stair truck and a short 50 yard walk into the new air passenger terminal at Ramstein AB, GE. **Colonel (O6) Hardknuckle USA (Ret)** is the ranking officer on our flight. He and his family will depart the aircraft first followed by a priority for deplaning designated by the flight cabin crew. In most cases, those families with children and other people in need of assistance during deplaning will be the last to exit. (**NOTE: Some terminals may no longer follow the DV/VIP ranking officer boarding and deplaning procedures.**)

IMMIGRATION: Next we must report to the immigration processing station/desk, and present to the German/US authorities our immigration/customs form and other travel documents. Sponsors will need their ID cards. Retired sponsors will also require a passport. Dependent family members will need their ID cards and passports. **All passengers must be present for this processing to verify their identities.** The authorities will examine your travel documents carefully. As part of the processing, they may also check for persons barred entry and other wanted persons. Passengers may be questioned about previous visits to Germany, the purpose of their visit, places to be visited and accommodations (place of residence) in the country.

We are delighted to find that all is in order for our family; our immigration forms and passports are stamped, and we are instructed to claim our baggage and report for customs clearance. We are lucky; our four bags are waiting for us on the carrousel. Colonel Hardknuckle has allowed us only one bag, that can be rolled or carried, per person. We move with ease to Customs Inspection.

CUSTOMS: The customs inspection is a breeze. We are not bringing any dutiable or prohibited items such as tobacco, coffee, tea, or alcoholic beverages into the country. Our

Military Space-A Air Basic Training - 21

customs documents are stamped, and we are now cleared to leave the terminal. Before we leave for our vacation, a very important task regarding our return Space-A trip should have our top attention.

REGISTRATION FOR RETURN SPACE-A AIR OPPORTUNITIES: We should verify our fax application for departure back to CONUS from Ramstein AB (RMS/ETAR), GE, if this is our planned return departure terminal (**it is a good idea for the sponsor, with everyone's travel documents, to verify our application for return air transportation while other members fetch taxis or attend to other arrival chores**). We can also apply at Rhein-Main AB, GE, or at any other terminal in Europe (Ramstein AB and Rhein-Main AB have joint sign-up). **A special caution! If you apply to return to CONUS from any European terminal (i.e., Ramstein AB, GE), and subsequently take a local flight from Ramstein AB, GE, (for example, a visit to Aviano AB (AVB/LIPA), IT, your application for CONUS and any other applications from Ramstein AB, GE, will be deleted from the computer based Space-A list.** NOTE: Under the new remote sign-up procedures Colonel Hardknuckle has signed up in advance by fax for his party's return air travel prior to arriving at Ramstein AB. This rule is in the Space-A DoDD and applies at any station worldwide. Once you depart on any flight from a station, all of your other applications for flights from that station are deleted from that station's Space-A roster system.

"Do you hear me George? I said take those stupid ear plugs out until we get on the plane!"

RETURN FLIGHT TO CONUS

As told by Linda Sue Hardknuckle, daughter: We took a local taxi at the terminal to the temporary lodging facility. We enjoyed dinner in the Officers' Club and a comfortable night in two adjacent rooms in the temporary military lodging (TML) facility, Bldg 305 Washington Avenue, C-011-49-6371-47-7345/7864. We had signed up immediately upon arrival at Ramstein AB, GE, for flights to Italy and Spain in order to retain our Dover AFB, DE, initial registration time and travel priority. The priority can be retained and is effective for a trip which continues in the same general direction from CONUS. In this case, we are continuing southeast to Spain/Italy. The countries must be on our CONUS sign-up and if active duty, we must be on leave.

SIDE TRIPS: We took the early morning "blue" bus to Rhein-Main AB because the Ramstein AB passenger personnel told us that there was a flight to Rota NAS

22 - Military Space-A Air Basic Training

(RTA/LERT), SP, with many open seats. We were fortunate to get this flight to Cadiz, Spain. On arrival **we were careful to obtain a "Letter of Entrada and a Base Pass" from passenger service personnel before leaving the base to insure our easy reentry**. This is a Spanish NB where the USN is a tenant under our Status of Forces Agreement (SOFA) with Spain. We also signed up for a flight to Capodichino Airport (NAP/LIRN) in Naples, Italy, which we took after our four-day visit to the Cadiz area.

The flight to Naples was aboard a C-130E aircraft with bucket seats along the side and cargo in the middle of the aircraft. The aircraft was very noisy, particularly on takeoff and landing/braking. The crew chief passed out **formable wax ear plugs to decrease the noise**. The ride was short, and it was a new and interesting experience. After two days of shopping in Naples, we departed Naples for Ramstein AB, GE, on a **C-009A/E Nightingale aircraft, MEDEVAC flight**, which was a special experience for my sister Loren who is studying nursing.

At Ramstein AB, GE, we checked our progress on the waiting list for CONUS. Our names had only moved up the Category VI waiting list from number 404 when signing up to number 314; however, our plan was to leave in approximately one more week's time, so we continued with our travel plans.

After a week visiting the Rhein and Mosel River areas via a major company rental car (Ramstein has Budget, Hertz, Powell's Auto, and Raule), we returned to Ramstein AB, GE, to discover that we were number 273 on the waiting list for CONUS.

There were two flights scheduled for the next day. The first was a flight to RAF Mildenhall (MHZ/EGUN), UK, and then on to Charleston AFB, (CHS/KCHS) SC. The second scheduled flight was to go directly to Dover AFB, (DOV/KDOV) DE, where we had left our car, and was exactly where we wanted to go. We stood by for the Space-A call for both flights, but there were a lot of emergency leave people in Category I, Emergency Leave Unfunded Travel, some active duty leave people in Category III, a few military personnel on permissive no/cost TDY in Category III and only 10 retirees in Category VI who were ahead of us on the list. Some of these retirees obtained Space-A transportation. We did not!

CIRCUITOUS ROUTING: After this failure and armed with tips from **Military Living Publications,** we discovered a flight scheduled for the next morning which was routed from Ramstein AB, GE, to Incirlik Airport (Adana) (ADA/LTAG), TU. The flight was scheduled to depart Ramstein AB, GE, at 1015 hours local time and arrive at Incirlik Airport (Adana), TU, at 1415 hours local time and remain at Adana for a 15-hour crew rest after arrival. The schedule for this mission was to fly the next day from Incirlik Airport, TU, back to Ramstein AB, GE, where the aircraft would remain three hours on the ground and then continue on to our desired destination, Dover AFB, DE. If we can be manifested, we will be flying our favorite C-005A/B/C Galaxy aircraft. (*We are manifested, with a new sign-up date because TU was not on our original sign-up at Dover AFB, DE. There are a few active duty Space-A passengers on leave who are returning to duty at Incirlik Airport, TU.*)

"We're going to NBO by way of NGU, TON, and SIZ."
We have learned another principal of Space-A Basic Training: **a straight route may not be the best route for Space-A Air Opportunity travel.** Circuitous routing is often used to get to your destination on Space-A. We are eager, risk-taking, Space-A travelers, so we go for it! **Please recall that our registration for CONUS from Ramstein AB, GE, will automatically be deleted from the system when we take the flight to Incirlik Airport, Adana, TU.**

Once we arrived at Incirlik Airport, TU, and signed up for our return flight to Dover AFB, DE, we lost our original Ramstein AB, GE, date/time sign-up and **picked-up a new date/time at Incirlik since we were changing direction completely and heading back to CONUS.** We remembered to list Dover AFB, DE, as our final destination. **Incirlik Airport was able to manifest us all the way to Dover AFB, DE, thereby allowing us to bypass having to terminate our flight at Ramstein AB, GE, and reapply for Dover AFB.** Otherwise, we would have been back where we started before going to Incirlik Airport, TU.

Gosh! The first leg of the trip worked as planned. After about four-hours flying time, we arrived at Incirlik Airport at 1415 hours local time. We departed the aircraft first. After showing our travel documents to Turkish and US Officials, we moved smoothly through immigration, claimed our bags and cleared customs. Colonel Hardknuckle, USA (Ret), applied for air travel for our group for the return to CONUS. We were 20-23 on the Category VI list for CONUS. We concluded that we had a very good chance of obtaining travel on this flight, which was scheduled to depart at 0445 hours the next day. This flight had an early show time of 0245 hours.

We had called from Ramstein AB, GE, after we were manifested to reserve our temporary military lodging so all was set. We took a taxi to our temporary lodging facility, Bldg 1081, 7th Street at Incirlik Airport, C-011-90-322-316-6786 (billeting office). Again,

24 - Military Space-A Air Basic Training

we found Incirlik Airport (the USAF is a tenant on a Turkish AB) to be a well-appointed facility with a splendid consolidated club complex for drinks and dinner and a very comfortable temporary military lodging facility.

The next morning we called the Space-A desk about one hour before show time to discover that our flight would not be departing until 1700 hours due to changes in cargo and other space-required needs. There were no other flights to Ramstein AB, GE, or CONUS prior to this time. So on the bright side, we had most of the day to spend as we pleased. The new show time was 1500 hours, but my dad, Colonel Hardknuckle, wanted to maximize our chances for travel; he set our personal show time at the terminal for 1400 hours.

In order to spend the day wisely and have some fun, different members of our family group planned the day's activities. Dad set up a day of tennis. Other family members arranged tours with the USAF Ticket and Tour Office of archaeological ruins and museums in the local area. A relaxing travel day was had by all.

We arrived at the passenger terminal promptly at 1400 hours. Our flight was posted as follows: leave LTAG/ADA, 180/97/1700, arrive ETAR/RMS, 180/97/2210. We knew from our **Space-A Air Basic Training** that we were scheduled to leave from Incirlik Airport (Adana), TU, at 1700. local time on Sunday, 29 June 1997.

"We went for broke. Quad fifties, twin forties, the works. Like I told ya yesterday, somebody's got to lead the troops. Remember Ike? That's what I told him. Know what he said" 'Go get 'em soldier.' How about that?"

RETURN FLIGHT: Luck and good planning were with us. The Space-A flight call was made and we were on the flight to Ramstein AB, GE. We had paid the $2.75 per person fee for the sandwich menus we ordered for this leg of the trip to Ramstein AB. Aware that we would have about seven-and-a-half hours' ground time at Ramstein AB, GE, before our flight continued on to Dover AFB, DE, we attempted to obtain billeting at Ramstein AB, GE, but nothing was available.

We were very fortunate to obtain temporary military lodging (TML) space at the Kaiserslautern East Community (Vogelweh) -Tel C-011-49-6371-47-7345/7864. Our best transportation option was a taxi, which we took straight to the Vogelweh lodging office. We rushed to bed because we had to be back at the airport for an 0400 Space-A call. We were smart travelers; we brought our toilet articles, sleeping attire and a clean shirt/blouse in our carry-on luggage, so we were prepared for the overnight in Vogelweh, GE, as our luggage was checked through to Dover AFB, DE.

Being cautious types, we made arrangements with the desk clerk for a wake-up call. All went well, and we met our early morning Space-A call. Since we were continuing on the same flight on which we arrived, we checked in with Passenger Service, signed up and paid for the in-flight meals, and received our boarding passes. We recognized some of the faces of Category VI people who were still waiting for transportation to CONUS at Ramstein AB when we departed for Adana, TU. They met the Space-A call but were not boarded on our flight to CONUS due to lack of available seating. We enjoyed our trip to Turkey and were now on our way home. If we had been unable to obtain military lodging, we would have had to use, if available, a pensione (small hotel) in the local area.

ARRIVAL AND CLEARING: The flight to Dover AFB, DE, was uneventful. **Before landing we were given immigration and customs forms to complete as a family group.** We completed the immigration forms for our passports and ID cards as a family group. Likewise, we completed the customs declaration as returning residents and we made an oral declaration since the value of goods which we brought into the country did not exceed $400 per person. **We were not bringing in tobacco, tea, liquor or any other exempted items. Also, we were not bringing in items for other persons.** We arrived on time at 182/97/1505L (also known as Tuesday, 01 July 1997, 1505). We checked through immigration, claimed our four bags and cleared customs.

In a stroke of good luck, my dad, Colonel Hardknuckle, obtained a local ride to claim our station wagon located in the long-term overflow parking facility. He met a Space-A passenger who wanted to hear of his Space-A experiences and who still had his car at the main terminal.

We met one of our friends, LtCol Zachary Sadbag, USAF (Ret), whose bag did not arrive with his flight. As a matter of interest, we inquired as to how this loss is handled. He told us that the Dover AFB, DE, Passenger Service personnel were most helpful. The procedure was similar to passengers who have lost baggage on commercial airlines. **He was requested to fill out an AMC Form 134, BAGGAGE IRREGULARITY REPORT. A copy of his baggage claim check (USAF Form 94) was secured to this form.** He was also requested to fill out an AMC Form 70, **RUSH BAGGAGE MANIFEST, specifying whether he wanted them to hold the bag for pickup when it came in or forward it to his home in the Washington, DC area at his expense.** LtCol Sadbag elected to wait for his bag which was scheduled to arrive on the very next flight from Germany in about two hours.

POST SPACE-A TRIP REPORT: We departed the terminal for a short, 2-and-3/4-hour trip via car to our home in Falls Church, VA. On the way home we compared notes on our trip which are to be submitted the next day to our dad, who will be preparing an **After Trip Report.** It will emphasize the Space-A lessons we have learned and will be circulated among our friends. We will also send it to *Military Living's R&R Space-A*

26 - Military Space-A Air Basic Training

Report® for possible publication in their reader report sharing section. This information will be very useful to us and others on future trips.

Linda Sue Hardknuckle

LESSONS LEARNED: The following key lessons were learned from the above overseas Space-A air trip with the family:

A. Plan your flight ahead of time to include information about desired departure location/station, destination/countries, routes of Space-A travel, schedules including overnight stops and flight conditions.

B. If you have a definite/required return date, a commercial backup ticket is essential.

C. Applications for Space-A air travel can be made for four countries plus "all" 60 days before travel is desired and at multiple departure stations in CONUS and overseas for both departure and return travel.

D. If you are in the station terminal and "travel ready" your chances of obtaining Space-A air transportation are considerably improved over reporting to the terminal only when flights are scheduled.

E. Travel light; each person should be able to carry his or her bags for at least 1/2 mile. Bags should have built-in wheels or strap on wheels. There are limited-to-no porters in the terminal area.

F. Buy in-flight meals or bring your own snacks. They keep you busy and help pass the time.

G. Wear loose fitting clothes in layers and ear plugs for comfort.

H. Verify your return registration at your destination station before departing for your travels.

I. Circuitous routing may be required to get to your desired destination on Space-A.

ONLINE?

One may reach AMC sign-up locations on the world-wide web at Military Living's homepage:

http://www.militaryliving.com

Click on "Friends on the Web" which will lead you to Space-A sign-up.

SECTION II

AN IMAGINARY SPACE-A AIR TRIP BY CONUS MEDICAL EVACUATION (MEDEVAC) FLIGHT

BACKGROUND

MEDICAL EVACUATION (MEDEVAC) FLIGHTS: These flights are flown all over the world in support of the medical programs of the Uniformed Services. The vital United States Air Force, Air Mobility Command (AMC) aeromedical airlift mission is implemented by highly trained medical technicians, flight nurses and aircraft crews which moved nearly 70,000 DoD patients on some 4,500, C-9, C-141 and C-130 missions during 1996. Medical evacuation missions include both litter and ambulatory patients. In addition to these patients, **thousands of Space-A air opportunity passengers were also served by the MEDEVAC system worldwide.**

THE MEDEVAC SYSTEM: There are several elements of the worldwide MEDEVAC system which operate in CONUS. Next, each major overseas theater of operations, i.e., Europe and Pacific, has its own internal and intra-theater MEDEVAC system. Lastly, there is a MEDEVAC system which operates between CONUS and overseas theaters. We have discussed Space-A travel between CONUS and overseas with return and travel in the European theater. In this section we will only discuss Space-A air opportunities in CONUS via MEDEVAC missions. **As our example, we will use an active duty Uniformed Service Member, First Lieutenant John A. Hardcharger, USAF, stationed in Northern California.**

CONUS MEDEVAC FLIGHT EQUIPMENT: The major aircraft used in CONUS MEDEVAC is appropriately named the **C-009A/E NIGHTINGALE.** This aircraft has been derived from the DC-9, Series 30 commercial airliner. The C-009A/E has been configured as an aeromedical airlift transport. This aircraft in this configuration has been in service in the USAF since August 1968. The aircraft accommodates a crew of three, medical staff of five, 40 litter patients or 40 ambulatory patients or a combination of both. More details regarding the specifications and performance of this aircraft are in **Appendix M. Two other aircraft, the C-130A-J Hercules and the C-141A/B Starlifter, have also been configured for aeromedical airlift and are used for long distance Theater and Intra-Theater aeromedical airlift missions.** Specifications, Configuration and Performance of these aircraft are also at **Appendix M.**

WHAT IS DIFFERENT ABOUT SPACE-A ON MEDEVAC FLIGHTS?

We will answer this general question by taking another round-trip on the Space-A system. With the help of **1Lt Hardcharger**, we will take another one of those favorite Space-A air opportunity trips. First, let's examine the special aspects of Space-A travel on aeromedical airlift (commonly known as MEDEVAC) flights. The seating for Space-A passengers on the C-009A/E Nightingale MEDEVAC flights is commercial airline type - reclining chairs facing the rear of the aircraft. **The C-009A/E is a very smooth-riding aircraft; however, for patient comfort, the temperature is kept at approximately 75 degrees and may be kept even higher for patient needs. Caution: wear clothes in**

28 - *Military Space-A Air Basic Training*

layers that you can take off or add as needed. **The temperature will only be adjusted for the comfort of patients.**

"Air Mobility Command announces the immediate loading and departure of flight number one to Kitty Hawk."

The Space-A seating is away from the litter patients, frequently in the front part of the passenger cabin. Litter patients are boarded first followed by ambulatory patients, Space-required (if any) and Space-A passengers. **A key item to remember is that at any time MEDEVAC flights can be diverted from their planned flight schedule without notice to pick up or discharge MEDEVAC patients.**

PLANNING YOUR CONUS MEDEVAC FLIGHT: The CONUS MEDEVAC system is **based on a revolving monthly (sometimes up to six months) proforma schedule which includes many stations.** These stations are visited on different days of the month depending upon station need for MEDEVAC (Aeromedical) Services. For specific details, please see *Military Space-A Air Opportunities Around The World Air Route Map* (**Military Living's Space-A Map**) and *Military Space-A Air Opportunities Around the World* (**Military Living's Space-A Book**). With these valuable tools in hand, 1Lt Hardcharger is ready to take his Space-A air trip.

As told by 1Lt Hardcharger: My plan is to travel from Northern California (San Francisco, CA) area, where I am stationed, to the East Coast of the United States (Washington, DC) then to Florida (Orlando, FL, area) and return to the West Coast (San Francisco, CA). I examine the MEDEVAC schedule carefully and determine that my Space-A MEDEVAC travel plan is indeed feasible.

I note from **Military Living's Space-A Book and Space-A Map** that I can take a flight from Travis AFB (SUU/KSUU), CA, on Sunday or Thursday to Andrews AFB (ADW/KADW), MD. The purpose of my leave travel is to visit relatives, see some fun places and be introduced by cousins to their friends. **I have my Air Force leave form signed by Colonel Michael Q. Topmissile, USAF, my project manager, and it is valid for 20 days.** I register for only CONUS destinations at Travis AFB, CA, by fax the day that my leave is effective. This means that I am eligible for any flight that departs from Travis AFB, CA, to a CONUS destination. It is reassuring to know that I can travel on any mission on any Services' aircraft.

Military Space-A Air Basic Training - 29

REGISTRATION AND DEPARTURE: I have registered for Space-A travel on Saturday, my first day of leave, at Travis AFB, CA, for CONUS. I have a registration for one person, Category III (ordinary leave), CONUS destination with my Julian date and time of registration from my fax transmission receipt (**see Appendix B** for an explanation). To improve my chances for a Space-A flight out of Andrews AFB, MD, I also fax a Space-A Travel Request to Andrews AFB, MD. I report on Sunday for a Space-A call for Andrews AFB, MD. Fortunately, I am selected for the flight. Wow! I am on my way and it is free. I reserve the snack menu (healthy heart menus) for $1.75 which includes a deli sandwich, salad or vegetable, fruit and milk or a soft drink.

ROUTING AND REMAINING OVERNIGHT (LODGING): I had called ahead to check on temporary military lodging (TML) at Andrews AFB, MD, using **Military Living's** *Temporary Military Lodging Around The World* book. Since I have called 24 hours in advance, I am given a confirmed reservation (Gateway Inn, 1375 Arkansas Road, C-301-981-4614) using my credit card. The flight to Andrews AFB, MD, is smooth and uneventful. Immediately upon arrival, I verify my fax Space-A Travel Request for Space-A air to CONUS. Next, I claim my bag in the passenger terminal, Bldg 1245, tel: 301-981-1854. (NOTE: AMC is making an effort to use the same line number (extension 1854) as the air passenger terminal information number at all AMC bases. This may take some time to accomplish.)

Due to the late hour of arrival, the shuttle bus is not operating. I have two ways to reach the billets: walk the approximately one mile or call for a commercial taxi to come on base. In the interest of saving money and since I have only one small bag, I decide to walk. It pays to travel light. You will have more flying options when traveling in CONUS if you keep your baggage under 30 pounds. The baggage limit on the smaller executive aircraft is 30 pounds.

I arrive at the TML and check in at Bldg 1375 Arkansas Road, which is a 24-hour per day operation. I have dinner at the Officers' Club in Bldg 1352, which is a short walk from the TML.

I leave on Monday from Andrews AFB, MD, for Keesler AFB (BIX/KBIX), MS. **The flight to Keesler AFB, MS, is diverted from our scheduled route to pick up an emergency MEDEVAC patient at Moody AFB (VAD/KVAD), GA, and this makes it a very long day for everyone on board.** After arrival, I register in person for CONUS (MacDill AFB (MCF/KMCF), FL) and claim my bag in the passenger terminal, Bldg 8153. I hitch a ride with a SMSgt, who is

"I wanted to be a pilot, but my mother wouldn't let me."

30 - Military Space-A Air Basic Training

stationed on base, to the TML check-in at the Inns of Keesler, Bldg 2101, where I obtain a room for the night.

I join a friend for a short ride to Biloxi, Mississippi, where we have dinner and return to the base. The next day (Tuesday) I take a flight from Keesler AFB, MS, to MacDill AFB, FL. On arrival at MacDill AFB passenger terminal, hangar 4, **I claim my baggage and register in person for CONUS so that when I am ready to return, I will be much higher on the Space-A waiting list.**

I reserved a rental car by calling ahead to C-813-840-2303, located at Bldg 17, Dayton Avenue, on base. My rental car is ready and I depart to spend a few wonderful days visiting relatives and enjoying Florida sights.

After a week in Florida, I am ready to head home to California. I take the Tuesday flight from MacDill AFB, FL, to Keesler AFB, MS, where I remain overnight. On Wednesday I take a flight from Keesler AFB, MS, to Scott AFB, IL. On Thursday I take a flight from Scott AFB, IL, to Travis AFB, CA, and home.

THE SCHEDULED MEDEVAC SYSTEM: Careful planning and coordination was required to reach my desired locations. The MEDEVAC system has been very reliable and has met my needs. The requirement to stop overnight several times was a different experience for me but very enjoyable. **This is a wonderful system for the unaccompanied individual Service member, active or retired, to move about CONUS.**

Given a short period of time you can go to almost any area in CONUS and return to your station with minimum waiting time. Please also note that while you are registered for CONUS at a departure location, you can take any flight regardless of the type mission to any location in CONUS. **If you are patient, relaxed and flexible, any Space-A trip is easy.** If I had missed a leg on my flight schedule, I would have checked to see about other Space-A flight opportunities. Space-A air travel is not always a series of flights in a direct line. **It was a comfort to know that if all my Space-A plans fell through, I could use my active duty military ID card to get a big discount on a commercial flight.** Most military bases have travel offices, known as Scheduled Airline Ticket Offices (SATO), or you can call the airline direct.

1Lt John A. Hardcharger

LESSONS LEARNED: The following key lessons were learned from an imaginary Space-A trip by CONUS Medical Evacuation (MEDEVAC) flight:

A. The CONUS MEDEVAC system is comprehensive and reliable for Space-A travel and is ideal for sponsors flying in CONUS.

B. MEDEVAC flights are comfortable and smooth but tend to be warmer in the cabin than other flights. Wear clothes in layers.

C. These flights frequently require overnight stops to reach your desired destination.

D. You can intermix MEDEVAC flights with other types of flights in order to reach your destination.

Military Space-A Air Basic Training - 31

SECTION III

NATIONAL GUARD AND RESERVE PERSONNEL ELIGIBLE FOR SPACE-A AIR TRAVEL

NATIONAL GUARD AND RESERVE PERSONNEL: All National Guard and Reserve personnel are eligible for Space-A air transportation with the exception of those who are not receiving pay or have not completed their requirements for retirement. First, let us look at the seven Uniformed Services to see which Services have National Guard and Reserve components. There are Army and Air Force National Guard components; but there are no National Guard components in the other five Uniformed Services. There are active Reserve components in the Army, Navy, Marine Corps, Coast Guard and Air Force. There are no active Reserve components in the USPHS or NOAA.

ACTIVE DUTY STATUS RESERVE COMPONENT MEMBERS: In order to be classified as an active duty status Reserve component member, you must be a full-time member of a National Guard or Reserve Unit or drill independently and receive National Guard/Reserve pay. This means that you drill or train with your National Guard or Reserve unit on a regular basis, you are in active status and you receive pay for your attendance at drills or training sessions. You may be an officer, warrant officer or enlisted grade. This describes the active duty status Reservist of all the Uniformed Services (Armed Services).

RETIRED RESERVISTS (GRAY AREA): National Guard and Reserve members of the Uniformed Services (Armed Services) cannot receive full retirement status until they attain age 60. **When Reserve component personnel, who have not attained age 60, receive their official notification of retirement eligibility, they may continue to travel by Space-A air as Reservists.** The date that Reservists receive official notice of retirement eligibility until they reach the age of 60 and are officially retired is known as the "Gray Area." When the retired Reservist reaches age 60, he or she is fully retired and receives the DD Form 2, Blue ID card and begins to receive retired pay. At this point the retired Reservist has all the benefits of any retired member of the Uniformed Services. Family members (Dependents) of active duty status Reserve component members and retired Reservist (Gray Area) are not eligible to fly Space-A until their sponsors are fully retired at age 60 and receiving retired pay.

DOCUMENTATION REQUIRED FOR NATIONAL GUARD AND RESERVE COMPONENT PERSONNEL TO FLY SPACE-A: First, Reserve component personnel must have their DD Form 2, Red ID. Second, they must have a copy of **DD Form 1853, AUTHENTICATION OF RESERVE STATUS FOR TRAVEL ELIGIBILITY, signed by their unit commander within the past 180 days (Appendix H is a copy of DD Form 1853).** Gray Area retirees must have their DD Form 2, Red ID card and a copy of their official notification (letter) of retirement eligibility. **A copy of DD Form 1853 is not required for Gray Area retirees.**

32 - Military Space-A Air Basic Training

NATIONAL GUARD AND RESERVE TRAVEL - GEOGRAPHY AND DEPENDENTS: National Guard and Reserve component members may travel in CONUS and between Alaska, Hawaii, Puerto Rico, the US Virgin Islands, American Samoa and Guam (Guam and American Samoa travelers may fly via Hawaii). **Except for National Guard and Reserve retirees aged 60 and above, National Guard and Reserve personnel may not travel Space-A to a foreign country.** The above geographic restrictions on Reserve component personnel travel also apply to the Gray Area Reserve component retiree.

National Guard and Reserve component personnel cannot be accompanied by **dependents** (as a minor exception, when Reserve component personnel are on active duty for training overseas, which is a regular active duty status, their dependents may accompany them on Space-A air travel within the overseas area). Gray Area retirees cannot be accompanied by their dependents prior to attaining age 60 and receiving full retirement and their DD Form 2, Blue ID card. **At this point their dependents will also be eligible for the DD Form 1173 Uniform Service Identification and Privilege Card reflecting the retired status of the sponsor.**

THE SCOPE OF NATIONAL GUARD AND RESERVE SPACE-A TRAVEL: Although there is a restriction against National Guard and Reserve personnel traveling to foreign countries, there are many exciting places to visit. Also, from these overseas (OCONUS) points, you can continue your travels to many foreign countries at a minimum expense. For example, American Samoa is 3/4 of the way to Australia/New Zealand. Likewise, Puerto Rico and the US Virgin Islands open up to you the entire Caribbean area. Guam is on the doorstep of Asia; Japan, the Philippines, Taipei, the Pacific Islands and Indonesia are nearby. A Space-A flight to Alaska places the traveler near to Japan and Korea in the northern Pacific. Of course, there are also the foreign countries bordering CONUS which you can easily visit.

AN IMAGINARY SPACE-A AIR TRIP BY NATIONAL GUARD AND RESERVE PERSONNEL

TRIP PLANNING

AN IMAGINARY SPACE-A AIR TRIP BY NATIONAL GUARD AND RESERVE PERSONNEL: This Space-A trip will be taken by **Sergeant (SGT), E-5, Roy L. Straitlace, USANG**, DC National Guard (who lives in Washington, DC) and **Staff Sergeant (SSgt), E-5, Kathleen L. Truelove, USAF Reserve**, Pope AFB, NC (who lives in Fayetteville, NC). They met during Operation Desert Storm at a United Services Organization (USO) canteen and have stayed in close contact since that time. Now they have planned a Space-A air trip to Puerto Rico where they will have a joint vacation and hopefully get to know each other better under more normal conditions.

ROUTING: SGT Straitlace checks **Military Living's** *Military Space-A Air Opportunities Air Route Map* and *Military Space-A Air Opportunities Around the World* **book** and finds that there are almost daily flights from the **Washington Naval Air Facility (NAF) (NSF/KNSF), DC, located at Andrews AFB, MD, to Norfolk NAS**

Military Space-A Air Basic Training - 33

(NGU/KNGU), VA. His review of Space-A air opportunities reveals that there are also numerous flights from **Norfolk NAS, VA, to Roosevelt Roads NAS (NRR/TJNR), PR.** As he continues to scan his Space-A Air Opportunities book, he sees that there are two flights each month from Andrews AFB, (ADW/KADW), MD, via Norfolk NAS, VA, to Roosevelt Roads NAS (NRR/TJNR), PR. There is also one direct flight each month from ADW/KADW to NRR/TJNR. Knowing the value of prior planning, SGT Straitlace also checks return flights because he must return within 10 days to his civilian job as a Federal Security Guard at a DoD agency in Washington, DC. He notes that there is a MEDEVAC flight from Roosevelt Roads NAS, PR, through Norfolk NAS, VA, to Andrews AFB, MD, arriving on the first and fourth Wednesday and the second Tuesday. Also, there are numerous flights from Roosevelt Roads NAS, PR, to Norfolk NAS, VA. To reconfirm the non-scheduled Navy link of his planned route from Washington NAF, DC, to Norfolk NAS, VA, and return, **SGT Straitlace calls the Washington NAF at Andrews AFB, east side, Bldg 3198, tel: 301-981-2740-2744, where he speaks with PO1 Norman Scuppers, USN, who assures SGT Straitlace that there are frequent flights with numerous Space-A seats on this route.** SGT Straitlace discovers that most of the aircraft on this route are the following types: C-009 A/E Nightingale, C-21A Executive Aircraft, C-130 A-H Hercules and P-3C-Orion.

Using **Military Living's Space-A book and map, Staff Sergeant Truelove finds that there are many flights each month from Pope AFB (POB/KPOB), NC, to Norfolk NAS, VA, which continue on to Roosevelt Roads NAS, PR.** Most of these flights are via C-130E mixed passenger/cargo missions. As the result of her active duty in the Persian Gulf area, SSgt Truelove has her own form-fitted ear plugs and also has some experience flying the C-130E aircraft. At SGT Straitlace's insistence, she checks the return flights because she, too, must be back in 14 days to report for a new job that she has obtained as a medical technician at an area hospital. Luck is with everyone, and there are many return flights from Roosevelt Roads NAS, PR to Pope AFB, NC through Norfolk NAS, VA.

APPLICATION FOR SPACE-A TRAVEL: The two sergeants apply for air travel at their respective locations. SGT Straitlace applies in person for air travel at both the Washington NAF, DC, and at Andrews AFB, MD. SGT Straitlace has learned from **Military Living's Space-A book that Space-A seats not used by the NAF are offered to Andrews AFB, and vice versa.** In order to cover any destinations that he may need, SGT Straitlace applies for travel to CONUS, Puerto Rico and the US Virgin Islands. He also lists "ALL" as one of his five possible destinations as protection to provide for any circuitous routing which will get him to his desired destination.

Following SGT Straitlace's lead, SSgt Truelove applies in person for air travel at Pope AFB, NC. She applies for travel to CONUS, Puerto Rico, the US Virgin Islands and "ALL."

Both sergeants also send a fax of their Space-A Travel Request (AMC Form 140, Feb 95) with a copy of their authenticated DD Form 1853, Authentication of Reserve Status for Travel Eligibility, to air passenger terminal Roosevelt Roads NAS (NRR/TJNR), PR, for registration for return travel to CONUS. This will give them a higher position on the Space-A register than if they wait until they are in Puerto Rico to apply for return Space-A air travel to CONUS.

34 - Military Space-A Air Basic Training

THE OUTBOUND TRIP

Our sergeants are all set to go. It looks like Tuesday is the best day to travel from Norfolk NAS, VA, to Roosevelt Roads NAS, PR. SSgt Straitlace reports to the Washington NAF, DC, early on Monday for four flights that will be departing during the day for Norfolk NAS, VA. SGT Straitlace obtained the above flight departure information by calling the Washington NAF after 2200 hours on Sunday. **An early morning flight is his on a C-009A/E Nightingale which delivers him to the Norfolk NAS, VA, before 1000 hours on Monday. Before leaving the terminal, he registers for Puerto Rico and is told that there will be two flights on Tuesday.**

OVERNIGHT: SGT Straitlace obtains billeting at the enlisted billeting office, Bldg 1-A, Pocahontas and Bacon Streets, tel: 757-444-2839 for one night. He calls SGT Truelove from the NCO Club, where he has dinner and tells her about his trip to Norfolk, VA. SSgt Truelove plans to report for both flights at Pope AFB, NC, to Norfolk VA. Of course, SGT Straitlace will be at the Norfolk NAS to meet her.

MEETING: SSgt Truelove is not on the first flight, a C-130E. Meanwhile, a flight to Roosevelt Roads NAS, PR, arrives. SGT Straitlace, a good Space-A traveler, follows the rule of **"see flight, take it,"** and he arrives in Puerto Rico before she does! SSgt Truelove does make the second flight, another C130-E, and continues on to Puerto Rico. SGT Straitlace is waiting to take them to San Juan (about 50 miles northwest) by bus. **Before leaving the airport, they both confirm that the passenger terminal has received their fax application for return flights to CONUS and that their requests have been entered into the Space-A register.**

VACATION: They have reserved adjoining rooms for the first three nights in a San Juan hotel, which grants special military rates. After they become oriented to the island, they plan several trips to the interior rain forest and beautiful beaches. **They have an enjoyable vacation and discover a greater than expected renewal of their friendship. In that vein, they also plan their engagement announcement.**

RETURN FLIGHT

The two sergeants keep checking back with the Space-A desk at the Roosevelt Roads NAS and find that there is a flight one week from the following Tuesday. When they report to the passenger terminal travel ready, they find that their names are near the top of the waiting list. They are both selected for the flight, which is another C130-E. The flight is routed from Roosevelt Roads NAS to Norfolk NAS, VA, and on to Pope AFB, NC. SGT Straitlace departs the flight at Norfolk NAS, VA. He registers for a flight which departs the next day to CONUS and remains overnight at the Naval Base BEQ. **The next morning, Wednesday, SGT Straitlace catches a C-21 flight directly to the Washington NAF, DC. He was able to take this flight on a small executive aircraft because his luggage did not weigh more than 30 pounds.**

Military Space-A Air Basic Training - 35

REFLECTIONS: National Guard and Reserve members and their dependents are not allowed to fly Space-A to foreign counties until they reach age 60 and are retired; however, they can have lots of fun flying by Space-A in CONUS and to and from United States Possessions overseas, such as Puerto Rico, "the star of the Caribbean."

Ed's Note: The following legislation has passed the US House of Representatives. A similar bill must be introduced by the US Senate and passed, submitted to Joint Conference, approved and sent to the president and approved for this legislation to become law. Subscribe to Military Living's R&R Space-A Report® to track the progress of this legislation.

H.R. 1119

National Defense Authorization Act for Fiscal Year 1998 (Passed by the US House of Representatives)

SEC. 656. SPACE AVAILABLE TRAVEL FOR MEMBERS OF SELECTED RESERVE.

(a) IN GENERAL-Chapter 157 of title 10, United States Code, is amended by adding at the end of the following new section:

Sec. 2646. Space available travel: members of Selected Reserve

(a) AVAILABILITY-The Secretary of Defense shall prescribe regulations to allow members of the Selected Reserve in good standing (as determined by the Secretary concerned), and dependents of such members, to receive transportation on aircraft of the Department of Defense on a space-available basis under the same terms and conditions as apply to members of the armed forces on active duty and dependents of such members.

(b) CONDITION ON DEPENDENT TRANSPORTATION-A dependent of a member of the Selected Reserve may be provided transportation under this section.

LESSONS LEARNED: The following key lessons were learned from an imaginary Space-A air trip by National Guard and Reserve personnel:

A. In addition to ID cards, Reservists require DD Form 1853, Authentication of Reserve Status for Travel Eligibility or Letter of Retirement Eligibility if in the "Grey Area."

B. Reservists cannot travel to a foreign country until they are age 60 and receiving retired pay.

C. Reservists can fly to US Possessions which position them near foreign countries at considerably reduced cost.

D. A law is pending to allow Reservists to travel on Space-A under the same terms and conditions as active duty.

E. If there is a flight going in the direction of your destination - TAKE IT!

36 - Military Space-A Air Basic Training

SECTION IV

AN IMAGINARY SPACE-A AIR TRIP TO AUSTRALIA AND NEW ZEALAND

TRIP PLANNING

The trip from CONUS or Hawaii to Australia and New Zealand has become a highly valued and sought-after travel experience by an ever increasing number of Uniformed Services members and their eligible family members. When one thinks about the Australia and New Zealand travel destination it brings to mind time-consuming travel and long distances between modern cities; however, it also brings to mind English speaking countries with unique customs and culture, exotic plants and animals, vast deserts and alpine mountains, 20th to 21st century modern infrastructure, industry, commerce and capitalism and best of all, democratic republics based on the rule of law. Does this sound like a place you would want to visit? There is much more to come. Let me mention up front, **the airfare via Space-A air opportunities is free.** We will discuss specific exciting travel sites and activities as we move along in this imaginary (near true) Space-A journey.

The routes on the Australia and New Zealand routing (stations visited) are stable and change infrequently. This route is flown to Australia in support of US Air Force satellite tracking and related missions and to New Zealand in support of US Navy Antarctica research and related matters. All of the stations along this route are small in size, remote (except Christchurch Naval Station) and have very limited support facilities. Travelers on this route should take special note of the above point and not expect extensive local military logistical and related support.

This trip is being made by Sergeant First Class (SFC) John Q. O'Neary, US Army (USA) (Ret) and his new bride of one year Donna Lasagna-O'Neary. When SFC O'Neary was on active duty, he traveled extensively in CONUS, Europe, Hawaii, Japan, Korea and Vietnam. Donna has never traveled outside the CONUS. They are both looking forward to a new adventure together to celebrate their first wedding anniversary. The following is the O'Neary's account of their trip to Australia/New Zealand:

We both study carefully the *Military Space-A Air Opportunities Around The World* book, primarily using the Location Identifiers and Cross-Reference Index, and the *Military Space-A Air Opportunities Air Route Map*. Our study disclosed that the best departure locations/stations in CONUS for Australia and New Zealand are McChord AFB (TCM/KTCM), WA, and Travis AFB (SUU/KSUU), CA, in terms of favorable routing and frequency of flights.

We discover that there are two distinct routes from the west coast of CONUS to Australia and New Zealand. The flights that depart McChord AFB (TCM/KTCM), WA, each Sunday fly the following route: McChord AFB, WA, to Travis AFB (SUU/KSUU), CA, to Hickam AFB (HIK/PHIK), HI, to Pago Pago IAP (PPG/NSTU), AS, to Christchurch IAP (CHC/NZCH), NZ, to RAAF Richmond (RCM/YSRI), AU, to

Military Space-A Air Basic Training - 37

Woomera Air Station (UMR/YPWR), AU (mission turn around point), to RAAF Richmond to Christchurch IAP to Pago Pago IAP to Hickam AFB to McChord AFB. The entire mission is accomplished over an eight day period. For identification purposes we will call this route #l.

The second route departs Travis AFB, CA, each Friday and flies the following route: Travis AFB to Hickam AFB to Pago Pago IAP to RAAF Richmond to Alice Springs Airport (ASP/YBAS), AU (mission turnaround point), to RAAF Richmond to Pago Pago IAP to Hickam AFB to Travis AFB. The entire mission is accomplished over a seven day period. For identification purposes we will call this route #2.

We have been advised by previous travelers to Australia/New Zealand to travel first to Australia then to New Zealand as part of the return to the United States; therefore, we elect to pick up our flight on route #2 at Travis AFB, CA. We note that trips to Australia/New Zealand originate at Travis AFB on Fridays (route #2) and Sundays come through Travis AFB (route #1), another reason for selecting Travis AFB as a starting point. This departure location will give us two chances at a Space-A departure for our desired travel destination within a three day period.

We note that Appendix B: Personnel Entrance Requirements of the Space-A Air Opportunities book, shows that a passport and Australian Electronic Travel Authority (ETA) is required for Australia and a passport without visa is required for New Zealand (if staying less than 90 days). The ETA is obtained by calling the immigration section, Australian Embassy C-202-797-3145 and giving the information from the title pages of your US passports. The address is: Embassy of Australia, 1601 Massachusetts Avenue NW, Washington, DC 20036.

We live in San Clemente, CA, which is midway between Los Angeles and San Diego. Since dependents cannot fly point-to-point in the CONUS (except with the active duty sponsor when on emergency leave or house hunting incidental to a PCS), we are required to utilize a flight which will transport our dependents outside of CONUS. We check the Space-A Air Opportunities book and find that there is a flight which departs March Air Reserve Base (RIV/KRIV), CA (near Riverside, CA), each Tuesday and flies to Travis AFB, CA, and the same aircraft and mission continues on to Hickam AFB, HI, in route to other Pacific area stations. Also there are infrequent flights to Hawaii from North Island NAS (NZY/KNZY), CA (near San Diego, CA). These flights meet the requirement to transport our dependents outside of CONUS. Once outside of CONUS, dependents may move around in the overseas theaters freely with their sponsors.

If we can get a flight from Southern California to Hawaii, we can join the Australia/New Zealand flight at Hickam AFB, HI. We will also need to get a flight from Hawaii to Southern California on our return to CONUS. We learn from Military Living Publications that it is more difficult to join the Australia/New Zealand flight at Hickam AFB, HI, than Travis AFB, CA, or McChord AFB, WA. In order to reduce the risk of not obtaining a flight to our target destination and also have more flexibility at the departure location, we decide to drive from San Clemente, CA, to Travis AFB, CA, with an overnight stop in San Francisco, CA. We have not been to San Francisco in many years and look forward to a renewed visit. It is 61 miles from San Clemente north to Los

38 - Military Space-A Air Basic Training

Angeles and 379 miles from Los Angeles north to San Francisco, or a first-day drive of 440 miles or about 8.5 hours including brief rest stops and changing drivers. Travis AFB in Fairfield, CA, is 50 miles northeast of San Francisco.

We fax our Space-A Travel Request, AMC Form 140, to McChord AFB, Fax: C-206-984-5659; Travis AFB, Fax: C-707-424-2048 and Hickam AFB, Fax: C-808-448-1503. We list the five countries (and overseas locations) in order of priority: Hawaii, American Samoa, Australia, New Zealand and "ALL" (we will take any flight going in our direction). This action is taken about 55 days before we plan to fly. We also send our Space-A Travel Request to the above countries for our return to CONUS. The faxes to the overseas return countries and areas (Australia, New Zealand, American Samoa and Hawaii) go out about 50 days before our desired return from overseas. The fax numbers are in the *Military Space-A Air Opportunities Around The World* book.

In order to become more familiar with the Australia/New Zealand area, we have, on the recommendation of Military Living Publications Editorial Staff, purchased the two Maverick Guides to Australia and New Zealand, both authored by Robert W. Bone, and published by Pelican (we could have also obtained these on library loan, but we wanted them for our trip). Roy Sr., an editor at Military Living Publications, evaluated the Maverick titles on a trip to our target area in 1989 (more recent editions are available). He found them to have extensive coverage of key travel locations and to be almost flawless in accuracy. We find that Australia and New Zealand are in the southern hemisphere and have reverse seasons to North America. We have planned our travel for late October which will be Spring in our destination area.

For the map enthusiast, RAAF Richmond, AU, is 45 miles northwest of Sydney, AU, and the coordinates are 151 degrees and 30 minutes east longitude and 33 degrees and 48 minutes south latitude. Christchurch, NZ (located on the eastern shore of the south island) is at coordinates 172 degrees and 30 minutes east longitude and 43 degrees and 35 minutes south latitude. The corresponding location in the northern hemisphere to RAAF Richmond, AU, is located in the North Pacific Ocean, 750 miles east of Tokyo, JA. The corresponding location in the northern hemisphere to Christchurch, NZ, is located in the Northern Pacific Ocean 500 miles south of the Aleutian Rat Islands, AK, and 1000 miles southeast of the port city of Petropavlovsk in Siberia, Russia.

We depart San Clemente very early on Tuesday in late October and arrive in San Francisco at the Marines' Memorial Club, 609 Sutter Street, where we have advance reservations. (We are the guest of a friend who has a life membership at the club.) Room prices are low here compared with other hotels in the area. There is a great rooftop restaurant and bar, theater, museum, library, athletic center with indoor pool, one block to the Powell Street Cable Car, Union Square and much more. After registering and obtaining a car pass, we park our car in a garage a half a block away on Sutter where the club has a discount. Our queen-size room on the 7th floor is newly decorated and very comfortable.

We take a cab to Tadisch Grill, our favorite seafood restaurant in San Francisco. Service is efficient and friendly with old world waiters. The fish is large portions of

Military Space-A Air Basic Training - 39

natural charcoaled west coast fish varieties—delicious beyond words and prepared just right. After dinner, we take a cable car (California Street line in front of the restaurant and transfer to the Powell Street line) to Fisherman's Wharf. We walk around a bit on the wharf to loosen up and listen to the street music. We end up at the Buena Vista on Bay Street overlooking the Bay for a few late night Irish coffees, which are reputed to be the very best in the world—after two it's the fog, big crowd of happy people that makes your head swim. The cable car turns around in front of the Buena Vista, so we queue up and are on the first car back to the corner of Powell and Sutter. It is a very short hike one block up the hill to the Marines' Memorial Club and to bed.

PRE-FLIGHT

After a great night's rest (Wednesday) and a good breakfast in the coffee shop on the first floor of the club, streetside, we check out, pick up our car, store our bags and head north over the Oakland bridge for Travis AFB. After entering the base, where we pick up a base map at the gate, we head for the Lodging Office, Bldg 404 Sevedge Drive, C-707-424-4779. We called on Monday and obtained a reservation starting today, Wednesday, through Friday. We will try to renew if needed. After check-in, we head for the Passenger Terminal, Bldg 3, open 24 hours daily, to check the status of our Space-A Travel Request and the flight to Australia.

We learn that the flight to Hickam AFB (continuing on to Australia) on Friday is on schedule. In Category VI (retirees and others) we are number 3 and 4 with only one couple ahead of us in this category. There are no emergency leave passengers in Category I, no EML leave in Category II, 20 active duty on ordinary leave, two on house hunting to Hawaii and one Medal Of Honor holder for a total of 23 in Category III. There are no Unaccompanied Dependents on EML in Category IV; there is one passenger on Permissive TDY in Category V. In our Category VI there are a total of 14 passengers. This means a total of 38 passengers. The Space-A desk clerk tells us that the terminal expects to receive about 48 to 54 seats. As indicated, our flight is a C-141B Starlifter, cargo mission (primary), which will be mixed passenger and cargo. We know that flights fill up as the departure time approaches, but we feel good about our chances for making the flight.

We decide to travel (about 20 miles) to the Napa Valley area. Our car seems to know its own way to the Robert Mondavi winery just north of the town of Napa. We arrive in time to visit the cellar tours, taste some wine and visit the wine shop where we buy a bottle of Coastal Chardonnay for our TML room. On the way back to Travis AFB, we stop on CA-29 two miles south of the winery and north of Napa at Mustard's, a trendy restaurant with delightful American and European food (mostly grilled). There is an extensive wine menu and the service is good and prompt. Try the garlic mashed potatoes. The charcoaled quail with mustard sauce in season is terrific. Home to bed after a great day.

We have breakfast at Burger King, Bldg 685 (Thursday) and then go to the passenger terminal to check on events of the night and our status. There are now two Emergency Leave passengers in Category I, but they may get transportation on other flights bound for Hawaii. There are now over 50 passengers in Category III, but two flights have been added for an early departure on Friday to Hawaii. Things are now getting more complicated, but

40 - Military Space-A Air Basic Training

we have faith in the system and hope for the best. Along with many others, we spend the afternoon doing laundry and writing letters to friends. We have a light dinner at the Enlisted Club and see an old movie on the VCR in our room. Early to bed for an early start tomorrow.

We are up early on Friday. I drop Donna off at the terminal, and I drive to long-term parking at the MWR Bldg 741, Ellis Street; the fee is $5 per week. I am fortunate to get a ride back to the terminal with a passenger picking up his car after arriving Space-A from Alaska. Donna has completed her breakfast at the terminal cafeteria and tells me that she has learned the good news that many of the Category III active duty passengers have moved during the night or early morning. The Space-A call for our flight is expected around 1000 local time. We visit the comfortable USO which is across the hall from the cafeteria in the passenger terminal building. The coffee and donuts are good, and we leave the USO a generous donation.

FLIGHT PROCESSING

Before we know it, the Space-A call is announced to begin in waiting area II promptly at 1000 hours. We have learned that there are 60 seats to Hickam AFB, HI. Of course we want to be booked all the way to RAAF Richmond, AU, if possible. The call moves right along. When it gets to Category VI, there are only eight seats left, and we are luckily booked to RAAF Richmond. We order and pay for our meals, our travel documents are carefully checked (passports must be good for at least six months) and we have visas for Australia. Our weight is recorded and our bags (with wheels) are weighed (tight cargo limits on this flight). We are released to report back in 30 minutes for boarding at 1120 hours local time.

"If we don't get out of here by tomorrow you take commercial to San Francisco and Honolulu, and I'll meet you sometime next month at RAAF Richmond."

IN-FLIGHT

We board a blue bus for the strip to the aircraft which is parked down the ramp about a mile. Colonel Stanford B. Leavenworth, USA (Ret) (descendent of the Leavenworth that the Fort is named for) is the ranking officer on today's flight. Families are boarded first and then Colonel Leavenworth followed by everyone else. We are seated near the pallets of cargo in seats facing the rear of the aircraft (for safety considerations). We hit our block time (when the aircraft starts its taxi for takeoff) of 1155 hours, and the aircraft is rolling down the taxiway. We are airborne precisely at 1215 hours as scheduled. The aircraft is very comfortable, and we are served lunch after about one hour of flying. Today's flight leg to Hickam AFB, HI, is scheduled for about five hours flying time.

We arrive in Hawaii on time and are told that we will have a longer than usual ground time of 33 1/2 hours. We will depart at 0110 Local Standard Time (LST) which is days out +2 or Sunday. We are fortunate to get a room at the Hale Koa Hotel (we spent our honeymoon here). It is now greatly expanded (new Maui tower with 500 rooms) and as wonderful as we remember. The beautiful beach is a great place to spend a layover in travel to our destination.

We get airborne on time for a scheduled five-hour and 50-minute flight to Pago Pago IAP (PPG/NSTU), AS. We arrive a few minutes late due to head winds and are met by the AMC ground service commercial contractor (Pritchard Airport Service), who gives us bus service to the Rainmaker Hotel (largest hotel on the island) for our estimated two hours and 15 minutes of ground time. We depart Pago Pago at 0915 local time for a six hour and 35 minute flight to RAAF Richmond, AU. When we arrive in Australia, we will have logged over 17 hours of flying time, days out +3 or the fourth day, and it will be 1210 hours on Monday (we have gained one day by traveling west across the International Date Line). Of course, we will lose this day when we return across the date line to Pago Pago, AS.

POST-FLIGHT

We clear immigration and customs at RAAF Richmond with little effort. Later in our trip, we will be leaving from here to fly over (east 1,000 miles) to Christchurch IAP (CHC/NZCH) -NZ. This is a Royal Australian Air Force Base where the USAF is a tenant. Everyone is very friendly and eager to be of assistance. We pick up a cab at the terminal for Windsor train station (about two miles). The train station is open from 0500-2400 hours daily with several trains into Sydney. We are in luck and get a train within the hour for a fare of $8 AU each.

OUR VISIT TO AUSTRALIA

We check the hotel board in the Sydney train station and pick a medium-priced hotel (The Russell) near the Rocks Area (old town Sydney) and waterfront which is also near the renowned Opera House. After a short taxi ride, we check in the hotel and select a nice room at $80 AU or about $59 US ($1.00 US=$1.35 AU). After we freshen up, we dress for a walk to the Rocks Area and dine at one of the excellent seafood restaurants in that area.

Australia is a very large country. In fact, Australia is almost as large geographically as the USA. It is clear that we cannot see the entire country in one visit. We decide on visiting the Great Barrier Reef near the northern tropical city of Cairns. I have been an avid diver since my first tour in Vietnam. We will also be visiting Alice Springs and Ayers Rock, which are Donna's view of the real Australia. We book our airline travel to start on Friday with the popular Ansett Airlines of Australia to Sydney-Cairns-Alice Springs-Sydney.

We enjoyed the QUICKSILVER catamaran on the Outer Barrier Reef Cruise out of Port Douglas. The trip on the Kuranda Rail up to the 2,000-foot-high Atherton Tableland (home of fruit and vegetable farms) was also exciting and colorful. Driving through the rich sugar cane fields on the way back to Cairns was very interesting. It is now Monday and the flight from Cairns out west to the center of the continent at Alice Springs is over a very sparsely populated area of Australia. Among other things, we visit the Royal Flying Doctor's Service headquarters in Alice Springs and a Camel Station on the bus (coach) ride to Ayers Rock, which is as big and all-imposing as we had imagined. As we head (fly) back to Sydney, it is Friday.

We call RAAF Richmond (as we have learned from the Space-A Air Opportunities book that we can telephone in for seats, Tel: C-045-88-5101) for seats to Christchurch IAP, NZ, and learn that the flight will be departing on Thursday and that we are near the top of the Category VI list. There is time for a side trip to the Blue Mountains, about 60 miles from Sydney. We take the train up to Windsor on Wednesday and spend the night as our flight is due to depart at 0845 hours on Thursday. We make the flight which is three hours flying time. Immigration and customs clearance is a snap, and we are on our way within the hour.

OUR VISIT TO NEW ZEALAND

We plan an overnight in Christchurch and have reserved a hotel there before leaving Sydney. This is the most English city outside of England, and it is true to its reputation. Again we realize that we can't see everything on this, our first trip; so we plan to stay on the south island of New Zealand and concentrate our fun there, which is still a large place. We plan to tour the Queenstown area, Milford Sound, Mount Cook and the Farley sheep farm country.

We map out a bus (coach) itinerary, which will allow us to see more of the countryside, and visit a travel agent. When we leave the agent, we are equipped with an exciting tour which will put us back in Christchurch a week from Thursday to catch the Friday flight to Pago Pago IAP, AS.

The all day coach run from Christchurch to Queenstown costs about $50 NZ and is about 25% of the airfare. The coaches are very comfortable with restrooms and music. Take your own reading materials and games. There are rest stops about every two-and-a-half hours. The scenery is wonderful. Our lodging was in a neat small motel right on Lake Wakatipu, a large S-shaped lake scooped out by glaciers millions of years ago. We got in town in time to take the cable lift to the Skyline Restaurant on Bob's Peak (great view, wonderful live music for dancing and good buffet food).

We took one of the first buses to Milford Sound, a memorable 75-mile trip to New Zealand's most famous natural feature. Milford Sound is an awesome fiord that resulted from prehistoric glaciers which melted and let in the sea to form the sound. We took one of the two-hour narrated boat tours with lunch for about $25 NZ. The boat goes all the way out to the mouth of the fiord and turns around in the Tasman Sea on the west coast of New Zealand. On the trip back to Queenstown we saw helicopters with nets catching wild deer in the area and placing them with sling loads in waiting 18 wheelers for movement to ranch patties and domestic ranching. We are reminded that Queenstown is a major snow skiing area during the winter months of July and August. It is Saturday night, and we leave tomorrow for Mount Cook.

Military Space-A Air Basic Training - 43

We are now traveling up the backbone of the south island. There are many hydroelectric dams on lakes and streams in this area which is the Alps of New Zealand. EnZed's peak in the Mount Cook National Park is over 12,400 feet above sea level. From the hotel at the base of Mount Cook, 5000 feet, we saw helicopters ferrying people to the summit for a day of skiing down the mountain. We journey on to Farley where our host for the Sheep Farm Stay meets us.

The sheep ranch is wonderful, and we go trout fishing in a lake for a big trout to cook in the smoker for lunch the next day. We help with chores such as checking the paddies for strays, fallen sheep, etc. The rancher sometimes makes his rounds from pattie to pattie in a Volvo with an electric flicker to open gates. Dogs play a big part in working the sheep. The rancher's wife is a great cook. All meals are served family style and very informal. The rancher's wife takes us on a shopping trip at a delightful ski sweater shop. One is impressed with the clean and pristine nature of the country. The lifestyle here is simple, uncomplicated, peaceful and very straight forward. Great country.

RETURN FLIGHT TO CONUS

We make it back to Christchurch on Thursday night. We check on our Friday flight and find that all is A-OK; we are on the flight all the way to Hickam AFB, HI. The flight goes directly from Hickam AFB to McChord AFB, WA. Our car is at Travis AFB, CA, and we have a request in at Hickam AFB for Travis AFB, CA. The flight to Pago Pago IAP, AS, is five hours and 35 minutes with two-and-a-half hours of ground time and then on to Hickam AFB with a flying time of five hours and 50 minutes. We spend the next two nights in the Hickam AFB, BEQ and get a C-005A/B/C flight out to Travis, AFB.

We pick up our car from long-term parking and head home. Wow! What a trip and the price was right. The destination and return airfares were free. We would do it again. See you in the terminals!

LESSONS LEARNED: The following key lessons were learned from an imaginary Space-A air trip to Australia and New Zealand:

A. Pre-flight planning to include research on the countries to be visited and attractions is indispensable to a good visit. Knowing where you are going, how to get there, what it costs and what to expect are all important to travel planning.

B. Pre-position your return request for Space-A travel at several locations in order to increase your chances of returning to your desired location.

44 - Military Space-A Air Basic Training

SECTION V

AN IMAGINARY SPACE-A AIR TRIP TO SOUTH AMERICA (CHILE AND ARGENTINA)

TRIP PLANNING

The trip from CONUS to South America and return is a very popular and unusual trip. This military airlift route has been established to support United States Embassies and political and economic interests in the region. Spanish is the official language in all of the South American countries with the exception of Brazil where the national language is Portuguese; however, English is a popular second language in the South American Region. Flights are less frequent on this route than, for example, the Central European and Middle Pacific routes. The routing (stations visited) on the South American trip is stable and changes very infrequently.

This trip is being made by **Hans Maltsmittle, Master Warrant Officer (MW-5), USA (Ret) and his lovely bride of over forty years, Gretchen Maltsmittle**. They have traveled extensively in Western Europe and the United States. Neither of them has ever traveled to the Caribbean, Central or South America. Both of them are very fluent in German and Polish. They both read and speak very limited Spanish. Their general health and physical mobility are good for their 65 years. The following is the Maltsmittles' account of their trip to South America:

The major personal objective of this trip is to locate relatives and friends who immigrated from Germany to the Lake Districts of Chile and Argentina during the 1920s and 1930s. The broader overall travel objective is to visit and learn firsthand about a new area of the Americas.

We carefully study the *Military Space-A Air Opportunities Around the World* book primarily using the Location Identifiers and Cross-Reference Index and the Space-A Air Route Map. Our study discloses that the best departure location/station in CONUS for Central and South American flights is Charleston AFB (CHS/KCHS), SC, in terms of favorable routing and frequency of flights among other things. The second-best CONUS departure location to reach our destination is McGuire AFB (WRI/KWRI), NJ.

Our primary destination is the Lake Districts of Chile and Argentina. The major towns on the Chile side (west) of the lakes are Puerto Varas and Puerto Montt; on the Argentina side (east) of the lakes are San Carlos and Nahuel Huapi. This lake area is approximately 580 statute miles south of Santiago, CH, and 875 statute miles southwest of Buenos Aires, AG. For the map enthusiast, the coordinates of Puerto Montt is 73 degrees and five minutes west longitude and 41 degrees and 50 minutes south latitude. For a reference, the corresponding coordinate in the northern latitude and longitude, is Torrington, CT, which is located in northwest Connecticut near the Massachusetts border. With this essential geographic information in mind, we are prepared to select the best routing.

Military Space-A Air Basic Training - 45

We can access the Lake Districts by flights which originate at McGuire AFB (WRI/KWRI), NJ, and fly to Charleston AFB (CHS/KCHS), SC, to Jorge Chevez IAP (LIM/SPIM), Lima, PE, to Arturo Merino Benitez (SCL/SCEL), Santiago, CH. This approach will take us south from Santiago to Puerto Montt and then east through the Lake Districts to Argentina. We also have the option of starting our trip via flights which originate at Charleston AFB (CHS/KCHS), SC, and fly to Brasilia Airport (BSB/SBBR), BR, to Ezeiza Airport (SAEZ/BUE), Buenos Aires, AR. We could then proceed southwest to San Carlos. Since we want to spend more time on the Chile side of the Andes mountains, we have selected Charleston AFB, SC, as our point of departure for Santiago, CH. As residents and natives of Lancaster, PA, this trip will require an approximate 625-mile automobile drive of about 14 hours, including brief rest stops.

We note that our entry and exit point in Chile is Arturo Merino Benitez Airport (SCL/SCEL) (Santiago), CH, and in Argentina is Ezeiza Airport (BUE/SAEZ) (Buenos Aires), AR.

We fax our Space-A Travel Request, AMC Form 140 to Charleston AFB, SC, C-803-566-3060/5808 and also to McGuire AFB, NJ, C-609-724-4621. We list the following five countries in order of priority: Chile, Argentina, Peru, Uruguay and Brazil. This action is taken about 55 days before we plan to fly. We also send our Space-A Travel Request to the above countries for our return to CONUS. The faxes to the overseas return countries go out about 50 to 55 days before our desired return from overseas. The overseas fax numbers are in the *Military Space-A Air Opportunities Around The World* book.

"Hello. Twenty-fifth Battalion? This is Corporal Atkins in CONUS. I'll have to extend my leave. All overseas flights have been cancelled."

We begin our car trip to Charleston AFB early on the fourth Saturday in October in order to provide time for any unforeseen delays in road travel. We have planned our trip for late October/November because the seasons in the Southern Hemisphere, where we will be traveling, are the opposite of those in the US; therefore it will be Spring in November. Several calls ahead to the Charleston AFB passenger terminal information office at C-803-566-3082/3083/3048 have indicated that the flight originating on the fourth Monday at McGuire AFB is on schedule and will depart Charleston AFB on days out +1 or the fourth Tuesday. The terminal has our Space-A application and reports to us that we are numbers two and three in Category VI. We trade off the driving assignment and arrive at the temporary military lodging (TML), The Inns of Charleston, 102 North Davis Drive, Charleston AFB, SC, C-803-552-9900, Fax: C-803-566-3394, reservation hours 0800-1700, where we have reserved accommodations for three nights. Our reservations are confirmed with a credit card for a late (after 1800 hours) arrival on Saturday.

We are early risers on Sunday and head for the terminal to confirm our Space-A application because among other things, we want to see what the overall waiting list looks like. Again we confirm that we are at the top of the Category VI list. There are no emergency leave passengers, seven active duty Marines returning to duty at various stations on our scheduled route, three foreign officers and their families (for a total of 12 seats), one retiree ahead of us in Category VI and four retirees below us in category VI. We calculate a total passenger load (manifest) of 26 seats. There may be some Space-A passengers from McGuire AFB, NJ, continuing on to South America. Looks like there will be a lot of room as our aircraft is scheduled to be a C-141B Starlifter cargo mission which is to be configured at McGuire AFB with airline passenger type seats, up front and facing to the rear plus many wrapped pallets of cargo.

We have a quick breakfast at Burger King and attend services at the Protestant Chapel on base. After Church we head for the golf course where I rent clubs and shoes and play a round of golf while Gretchen reads the Sunday Atlanta Constitution, "which covers Dixie like the dew," or something like that! After nine holes of golf, we have delicious hamburgers and beer for lunch at the club. We take a quick orientation drive around the base using the map which we picked up from the security guard on entering the base on Saturday night. We find the long-term parking, where we will be leaving our car, at Scott Street and Davis Drive across from the Child Care Center. The long-term parking is four blocks from the passenger terminal. We decide on a light dinner at a local restaurant, which was recommended by the golf pro, and afterwards head for our room to watch TV then early to bed.

On Monday morning we check the passenger information and our status at the terminal. There are no material changes. Confident that we have a good chance of making this trip, we leave the base to tour old town Charleston and lunch in one of the many seafood restaurants. After a super seafood luncheon, we take one of the walking tours outlined in a brochure which we picked up in the passenger terminal. This is real inexpensive sightseeing and healthful fun. We return to the base passenger terminal to check our status. The clerk tells us that all is the same except that eight government civilian employees with a lot of strange looking equipment signed in and will be accommodated as Space-Required passengers on our flight. The passenger load is growing, and we are told that we should expect the passenger list to increase as we near the departure time.

The early afternoon is spent in a laundromat doing our laundry and picking up some last minute supplies at the base exchange. About 1430 hours we go back to the terminal to see if our C-141B from McGuire AFB has arrived. The flight arrived at 1100 hours local time, and the aircraft crew will have a minimum 15 hour rest here before beginning our flight to South America. We learn that the show time is 0015 hours (Tuesday) which is three hours before the scheduled departure time of 0315 hours. We are told that three hours rather than the customary two hours of show time (reporting time before departure) is due to increased security for the flight; so we are early to bed at 1530 hours to make our show time of 0015 hours, Tuesday.

On Monday night we are awakened at 2300 hours by the 24-hour desk. We had packed before going to bed, our toilet articles are added to our carry-on bags, we grab a cup of coffee in the billeting lounge, check out and drive to the passenger terminal where I drop off Gretchen and the bags. I drive to long-term parking, find a spot under a light, lock the car and see a security guard car which I hail. He can't give me a lift due to police regulations, but he does point out the shortest route to the passenger terminal.

PRE-FLIGHT

"They sure have tightened security since I was here last."

I get to the passenger terminal by 2400, and we have time for a cup of coffee. We learn that there are 48 seats on this flight. The Space-A call begins promptly at 0015 with the familiar Space-A refrain "anyone desiring transportation to Lima, PE, Santiago, CH, etc., please assemble at the Space-A desk in the main passenger terminal." The NCOIC of passenger services, SMSgt Gomez, is managing the call. The Space-Required passengers, eight government civilian employees are processed first and given their boarding passes. Next there were four passengers from McGuire AFB who are processed, turning in their old boarding passes for new passes. There are no emergency leave passengers, Category I, no EML passengers in Category II, seven active duty passengers, Category III, no unaccompanied EML passengers, Category IV, 12 foreign officer passengers, Category V and the passenger who was ahead of us in Category VI did not show; we are processed next. Also there are six more passengers in Category VI who are processed for a total passenger load of 39. As you can see there are six Space-A lists, one for each of the six categories of travel.

During the in-processing, we have checked our two pieces of luggage with wheels, each weighing less than the maximum 70 pounds each. Also, we paid $2.75 each for breakfast and lunch meals in route to Santiago, CH, or a total of 4 x 2.75=$11.00. The paid meals information is recorded on our boarding passes along with our Julian sign-up date (retain all boarding passes until your trip is over). The flying time to Santiago is approximately six hours and 45 minutes. We go through a pre-boarding security check of both our checked bags and our carry-on bag; all is well. We have about 40 minutes to wait before boarding. Families with children are boarded first followed by an LTC from the Peruvian Army who is the ranking passenger on today's flight. There is a short walk from the passenger terminal to the waiting C-141B aircraft. About 15 minutes after boarding, we depart the ramp (block time) and move to the taxi-way entering the main runway to wait behind two other aircraft. We are airborne at about 0315 as planned.

IN-FLIGHT

Our breakfast meal is served at 0415 US EST. The aircraft has fresh coffee and water in the galley. The rest rooms are unisex and more than adequate. There are also blankets and pillows for our comfort. We have brought along our own reading materials and games (non-electronic), Gretchen has movie magazines and I have crossword puzzles. At 0900 we are served our lunch meal. The ride to Lima, PE, is smooth and relatively uneventful.

We arrive at 1000 hours local time (GMT-5, same as US EST) at Jorge Chevez IAP (LIM/SPIM), Lima, PE. There is no immigration and customs processing for us because we will not be leaving the airport. Our continuing flight to Santiago, CH, is scheduled to depart at 1315 local time with a gate call of 1215 hours.

We expect less jet lag since we are traveling north to south rather than east to west or west to east. In fact, from Charleston AFB, SC, to Lima, PE, we have remained in the same time zone, GMT-5. When we depart today (Tuesday) for Santiago, we will be traveling southeast from the GMT-5 time zone to the GMT-4 time zone.

We are checked in with our boarding passes from the incoming flight. Our bags are already on the flight, checked at Charleston AFB for Santiago, CH. In case of an unexpected stopover, our carry-on bags contained toilet articles, medications, night-shirts and clean shirts and underwear for the next day. Checking bags through is advisable anytime that you have an overnight in route to your destination.

POST-FLIGHT

After a flight of three hours and 15 minutes, we arrive at Arturo Merino Benitez Airport (SCL/SCEL) (Santiago) around 1630 local time; we have lost an hour as we are now in GMT-4 time zone. The immigration and customs processing is fast and courteous. We line up for a taxi into the city. Santiago is located in the center of the country and set between the Pacific Ocean and the Andes Mountains. The city has evolved as the country's political, commercial and cultural capital. The city's history and heritage goes back to the 16th century. Our hotel is small and near the 18th century cathedral and the main square.

After settling in our hotel, we take a walk through the city central, select a seafood restaurant from several recommended by the hotel. The shellfish cocktails (shrimp/lobster) are wonderful and cheap by US standards. The grilled game fish (probably tuna) is outstanding, and the chocolate pie is also wonderful with very dark coffee. The premium Chilean chardonnay with a medium oak cast is cheap and wonderful. The TV in the hotel lounge is in Spanish, so we retire for a long night's sleep.

Space-A is like a magic carpet!

OUR VISIT TO CHILE AND ARGENTINA

After a very restful sleep, (Wednesday) we have recovered from our mild jet lag, if any, and we go in search of a recommended English speaking travel agent. We learn of a tour through the Lake Districts of Chile and Argentina which terminates in Buenos Aires, AR - just what we want. The best part is that we can interrupt the tour at several points in the Lake Districts then continue on with a later tour. We buy the tour which departs the next day (Thursday) for Puerto Montt via air.

After a night in Puerto Montt, (Friday) we bus to Puerto Varas where we leave the tour to contact those relatives. Through leads we have, we are fortunate to contact two cousins, and they in turn know several other cousins and two uncles. A party is arranged for the next day (Saturday), and we are very excited. The party is a type of German festival with zither and accordion players (some dancing) and loads of German wurst, strudel, great Chilean wines and oh yes, beer. It is wonderful to establish contact with our distant relatives and best of all to be able to speak freely in our native German. We have invited our German cousins and uncles to visit us in the US, and we hope to host them there soon.

After three days (Monday), from our hotel along the festive rosebush-lined streets in the lakeside resort of Puerto Varas, we rejoin a new tour via motor coach which travels along the southern shore of Lago Llanquihue. We take pictures of the thundering Petrohue Rapids. We check the soaring Osorno Volcano as we cross Lago Todos los Santos by ferry. We continue by motor coach through an area of pristine wilderness adorned by emerald lakes, thick pine forests and snow-capped peaks. We stay overnight in the quaint village of Peulia which is on the Chilean side of the border on a lake at about 3,000 meters or 10,000 feet above sea level.

The next day (Tuesday) we continue our motor coach tour. We capture the splendid vistas of the surrounding lakes and mountains. This is a leisurely drive to Lopez Bay, Lago Moreno and the Llao Llao Peninsula. There was a brief stop at the border. Inspectors came on board the motor coach for a look around; the driver and tour guide had our passports and took care of the immigration and customs details. We arrived at the Chic alpine resort of Bariloche on the shores of fjord-like Lago Nahuel Huapi where we took an exciting chair-lift ride up to one of the lookout points at Gerro Campanario. This is the heart of Argentina's beautiful Lake District. We finish up the day's activities by admiring the famous chocolate factories - each built like a Swiss Chalet.

After a great night in the cabarets of Bariloche with a few great glasses of wine and some sleep, we are up and ready for our flight from San Carlos to Buenos Aires (Wednesday). We arrive by noon and immediately go on a leather shopping tour to seek out the best buys. After a night here in the hotel, our formal tour is over (Thursday). Now we are on our own for more travel and the return trip home.

Our return trip back to Charleston AFB, SC, is scheduled for departure the next Wednesday. On Thursday afternoon we call the AMC contact at the USMILGP, C-011-54-1-777-1207. We are assured that they have our fax and that it looks like there will be no problem in our making the flight. There is very little for us to do now except check the status of our flight again on next Tuesday and enjoy our visit.

We arrange a tour in our hotel to the pampas where we experience the atmosphere of Argentine country life as we visit an estancia (cattle ranch). We get acquainted with the lifestyle, folklore and traditions of the gauchos. An excellent barbecue lunch is served with the warm hospitality of the host before we return to the city.

For Saturday we have arranged a tour which starts at the Plaza de Mayo for a visit to the President's Pink House and the Metropolitan Cathedral. Also on the agenda is the historic San Telmo, the oldest neighborhood of Buenos Aires, the ornate Colon Opera House, the Recoleta district and the cemetery where Eva Peron is buried. The evening portion of the tour includes a typical Argentine steak dinner and a great performance of the latin tango.

Sunday is a day to attend church and rest. Argentina is a predominately Catholic country, so protestant churches are not easy to find. Our hotel recommends a church which is a short walk. We enjoy the singing in Spanish. In the afternoon we window-shop along the broad city boulevards.

We spend Monday and Tuesday searching for just the right presents for family members at home. The leather shops are plentiful, and the assortment of handcrafted leather goods is vast.

After enjoying several days of sightseeing, we are ready to go home. A call to the USMILGP in Buenos Aires confirms that all is well and that we will be on the flight departing on Wednesday for Montevideo, UG, Brasilia, BR, and terminating in Charleston AFB, SC. The flight to Montevideo, UG, is scheduled for only about 45 minutes. We are processed and join a passenger group of about 45 people. We depart on time at 1645 hours and arrive at Carrasco IAP (MVD/SUMU), Montevideo, UG, at 1700 hours local time. There is a 17-hour ground time/crew rest scheduled for Montevideo, UG. We are processed through immigration and customs. The processing team recommends a local hotel, a short ride from the airport. We have dinner in the hotel, read our pulp novels and retire early. After breakfast, we catch a taxi to the airport for a show time of 0900 hours and a departure of 1015 hours. We check in with our boarding pass of the previous day and pay for our meals in route to Brasilia, BR, and Charleston AFB, SC.

RETURN FLIGHT TO CONUS

We drop off passengers and pick up new passengers as we fly north back to the US. The longest leg of the flight is from Brasilia Airport (BSB/SBBR), Brasilia, BR, to Charleston AFB (CHS/KCHS), SC, eight hours and 45 minutes.

We arrive back at Charleston AFB, SC, at 0145 hours on Friday. We go through immigration and customs. We have a few leather items to declare, far less than our $400 per person duty free exemption.

I walk to long-term parking to claim our car. Gretchen waits at the terminal with the luggage. It is Friday. We will be home tomorrow, Saturday, just three weeks since we departed. Wow, what a trip! The price was right; most of the airfares were free.

LESSONS LEARNED: The following key lessons were learned from an imaginary Space-A air trip to South America (Chile and Argentina):

A. The most important step in successful Space-A air travel is to plan ahead.

B. Check frequently on the Space-A roster/waiting list. New people with higher priorities can and do join the waiting list. Know your chance of obtaining a particular flight; this gives you the flexibility to stay or not stay in the terminal and to join other flights at this or nearby stations.

C. Learn the local ground rules regarding registration via telephone, reporting times, Space-A calls, processing, block and departure times.

SECTION VI

READER TRIP REPORTS

Many readers have told us of their successful Space-A trips. The following Reader Trip Reports will provide a guideline for you on using Space-A to various locations throughout the world. *Please remember that prices, times, routing and other details in Reader Trip Reports should be viewed as things that can, and do, change.*

HOPS AND DREAMS
STAFF SERGEANT GOES ON VACATION MISSION 'SPACE-A' TO ALAMO COUNTRY

Andrews Air Force Base ... my hands perspired as I clutched the small slip of paper and waited for my name to be called. I wasn't alone; there were nearly 20 others in the room who were on pins and needles as well.

Once in a while we'd break the silence with small talk to help pass the time away. Finally, after many long hours of waiting, the word had come and the news wasn't good. I wouldn't be one of the lucky few to board the C-9 jet headed to sunny San Antonio, my summer vacation destination.

When choosing to take a military hop, one should keep in mind that the experience can be very rewarding or extremely torturous. It all depends on your lucky number. You make plans, pack your bags and wait.

Several other active duty and retired service members had gone to Andrews Air Force Base that morning, each hoping to get a seat aboard the MEDEVAC flight, but only a select few actually did.

Nevertheless, we all were on our own special missions: Rogelio, an air guardsman, wanted to visit his family for a week; Dave, a retired service member, looked forward to seeing his sister; and Mark, an active duty sailor, hadn't seen his family in nearly five years. As for me, I was going to visit my sweetheart. Regardless of the "mission," for most of us the mindset was "San Antonio or bust!"

Those of us who were left behind began searching for other routes to get to our desired destinations. After a tip from one of the passenger service representatives, we learned there was a Navy flight to Dallas leaving the following morning with a connecting flight to San Antonio. For most of us, that was good news.

However, Rogelio decided to go back to Delaware and spend what was left of the weekend with his wife, and Mark bought a ticket to California on an aircraft that was leaving later that evening.

All of us who were still interested in getting to Texas bid our farewells to one another and said, "See you in the morning."

Show time was set for 0700. That's when we would learn if there were to be any spare seats aboard the flight.

We felt confident that we'd be flying out of Andrews to Texas that morning. We had learned from flight operations that there were 10 seats available on the Navy flight. Soon the number was down to only two Space-A seats, and I was second in priority.I started thinking, "Wow, I know the others are going to be very disappointed that they won't get to go." But I was in for a rude awakening.

52 - Military Space-A Air Basic Training

We all were sitting on the edges of our chairs ready to grab our luggage when the announcement came that there were no Space-A seats on the flight.

"It's hard in the summer," explained Sgt. Victor L. Robinson. "It takes a little more time in the summer (traveling Space-available) than it does during the school year." He has worked at the Andrews terminal for a year now and says he's seen a lot of disappointed travelers. He also said it is hard to get a Space-A flight on holidays as well.

Robinson said one way to get around the long wait is to sign out on leave four to five days earlier than your desired travel date. This will give the passenger some priority. Because you can only sign up for Space-A travel after signing out on leave, the earlier you sign up the better.

Because I was an active duty soldier on regular leave, my chance of getting a seat was greater than for a retired service member but less than a soldier on duty, emergency leave or a funded TDY.

I, along with all the other active duty and retired service members, quickly learned perseverance is crucial to taking a Space-A flight. If at first you don't succeed... you know the rest.

Someone suggested we take the flight to Scott Air Force Base, IL, because they had scheduled flights to Kelly almost daily. We had only a matter of minutes to make a decision, check our bags and board the flight. All of us were on missions; all of us decided to go for it.

The flight was smooth, and there was little, if any, turbulence. When we landed, I gathered my belongings, thanked the pilots for a pleasant flight and fled off the plane onto a shuttle bus which took us to the passenger terminal. On the way over, I thought, "50 cents for a candy bar, 50 cents for potato chips and 50 cents for a soda. The flight from Andrews to Scott cost only $1.50 - what a bargain." I was starting to like this.

Once at the terminal, I immediately took that important step of signing up for a flight leaving the following morning for San Antonio. Show time was at 0600. Meanwhile, the trip to the billeting facility with our luggage loomed as a problem. There was no base transportation, and the commercial shuttle had already made its last run for the day.

Fortunately for the majority of us, Scott was the final destination for one of the passengers, and his wife had met him with the family car. We put our bags into his car, and two of us were able to squeeze in; the others walked the 3/4 of a mile to get rooms for the layover.

The rooms were very comfortable and cost a mere $8 per day. For some reason, my room was stocked with a large assortment of snacks and beverages, but I didn't mind.

By the time I got settled into my room, it was nearly 1320. I phoned my sweetheart to tell him that there had been a change in plans because I was unable to get a seat on the Dallas-bound flight, and instead was in Illinois. Plus, I was still uncertain as to what my chances were for getting a flight the next morning. By that time we were both tired of playing the odds, and we decided I should take a commercial flight the rest of the way to San Antonio. Even with that small fare, I would save over $300.

The only problem I faced was that the nearest airport was more than 20 miles away, the commercial shuttle was not due at billeting until 1400 and my flight was scheduled to leave in one hour and 33 minutes.

Well, just as always, someone in the "military family" came along to lend a helping hand. The retired gentleman was kind enough to take me to the airport, getting me there with 30 minutes to spare, help me with my luggage and keep me company until my flight departed.

As the plane took off, the sun appeared to shine much brighter. After a 20-minute stop in Dallas, I was off to my final destination. When the plane landed, I thought, "Mission accomplished!"

My week-long vacation in Alamo country was wonderful. I visited Sea World (a good friend told me to sit close so I could get pictures - I was splashed by Shamu!), toured the area Missions (I saw the famous Rose Window), took a stroll along the River Walk (how romantic), visited the wax museum (I saw Gen. Patton, Whoopie Goldberg, Elvis Presley...), and ate at some nice restaurants (Nacho Momma's has the best salsa!).

My return trip, again by military Space-A, was less eventful. First of all, I was no longer "on a mission." Second, everything just kind of fell right into place. It started with a smooth flight from Kelly to Scott and on to Andrews the following morning.

During my trip, I learned that patience and perseverance are key elements to getting where you want to go. For me, the trip reinforced the spirit of camaraderie that service members possess when they have a common goal.

by Staff Sergeant Tonja D. Batts
Staff writer Pentagram News
Washington, DC

PATIENCE AND FLEXIBILITY PAY OFF

Ed's Note: Although this letter is an old one, we're including it to show that perseverance really can pay off.

Dear Ann,

Our trip was to take two weeks by way of the Azores, Rota, Sigonella (Sicily) to Crete.

On September 23 (Thursday) my wife and I left for the Navy Lodge on the Philadelphia Naval Base. You can reserve a room 30 days in advance, the rate is $40 and excellent quarters. The base has a good-size BX, commissary and gas station. There is a long-term parking lot (can be used for flights leaving Philadelphia IAP) just outside the main gate. If you stay at the Lodge, you can leave your car in their lot.

Ed's Note: The Philadelphia Naval Base is now closed under BRAC. Try parking at Defense Personnel Support Center, 2800 South 20th Street. C-215-737-2411, no lodging here.

Friday morning, we went to the Philadelphia IAP by cab (seven miles from base) at a cost of $15. A flight was leaving for the Azores, Aviano, Bahrain that afternoon. Seats went from 14 to 39 during show time. No retirees (Cat VI) were called. In checking with the USO for a cab back to base, I was told a Navy shuttle bus stops at the USO (no schedule) 0900-1300-1500-1800-and 2200. If they have room, they will take other passengers back to the naval base. On base, if you need transportation to the airport, call TPU or the duty driver.

No quarters were available on arriving at Dover AFB because it was training weekend. Upon arriving at the terminal, there were 25-30 retirees. No retirees had left Dover in three weeks. Two flights to Rota NS, Spain, C-5s, 73 passengers each, were scheduled but later took no passengers for full cargo. Later, a flight was being boarded for Mildenhall RAF, England (six to eight retirees boarded). Two additional calls were made because of available seats. The early morning schedule had two flights going to Rhein-Main (Frankfurt) and then were cancelled. Later in the morning, a C-5 left for Rhein-Main with many empty seats. Many retirees were in the terminal but didn't care to go to Mildenhall or Rhein-Main. I believe the weather there this time of year had a lot to do with it. The temperature averages between 35-60 degrees, cool and rainy. It seems everyone was waiting for flights to the Azores, Rota, or Sigonella. There were three more flights, C-5s at 1230 to 2130, going to Rhein-Main. We didn't wait for these and headed back to the Philadelphia Naval Base.

At the Philadelphia IAP, a Space-A flight was scheduled for Rota, Sigonella, Bahrain at 2030. There were 25 seats but again, no retirees called. I was the seventh name on Category 6. We had quarters at the Navy Lodge.

There were no flights scheduled for Sunday at Philadelphia IAP, but Dover AFB had two flights to Rhein-Main and two flights for Mildenhall throughout the day. I do not know if flights were cancelled, number of seats or if any retirees (Cat 6) had left. With a chorus of "On the Road Again," the car headed for McGuire AFB, NJ. Stayed on base for $16. Room rates: VOQ/VAQ - $8 per night per person, TLF - $24 per night per person, DVQ - $14 per night per person, and Chiefs' Suites - $14. Check-in time is at 1400 with no exceptions and first come, first served.

In the morning, we went to the terminal for a flight to Andrews, Azores, Sembach. Seats unknown until show time, 20 seats - four for McGuire, 16 seats left open for Andrews. Informed next day, Andrews left empty seats. The PX and commissary on Fort Dix are massive.

Dover had a flight to Rota (no seats because of hazardous cargo) and one to Mildenhall RAF, England. On Tuesday, McGuire AFB had a flight to Pisa, Italy; Dover had two flights to Mildenhall, one to Rhein-Main; Philadelphia had a flight to Rota with six seats, and one flight to Rhein-Main. We didn't appear for any of these flights and stayed at Philadelphia Navy Lodge.

Wednesday showed no flights at Philadelphia or Dover. I gave up on McGuire AFB. Gayle and I decided to head south and visit Williamsburg and Norfolk area. We stayed at the Langley AFB, VA, in TLF for $24. TLF rates are: AB-AMN-2LT - $14, AIC-TSGT - $21, MSGT-CMSGT - $24, 1LT-COL - $24. Room rates are VOQ/VAQ - $8 per person, DV - $12 per person.

The Navy Lodge at the Norfolk NAS is the largest in the world and is excellent with a $40 room rate. Show time for KC-10 aircraft is three hours before departure; other aircraft is two hours. Philadelphia had a flight to Mildenhall RAF, but we did not appear. Stayed at the Philadelphia Navy Lodge Thursday night.

On Friday, 30 September 1994 out of Philadelphia IAP were two flights; one to LGS, Rota - 25 seats - no retirees boarded; one to Keflavik, IC - 65 seats. I didn't stay for this show time. McGuire had a C-141 going to Andrews, Keflavik IC, Azores - 25 seats (two places you could get bumped). We did not appear.

On Saturday, Philadelphia IAP had a flight scheduled from Norfolk, Philadelphia, LGS-DC-8 with six seats (did not appear) and Dover AFB had one flight to Mildenhall and one to Frankfurt (Rhein-Main).

My wife and I decided it was time to head for home. We had planned a warm weather trip overseas and nothing looked encouraging in that directions for retirees. As you can read by my report, there were many flights. We could have boarded on at least four flights to Mildenhall RAF or Rhein-Main just by walking into the terminal. This is the first time this has happened to us. I had a very good Julian date of 32 to 40 days as time went on. I had faxed stateside bases and also covered my return by faxing overseas bases in advance from home. All in all, we don't feel this time or money was lost. We made it a vacation and met some very nice people along the way. I'm planning another trip in the spring with a few changes from those we experienced this time. Space-A is a challenge but can be enjoyable if you make the most of it.

Griffiss AFB was our next destination. We shopped at the BX and commissary which are big and very nice. Billeting rates are: VOQ - $7 per person, VAQ - $6 per person, SNCO Suite - $8 per person, DVQ - $14 per person, TLF - $22 per person.

John A. Caruso
Lt Col USAF (Ret)
Getzville, NY

Ed's Note: Yes, it is always great to get a flight to your preferred overseas destination; however, taking a flight overseas to your desired theater, i.e., Europe, can be used to move around in the theater to your preferred destination. This is particularly true in the European and Pacific theaters which have local MEDEVAC and cargo/passengers assignment aircraft.

CHAPLAIN AND WIFE ENJOY CAMARADERIE

*Chaplain George R. Castillo is the author of **My Life Between the Cross and the Bars**, $25.45 (PST paid). For more info write POB 657, Shalimar, FL 32579 or call 850-651-3103.*

Dear Ann,

On June 27, we drove from Florida near Eglin AFB to Dover AFB, DE. On our first day out we couldn't get a plane to Ramstein, but the next day we got a flight to RAF Mildenhall. We were there for three days. One day was spent touring Cambridge. I had never been there, but in 1958 my husband was one of the lucky ones from Scultthorpe chosen to take a seminar at Cambridge. So, 37 years later we both enjoyed the city. The following day was spent at the terminal, but we didn't mind one bit because we met some wonderful, experienced Space-Aers who willingly shared all sorts of helpful hints. The third day all Category 6s made it to Ramstein.

For a month we enjoyed touring Italy, Turkey, Prague, Czech Republic, France and Germany. When it was time to return home, we expected to wait several days because it was summertime. However, we waited six days and didn't expect the nightmare we experienced; some of which is described in the attached letter. *(Ed's Note: The "attached letter" refers to comments sent to AMC which is not included in this publication.)* I didn't go into detail about broken unavailable lockers and families actually sleeping outdoors on the benches when the AMC terminal closed at 2200. Nor how we decided to return via the Azores and got all excited when Category 6s were called only to wait anxiously to learn that only one seat was left.

Despite the problems encountered, we plan to use Space-A again, however, not in the summertime to Europe. Next year we hope to go to Australia and New Zealand. When is the best time? *(Ed's Note: Weather is best Nov-Dec, AU summer; Space-A travel is best June-July, AU winter.)*

The tours were wonderful, but the most memorable part of the trip was the friends we made. Strangers who were tired and weary from living day and night at the terminal were wonderfully kind and encouraging to each other. It was a great experience and such an uplift.

> Very truly yours,
> Chaplain and Mrs George Castillo
> Shalimar, FL

CYBERTALK ON SPACE-A

Dear Ann and Roy Crawford,
Here's a report on our recent trip. Hope it is useful to you.

Along about March 1997 my wife Ruth and I decided it was once more time to plan a Space-A trip to Europe. We had missed out in 1996 due to some surgery I had to have done, but this year looked good. During the year I missed, I spent lots of time on my computer checking on what was going on. I can tell you now that this is the best way to plan for your trip. Here's how you do it.

How to use the World Wide Web to get information:

We planned on leaving from Dover AFB trying to get to Ramstein, Germany, so we got on the World Wide Web (www) and found that Dover has a homepage. For those of you who may not know, a homepage is simply a place that someone tells about themselves and refers you to other relevant places. There are a couple of ways to reach Dover AFB's homepage. Go to http://www.dover.af.mil/info/spacea/spacea.html on the World Wide Web or you can go to Military Living's web site, http://www.militaryliving.com/ and click on Our Friends on the Web. Don't worry if you forget this or if you can't do it; use any search engine on the web, such as Yahoo, Excite or America Online, search for Dover AFB and you will get to it.

Once at the Dover site, you will find that you can find out next month's schedule, flight schedules for the next few days with estimated seat availability and how many passengers in each category that moved in the last 24 hours. You can also find out what the last 30 days looked like. That's not all. You can sign up for Space-A travel right there on the net.

You will also find a list of other military installations that you can click on to find out what's going on there. Some of these are Travis, Aviano, Ramstein, Hickam, etc. By double clicking on one of these you can get all the details of that base. At Dover's homepage we found that Dick Pepperd's Space-A page with lots of detailed info was there as well as Doug Oard's Space-A page, which contains feedback from many Space-A travelers. Of course, Military Living Publications' homepage is also there. Click on any of these and you will find a world of detailed information. Everyone is using it. Between March 6, 1997 and May 25, 1997 a total of 15,437 people had been on the page!

Ed's Note: Dick and Doug can also be reached from the Military Living homepage at http://www.militaryliving.com.

I clicked on Ramstein and found the 623 AMSS Space-A info page which listed daily arrivals, departures, flight schedules, billeting reservations and loads of other travel links. About that billeting reservation business, there has been a new change and now ID card holders can make reservation at an Air Force lodging facility 24 hours in advance!! Also, if rooms are available, you can confirm reservations for stays as long as 72 hours. Click on the Ramstein page to get the details.

One of the Ramstein homepage items was "Other Space-A Links" which took me to a homepage for AFRC Garmisch and Chiemsee where you can make reservations by E-mail! It works!!
Another took me to an interesting homepage for Burg Reichenstein (http://www.caltim.com/reichenstein/) and another to the German Tourist Office (http://www.germany-tourism.de) where you can have your details in either German or English!

How Ruth and Ed Delong did it:

I signed up by E-mail at Dover for the outbound trip about 45 days before we wanted to leave and Ramstein, Mildenhall, Aviano and Sigonella for the return trip about three weeks later so I would have a high Julian date and still not be dropped. I signed up at Garmisch requesting reservations for a week in May and Chiemsee for another four days. There were some foul-ups in this system as Garmisch lost the request and by the time we exchanged E-mail messages six different times and they got things straight, I had four days at Garmisch followed by three days at Chiemsee.

I also called Heidelberg (phone - not yet on the net) *(Ed's Note: C-011-49-6221-795100)* and was told that retirees could only make reservations a week in advance but that things looked good for that period. We planned on visiting friends in Holland and Belgium too so got the tourism offices for those countries on the net and requested detailed maps and info. All came within a few weeks.

Now that we had all the information, all we needed to do was make the plan. We had tickets to "Oklahoma" in Virginia on Wednesday April 23 so planned to leave the next day and drive to Dover to wait for a flight. I went to AAA and signed up with Hertz for a car starting April 24. Good discount there and the rental agency is right on base. As it turned out, by watching the daily movement and schedules on the net, we found that Thursday was not as good a day as Wednesday to get to Ramstein. We gave our "Oklahoma" tickets away and drove up on Wednesday.

We got to Dover about 1500 and found there were a number of flights. I knew I was on the list because Dover had the list on the Internet!! All I needed to do was get the paperwork from the sign-up desk. It was a snap! They wanted to see passports and ID cards and all was great.

We were processed for a C-5 flight to Ramstein with a show time of 1830 and a 2130 departure time. At 2030 got checked in, baggage and all, and parked the car in the new long-term parking about half a mile away. (By the way, the new Dover terminal is looking good and should be ready soon.) While waiting, we were told the aircraft was waiting for cargo. By 2230 we were informed that the cargo had not yet arrived. By 2330 we were told that the C-5 was broken! They would schedule us on the next flight. We got booked on that one at 0030 and after a very long wait finally got airborne at 0100. As usual you must have patience and go with the flow for these flights. We met loads of interesting fellow passengers and swapped stories. Meal cost has gone up from $2.40 to $2.75 - inflation they said. Tough prices huh? They served us a steak dinner and after a beautiful and uneventful flight, we landed at Ramstein at 1430 (Ramstein time) - a 7-hour flight.

Hertz, as usual, did not have the car I requested but gave me a 1997 VW Passat for the same price.

We spent our first night in Trier then visited the military cemetery at Luxembourg, where General Patton is buried, Bastogne and other interesting BeLux areas before spending a few days with a retired Dutch Navy Captain friend and his wife in Uden. They showed us this beautiful country over three days, and even though it rained most of the

58 - Military Space-A Air Basic Training

time, the tulips were in bloom at Keukenhof Gardens. If you haven't visited this place, don't miss it. Bought wooden shoes for six grandkids and found that it cost as much to mail them back as it did to buy them. By the way, they are bought in hardware/grocery stores at about a quarter of the price you pay on tourist areas. While there I made the reservations by phone for a night in Heidelberg's Patrick Henry Village.

That Burg Reichenstein Castle I found out about on the net looked good so we stopped there for a night at 141 DM (about $81, including breakfast) and found that we were on top of a mountain near Bingen, Germany, on the Rhine in an 1100-year-old castle complete with ghosts! There were only three couples there and the view was magnificent. The food was even better.

We drove on down to Heidelberg and spent two days there. We found Patrick Henry Village a nice place to stay at $81 per night, but the only place you could get breakfast was at Burger King! Nothing else was available due to construction - we were told. I question this. They must have somewhere else for people to have breakfast, but the desk at Patrick Henry doesn't know about it.

The net had also told us about great places in the Black Forest, which we wanted to visit anyway. Drove through there and visited Triborg, where nearly all of the cuckoo clocks and grandfather's clocks are made, then on to Villengenm, a walled city where we spent the night.

Arrived in Garmisch after a beautiful drive along Lake Constance (Bodensee) and checked in at the General Patton Hotel. Prices there are going up too. $63 for an 0-4 and you buy your own breakfast (buffet at about $6). You can stay in a German Gasthaus or Pension for about $50 a stay. Very filled with conferees and Boy Scout Troops. These AFRCs are not supported by appropriated funds and must host these events to stay in business. We found several retirees (all of whom had spent two years on active duty and 18 years in the reserve doing weekend drills) who were upset because these people had priority over them. They complained a lot and said they would write letters.

Garmisch now offers a tour to Vipiteno, Italy, which is the northernmost city in Italy and is just over the Brenner Pass in Austria. We took it and found ourselves in a blazing snowstorm - on May 7th - with a bus that kept losing cooling water and had to stop for more at every station. Nearly a foot of snow on the pass and the salt spreaders and plows were working hard. What an experience! While we visited a museum in Vipiteno the driver managed to find a mechanic who fixed the bus and got us all back safely. This is really a great tour and I'd recommend it to all (without the snow and bus problems, of course).

Garmisch is still the best base from which to visit Neuschwanstein and Linderhof, two of mad King Ludwig's castles as well as Oberammergau. We had visited before but went again. If you take the tour, you can see more; but if you drive, as we did, you can stay as long as you like and stop wherever you want.

Chiemsee is as beautiful as ever, but there isn't really much to do except visit the other Ludwig Castle, Herrenchiemsee, this time of the year. The water is still too cold for swimming, and it rains a lot. We drove over to Berchtesgaden to visit. The old AFRC and General Walker hotels are closed, and there are no signs of the military at all. Berchtesgaden is still a great and beautiful place to visit. The Eagles' Nest was closed due to heavy snows until mid-May.

Called Ramstein by phone and found that there were several flights scheduled for the Saturday before Mother's Day, so we drove there to try to catch one. Unfortunately they were all cancelled, and since Ramstein has a "quiet period" on Sundays, none would leave until late Sunday evening. No problem; we found quarters at Vogelweh for $17 and spent the evening with some other Space-A travelers listening to their tales. We had kept the rental car until we were sure we could get out. We finally got a C-5 out at 2325 which was scheduled to RON at Keflavik, Iceland. When we arrived there, we had to park the plane miles away from the terminal since explosives were aboard. By the time we got into the terminal, the pilot had received permission to continue on without staying the night. We finally arrived at Dover about 0300. Customs was quick and we found our car in good condition and drove home.

As usual, Space-A is a great way to travel, but you have to be flexible and prepare for the unexpected - like RON's in Iceland. We'll do it again - soon I hope.

Edgar E. and Ruth DeLong
LCDR USN (Ret)
Virginia Beach, VA

DELIGHTFUL TRIP TO GERMANY BY SPACE-A

Dear Ann and Roy,

My wife, Kathy, and I recently (April-May '97) enjoyed a 5-week Space-A trip to Germany and Austria. We signed up 45 days in advance. Should sign up for Space-A return flight at the same time (60 days in advance is permitted). Took a leisurely drive to Dover AFB, arriving on April 15th and were immediately whisked off to Ramstein AB, Germany, four hours later. About 20 empty seats. Regular long-term parking at Dover is difficult, and I noticed they were repaving the overflow lot, so it may have been expanded. There was no charge for parking or anywhere to leave the $5 mentioned in *Military Space-A Air Opportunities Around the World*. *Ed's Note: Long-term parking #1 Dover/Lajes Streets, #2 Arnold Avenue: no charge.*

Overnight accommodations at both Ramstein North (officer) and Ramstein South (enlisted) were excellent. Several other military places, Sembach AB, Vogelweh AB and Landstuhl Army Hospital, all within 30-minute shuttle from Ramstein. Ramstein South is directly across from the AMC terminal and a little noisy but most convenient for Space-A travelers. New AMC terminal planned for construction near the flight line. Can take free base shuttle bus to North (about 1 1/2 miles away and close to Officers' Club, food courts, commissary/PX). On-base shuttle does not run on Sundays and holidays. Taxi fare is $5 from AMC terminal to BOQ. By the way, in accordance with Status of Forces Agreement, transient retirees cannot use commissary/PX or mini-marts. Many other eating places at Ramstein; Officers' and Enlisted Club bowling alley, Popeyes, Pizza, Italian, Greek, German (for lunch only), ice cream. Allowed to shop at German vendor stores on base. There were also two movie theaters on base.

Prearranged Hertz rental car awaiting at Ramstein North BOQ. Make prepayment from CONUS...considerably cheaper, especially with AAA discount. Gas expensive (about $4-$5 a gallon) and gas coupons not available for transient retirees.

Went to Stuttgart to meet German friends and stayed at Patch Barracks, an Army base. Robinson Barracks guest facilities were being renovated. Patch Swabian Inn was excellent with video rentals, fresh-brewed coffee (free) and professional reception staff. O'Club facilities were excellent. Cost for double was $39.

Traveled throughout southern Germany and Bavaria. Visit to Garmisch was lovely, but both General Patton and Von Steuben Hotels (room rate $63 for 0-5) were filled with

60 - Military Space-A Air Basic Training

military conferences and active duty tour groups. Stayed in a German pension, a bed and breakfast called Marlene Karg, very comfortable and quiet. Much cheaper than the Army facilities at Garmisch. Room and breakfast at B&B about $50. Ate dinner at Von Steuben Hotel and meal was excellent.

Spent two weeks at time share hotels near Salzburg, Austria, and loved the "Sound of Music" country. Every village and vista is a post card shot. Drove to Berchtesgaden to see "Eagles' Nest," Hitler's mountaintop fortress bunker, but couldn't get up there due to heavy snow barring access. Continued to Lake Chiemsee Army Recreation Area to check it out. It is a beautiful vacation spot...a bit pricey for spoiled travelers spending between $17-$43. Room rates varied by pay grade...0-5 was about $63 for a double room with beautiful lake view.

Not bad for what you got, but we were hurrying to rendezvous with more German friends. Someday, we'll return. Rooms were available, but many book months in advance. Tour office there is very active with forays in Bavaria, Austria and Italy.

Also stayed at Augsburg (Army) Kaserne Guest House. Base appears to be drawing down on facilities. O'Club is closed. Room was big and clean...cost $43. Then on to Ansbach (Army) Kaserne, home of the Big Red One. Base was busy with activity...eating facilities were good and familiar...ate at Burger King. Bamberg VOQ seemed very nice but our reservations got messed up, and we were "sans" room for the night. We found a room at a small base named Kitzingen. Cost was $35. Room was on second floor of Rod & Gun Club/Restaurant. Toilet and shower facilities down the hall (about 30 feet). Eating tip...look for German Cantina. Cater to German on-base employees, breakfast and lunch only. Food is considerably cheaper and excellent German cuisine. Ate there at Ramstein and Ansbach.

Then back to Ramstein, and there we bogged down. Waited four days to get out. Tried to arrange our return to beat the exodus of dependent wives and school children; however, many spouses took kids out of school early. Of course, they are higher priority than retirees, and that's the way it should be. The key to Space-A travel is patience and flexibility. We had an uneventful return to Dover; my awaiting chariot was dusty but unbowed and turned over with a roar. Dover overflow lot was closed to incoming vehicles, but had been relocated on base.

Tony and Kathy DeMarco
CDR USN (Ret)
Homestead, FL

SHARON AND JOE FELTS FIND
FREE ARMY LODGING AT FRANKFURT

Dear Ann and Roy,

Thanks for the complimentary road maps. We are sending you more handouts that you might be able to use.

Our advice to "Space-A" travelers - call ahead (use DSN phones) to other countries to obtain a room. Get an American Express to secure room. We didn't have American Express, but they were kind and reserved for us anyway. We found Heidelberg the most expensive at Patrick Henry Village - $50 for Joe, $30 for extra person ($80 for the two of us). Lovely rooms though.

We even lucked out and spent two nights in an Army transient barracks at Rhein-Main,

Frankfurt. So what if we had reveille and had to strip our beds and go get clean linen and remake beds - who can complain for free nights' lodging. We even had room inspection. No towels or washcloths were furnished, so we went to exchange and purchased towels. We carry two or three cheap washcloths on all trips, so we made out fine. We were told about this after we had ventured into Frankfurt via bus from international air terminal (free bus still goes to air terminal and picks up servicemen). We used the trolley, too, and spent one night at a youth hostel - $25 each with breakfast included. A good one-time experience. Enjoyed meeting youths and talking to them.

We flew into Philly, went through Customs and reboarded for flight to Atlanta where we rented a Budget vehicle for ride to Charleston, SC, where our vehicle was parked. Dollar does not allow drop-off to other states. I checked it since I had coupon and your book advertised it. I also checked with Dollar on overseas. They connected me with Euro Car which is very expensive. We found Hertz to be the best rate. I think I told you we called back to the states to rent it. If they'd had a Ford, we would have rented it because it can be taken into Eastern bloc countries. We got an Audi (only thing available and I guess they get ripped off in those countries).

Tolls and gas very high. Tolls all the way through Italy.

We saw the Leaning Tower of Pisa, visited the Italian Riveria, toured Carrara, Italy (Marlie country), ventured into a corner of France and all through Switzerland (all French speaking). Spent three days in Switzerland, high up in the Alps in a mountain village called Leysin. What a great experience!

Sharon and Joe Felts
SCPO USN (Ret)
Galax, VA

PLACES TO STAY

Dear Ann,

Recently (early June) spent three nights at RAF Club in London - very well-located - coat and tie club. Being a member of the Marines' Memorial Club in San Francisco (they have a reciprocal agreement) made it possible for my wife and me to stay there. Excellent restaurant - a little expensive but a lovely treat.

We also spent three nights at Cercle des Militaire in Paris. Very nice club with several categories of restaurants. Very well-located. $50 per night cheaper than the RAF Club. Booked very early. *(Ed's Note: See Military Living's **Temporary Military Lodging Around the World** book).* Would certainly recommend both Clubs to any and all. Would have liked to visit the Union Jack Club and Victory Club but time was too short. Keep perking up and keep up your good work.

Sincerely,
Louis C. Forget
Ft Pierce, FL

Ed's Note: A membership to the Marines' Memorial Club is a great investment. I gave Roy a lifetime membership when he retired from the Army.

The club offers reciprocal privileges at worldwide military clubs; the Army Navy Club in Washington, D.C., is a recent addition! The Marines' Memorial Club in San Francisco is a marvelous haven for military personnel of all ranks, active or retired, Guard or Reserve and their family members.

62 - Military Space-A Air Basic Training

For information write General Manager Mr. Harry Reiter, Marines' Memorial Club, 609 Sutter Street, San Francisco, CA 94102-5000 or call (415) 673-6672 or 1-800-5-MARINE.
Be sure and mention that Military Living's publishers, Ann, RJ and Roy Crawford, Sr., referred you!

LESSONS LEARNED FROM NAVY ENSIGN

Dear Ann and Roy,

Thank you so much for your book, *Military Space-A Air Basic Training and Reader Trip Reports*! I am both new to the military and to Space-A travel. Your book was such a help to me on my recent trip to Japan. I wanted to write you of my Space-A adventure and share with your readers the valuable lessons I learned.

I began my trip Saturday January 11 at Andrews AFB, MD. My ultimate destination was Yokota AB, Japan. My original flight plan was to catch a C-9 MEDEVAC from Andrews to Travis AFB, CA, that Saturday morning and from Travis catch one of their daily hops to Yokota. Space-A reality quickly set in when I learned there were zero seats on the MEDEVAC flight (typical of those kind of flights). After calling several nearby bases and alternate destinations, myself and several others trying to get to Travis decided on a 2300 flight that same day to McGuire AFB, NJ. McGuire is a main hub for flights out west, especially to Travis. We had no problem catching the late flight to McGuire. Due to both the time and the freezing temperatures when we arrived at McGuire, my travel companions and I decided to stay the night in the terminal. It was a long night, complete with a nap on the floor of the ladies' room.

There were two flights the next morning to Travis: a MEDEVAC (again zero seats) and a C-141. We had no problem getting on the C-141 and left for Travis around 1030. If the previous night's short hop on a C-141 didn't teach me, the six-hour flight to Travis awakened me to the further physical realities of Space-A travel. Cargo plane travel is cold and loud despite the blankets and ear plugs issued by the flight crew. We arrived in Travis Sunday afternoon. After a pleasant evening on the town and a much-appreciated night of rest at billeting ($10 per person), I was able, with much luck and a little help from above, to catch a flight the next morning to Yokota. The flight from Travis to Yokota, although relatively simple, had the potential to be the most challenging aspect of the trip. (See lesson #1.) I arrived in Japan around 1430 on Tuesday January 14th.

To help future Space-A travelers and to bring closure to my trip, I've compiled a short list of lessons I learned. I hope it is helpful to your readers!

Lessons I learned from my Space-A adventure:
1. It is important to ask not only how frequently a base has flights to your destination, but also how many seats they average on each flight. Ask for a realistic estimation. Case in point: Travis AFB, CA, has flights every morning to Yokota AB, Japan, but the flight is a "PAC Express" and therefore has 0-5 seats. In preparing my plans for this trip, I only thought to ask when and how frequently there were flights to Yokota, not how many seats were available on average on these flights. Being a Category III traveler there were about 20 Category I and II personnel in front of me (some who had been waiting three to eight days to catch a flight).

Military Space-A Air Basic Training - 63

2. Always wait until the flight actually departs before leaving the Space-A terminal. Sometimes the pilot or load master will reconfigure the flight shortly before takeoff and seats will open up. As with the example mentioned in lesson #1, I waited roughly one to one-and-a-half hours after the show time just to make sure no seats opened up. Thirty minutes before takeoff they issued another call for the same Yokota flight - 13 seats had opened up! All the Category II people had left in frustration shortly after the initial role call. I was able to get on the flight as were several retired service members. It was a true joy to see their excitement at getting on the flight as they had been waiting the longest to catch a hop to Japan!
3. Depending on the season in which you travel, be sure to dress appropriately. My flights were during the second week of January. Each of the three flights were on a C-141, which is not the warmest of planes. I was dressed for cold weather, but the temperature drops even further as the altitude increases. The crew issued us blankets, but sometimes that was not enough. If you travel with children be sure to bring extra blankets and dress them very warmly.
4. Scott AFB, IL, is a main hub for Space-A travel. It is a good place to call with routing and reservation questions. They also put out a monthly publication "AMC Passenger Travel Planner" which is filled with flight information. If you cannot acquire this booklet from your local AMC terminal, write for it: HQ AMC/DOJR, 100 Heritage Drive, Room 102, Scott Air Force Base, IL 62225-5002.

In reflecting on my trip, I am glad that I flew Space-A. Despite the rougher aspects of the trip, i.e., sleeping in AMC terminals, cold and loud flights and long waiting periods, I did get a chance to meet some great people, see some places I'd never been and share with my fellow adventurer the ups and downs of Space-A travel.

Thank you again for your book, *Military Space-A Air Basic Training and Reader Trip Reports*. It was an invaluable resource in planning and executing my Space-A trip! God Bless!!

Very respectfully,
Jamie Ann Fraser
Ensign USN

SPACE-A TO EUROPE FROM THE WEST COAST

Dear Ann and Roy,

I have just returned from Fairchild AFB, WA, doing a bit of research and documentation on the 92nd ARW KC-135 Space-A flights to Mildenhall, UK. Yesterday was a disaster as they were having a terrorist defense exercise and the base was tighter than a tick!

A very helpful airman at the Base Ops service counter indicated that the Wing initiates a large number of flights to Europe; as an example, the monitor today was showing a flight to Ramstein, GE; Mildenhall, UK; and Dover, DE, on the 25th and 29th of June, each with 10 seats showing. As for Space-A takers on these flights, the airman indicated that it was no problem getting on as the Wing generates so many flights.

Long-term parking for Space-A passengers is available in the lot between Omally Avenue and Bldg 2000, about a two block walking distance. The price is right; it is free!

Due to the exercise, I went for Space-A billeting. The billeting office is now called Fairchild Inn and last night main base housing was full, so I was sent over to the Survival

64 - Military Space-A Air Basic Training

School facilities. Attached is the Survival Inn info handout, which also includes floor plans of the VOQ and VEQ quarters.

This is apparently a rather new facility, and it is A-1 top notch as I judge all facilities based on my 1953 Scott AFB, IL, BOQ, which was brand new at that time and would only rate five on a scale of 0-10 by today's billeting.

The Survival Housing is located on a southern portion of the base, i.e., exit the Main Gate onto US 2, turn right on Rambo Road and continue through the manned security gate onto Thorpe Road to the main entrance and desk at the end of the street on your right.

The Officers' Club of old is no longer there, it is now a Consolidated Club located in Bldg 2452 on the right side of Fairchild Highway just past the main BX.

If you are not a Club member of any kind, they now charge a $3 per meal surcharge, which is still not a bad bargain with Mongolian BBQ going at $7.50 per person.

Sorry, no pictures of Fairchild as I shoot slides in my camera and the wife has hers in Tucson shooting the new grandson. In a week or so I will send you pictures of the Camp Rilea facility.

> Sincerely,
> Robert S. Furrer, Maj USAF (Ret)
> Lake Oswego, OR

FIRST SPACE-A TRIP

Dear Ann and Roy,

We have just returned from our first Space-A trip and wanted to share our experiences with you and others. We learned a lot about the procedures which will help us on future trips. We had studied your publications, and they were so helpful!

We took a room at Dover before we realized that we could get a flight out that night to Ramstein. (Not smart as we forfeited the cost of the room.) It pays to check the air terminal before taking a room! Our ultimate destination was Rota, Spain, and we had made reservations at the Navy Lodge to begin on 15 May. We took a C-5 to Ramstein on 12 May and spent two nights there before getting a C-9 MEDEVAC to Rota. We arrived right on time for our reservations!

Lodging at Ramstein was a bit of a problem. We learned that we might be told on the phone that there were no rooms available, but when we walked up to Ramstein North it was possible to get a room. Front desk personnel at Ramstein South were especially indifferent. They refused to make a reservation for Space-As.

Our experience in Rota was wonderful and we greatly enjoyed the Navy Lodge. Personnel there were cordial and helpful. We regretted not being able to use the exchange or commissary, but there was a mini-mart we could use and a nice bookstore. The Officers' Club is operated by the Spanish military, but there is a nice restaurant on base called Reflections where we had some excellent meals.

Our return trip was by C-9 back to Ramstein and C-5 on to Dover with one night in Ramstein. We were amazed that long-term parking at Dover is free!

Our trip was extremely pleasant and we shall look forward to planning another one soon. Our deepest thanks for the good work you are doing to help all of us prepare for our travels.

Sincerely,
Art and Ginny Hayes
LTC USA (Ret)
Greensboro, NC

THEY WERE FLEXIBLE!

Dear Roy and Ann,
Here's another article with three photos you might be interested in. I think the moral of the story is if you can't get to where you want to go then go somewhere else.

Since we had been unable to get a Space-A flight directly to Spain from centrally located bases, we decided on plan B. On April 4 there were seats available on a KC-135 out of the former Forbes AFB, Kansas, now an ANGB for Iceland. It sounded like a chilling idea to my wife, Mary, but realizing that Space-A flying on military aircraft would be a privilege lost if I croaked, she went for Iceland in April instead of Spain in the spring!

We were the only Space-A people on board so the pilot, Capt Ken Oliver, invited one of us to ride the jump seat on takeoff. I told Mary to go ahead since I had experienced this before. He said, "Well, she can ride it on takeoff and you can ride it on landing." During the flight we also went to the tail and the boom operator, SSgt Jamy Dunbar, showed us how he maneuvered the boom to refuel aircraft in flight.

On the approach to NAS Keflavik, Iceland, the whole island looked snow-covered like most people expect it to look, but as the plane neared the runway, one could see there were patches of land which had melted naturally and areas which had been snow plowed. We were met by a Navy airman named Shultze who drove us to the terminal and punched our names in the computer to make us eligible for all flights to the European continent.

We were thankful that Space-A military lodging was available for $17 a night. There is also a Navy Lodge, but the cost is $51 for a double. We had to use it one night during our six-day stay when military lodging was not available. We could also eat in the Navy mess hall, a privilege we had only experienced one other place - the Army mess hall in Panama.

We took a USO tour to Reykavik, the capital and largest city, and to the fishing village of Keflavik. The big thing to do in the Keflavik area is to soak and/or swim in the Blue Lagoon, a geo-thermal heated outdoor pool. So, been there, done that! It was fun.

One day after checking the Space-A monitor at the terminal, I decided I would jog to the mess hall about half a mile away. It was about 40 degrees and the sun was shining. When I was about half way to the mess hall, the wind came up and I was in the middle of a full-blown snowstorm. The wind was the strongest I have ever experienced. It, combined with my own locomotion, propelled me faster than I have ever run in my life... and that's no exaggeration. My body acted as a sail. I passed three sailors coming in the opposite direction leaning into the wind but making little progress. It was that strong. I didn't hear them say anything as I zoomed by, but I knew what they were thinking: "Wow! Look at that old man go!" It was quite a sensation.

While looking over the stock of the Icelandic sweaters which they are noted for - available in the BX - there was a chap who looked to be around 30 in civilian clothes also

66 - Military Space-A Air Basic Training

looking over the selection. We started talking and commenting on how expensive they were.

"I was going to buy my wife one of these, but they're so high I think I'll just wait until I get to Germany tomorrow and buy her a Scottish sweater in the BX," he reasoned.

If I had been asked to guess what rank the guy was I would have figured him to be a junior NCO trying to make ends meet by downgrading his wife's gift from Icelandic to a cheaper Scottish sweater. I make the offhand remark that we were hoping to get a C-141 flight to Ramstein Air Base, Germany, tomorrow also. "I'm the pilot for that flight," he said. "So, I'll be seeing you." Remembering that Mary had not seen Iceland from the air as I had, I quickly asked if Mary could ride the jump seat on takeoff. "No, but she can ride in the navigator's seat," he replied.

The next day when we saw him, no longer was he the nondescript, frugal shopper in search of the best sweater deal available. Now, in his flight suit backed up with captain's bars and senior pilot's wings, he had become the confident aircraft commander responsible for a three million dollar airplane and getting nine souls to Germany in one piece. He summoned Mary to the flight deck. She rode the navigator's seat for the whole flight while I occupied a web seat in the cargo area. I should say "seats" because I slept across four of them for about half of the flight.

At Ramstein we had hoped to get a flight to Rota, Spain. There was one flight, but they never got past Category III on the Space-A list. We stayed at the Ramstein Inn South, taking side trips to Ramstein village and Frankfurt. Having no luck at getting a flight to Spain, we decided to shift back to plan B - travel to Jolly Ole England.

The first plane we boarded was a C-17, but like Orville and Wilbur on their first attempt at powered flight, we never got off the ground! There was an electrical problem they couldn't find, so we deplaned and took the first of four scheduled flights, a C-130, to RAF Mildenhall, England, the next day.

The next morning we ate at the Galaxy Club on base which is a good place for breakfast.

We wanted to see the white cliffs of Dover. The people at the retiree office on the second floor of the terminal at RAF Mildenhall suggested the least expensive way to get there. Take the free military shuttle bus to Gatwick Airport and then take a train to Dover. There were two changes, but they were made without too much trouble. When we reached Dover we located a hotel, The Priory, that had been recommended.

At Dover we ran across the transportation deal of a lifetime. For a mere one pound ($1.66) we could take the ferry, round-trip, across the 26-mile English Channel to Calais, France. This included bus transportation to the ferry from downtown Dover and from the ferry to downtown Calais. The idea was to get you on board and, hopefully, you would spend money in their duty free stores and play the slot machines. We didn't think their prices were all that great, so the most expensive thing we bought was fish and chips ($6.58).

"Richard the Lionhearted" crossed here in the year 1190 on his way to The Crusades. Gertrude Ederle swam the channel in 1926 and in 1944 the band leader, Glenn Miller, crashed into it. And in 1997 William and Mary Hobbs were crossing it for a dollar and sixty-six cents... just for the heck of it!

Our original plan was to take the ferry one-way to get the panoramic view of the white cliffs and return via the tunnel, which the British call the "chunnel!" "Well, you can do that," one Dover resident told us. "But it'll be a bit expensive." It seems that the chunnel starts eight miles back from the shore. You have to take a taxi out there, and when you get to France, take another taxi to Calais to catch the ferry back to Dover. The idea sounds good but in practice it is, well, "a bit expensive." We took the $1.66 deal.

The next day we visited the Dover castle and the World War II underground hospital and command center in the white cliffs. That, we think, was the high point of our trip. Not in most people's imagination would they dream such a thing existed. There were miles of tunnels and rooms. It has only been open to the public for two years, and it is something to see.

Our next destination was Peterborough in the central part of the country for a planned visit with Ben and Pauline. We had met them on a boat trip on the Panama Canal back in November. They were an interesting couple. Pauline, now 56, had been a real beauty in her youth having played important roles in musicals in the local theater. They treated us to the one that was playing at that time, *Carousel.*

After a couple of days in Peterborough, we proceeded by bus to Oxford. The main thing out of the ordinary that we did in Oxford was to visit the grave of Rick Bunday, a former French Foreign Legionnaire, whom I had met in 1959 and was now in the process of growing a rose bush! His wife said that was the most productive thing he had done in years! The whole cemetery was for the *cremains* of people. While there were some mausoleum niches for ashes, most of the deceased there were represented by a rose bush of some variety on top of the ashes. Land is so expensive in England that this sort of thing is catching on.

Near Cambridge we visited the Imperial War Museum at Duxford. Here they have one and sometimes two of the aircraft used by both sides during World War II, most in flying condition. The day we were there they were flying a US Catalina Flying Boat.

After a couple of days in Cambridge, we proceeded on to Mildenhall where we hoped to get a scheduled flight back to Forbes Field the next day. But that was not to be. Because it was an in-flight refueling mission the pilot released only two Space-A seats. An active duty guy got one, so we didn't get to go. The plane left with one seat empty. Our next best bet was a KC-135 to McConnell AFB, Kansas, two days later, but it filled up with Category I, II and III people.

There were several flights going to the east coast but few to heartland bases so we decided to take a C-5 flight to Dover AFB, Delaware, and rent a car or, possibly take Amtrak back to the Show Me state. This wasn't the best deal but it looked like the only way we were going to get across the ocean. We climbed aboard and guess what? This would be the second time we never got off the ground. It seems they were having problems with one of the engines and couldn't get the thing going.

I asked Mary to take care of the bags while I made a dash for the billeting office. We were in luck. Rooms were available not only for us but for everyone on the aborted C-5 flight.

The next day we decided to take a KC-135 to Grand Forks AFB, North Dakota, of all places. The pilot asked if anyone would like to ride the jump seat on takeoff. There was a long hesitation so I said, "Mary, go for it." So she did. A lot of people fly Space-A for years and never get to do this. Mary had been able to do it twice on this trip.

After the plane landed late Friday afternoon, the pilot, Captain Bill Neitzke, came back, shook all the Space-A people's hands and thanked them for flying with the United States Air Force, which we thought was a nice gesture. The cargo door was opened and the rolling stairs were pushed up to the plane. One of the crew members said, "There are two lieutenant colonels down there, but they didn't send anybody to help with the baggage."

"Maybe they're running short on help and the two colonels are here to help with the baggage," I quipped.

Well, that's exactly what happened. The two LCs helped us put our luggage on the bus which came to take us to the terminal. It was great public relations which took about 60 seconds.

When we arrived at the terminal we found that our problems were just beginning. Nine days before the town had been flooded.

I phoned the car rental places and they wouldn't approve a car to be rented beyond a 75-mile radius let alone rent it one-way to Topeka, Kansas. Amtrak only ran east and west. The only way to get there by commercial air was to fly to Denver then to Kansas City, then Topeka, and that cost a mere $492 each... but you couldn't even do that on a weekend. The only means of escape from Grand Forks was by bus and there wasn't even a direct route to do that. You had to go to Minneapolis then cut back diagonally through Ames and Des Moines, Iowa, to Kansas City.

I called base transportation and asked if we could get a ride to the bus station. The man on the other end, TSgt Don Sandbothe, said he didn't have any vehicles going that way and the taxis weren't running. I felt between a rock and a hard place. But then Sandbothe said, "If you'll wait 'til I get off duty, I'll take you to the station in my personal vehicle." We had been lucky to talk to the right man at the right time while we were in the wrong place!

On the way to the bus station we expressed interest in the flood damage in Grand Forks. The bus didn't leave until 2145, so Sandbothe gave us a tour including that of his own house. The Red Cross was serving beef stew and the Culligan Man was giving out free water. I soon saw that my problem faded into insignificance beside his, yet there he was helping us.

As we viewed the devastation on both sides of the Red River, Sandbothe mentioned that he was going to visit his girlfriend in Gardner, and if we would like to go along, he would take us on to Fargo and see if we could catch a more direct bus south through Sioux Falls, Omaha and Kansas City.

"Look at it as an adventure," my old friend Lt. Col. Pat Patterson would have said. So, there we were, headed south with a guy we had known for little more than an hour to pick up his girlfriend in Gardner and catch a bus in Fargo.

The second leg of the journey from Minneapolis to Kansas City was, believe it or not, enjoyable. It turned out to be a backroads tour of Iowa farm country, not unlike the bus trip from Ramstein to Frankfurt. After the second stop we were able to move up to the front two seats on the right-hand side, adjacent to the bus driver. I believe these seats to be the best two on a bus if you are interested in seeing the countryside.

At Kansas City we were met by our daughter and son-in-law and proceeded on to Forbes Field, 80 miles west. There we picked up our car, which after one month started on the first turnover of the engine.

We never did get to Spain!

                        Best Regards,
                        William D. and Mary Hobbs
                        Maj USAF (Ret)
                        Columbia, MO

COMBINE LOW COST FLIGHTS TO EUROPE AND SPACE-A

Dear Roy and Ann,
My wife and I completed a good Space-A trip to Europe last month. Living in south Florida it is hard and costly to get to a departure point and wait for a Space-A flight to Europe. So when LTU airlines had a special fare of $199 round-trip between Fort Myers and Frankfurt, we took it.

We arrived in Frankfurt at 0700 on December 14 and got a military bus at the USO to the Rhein-Main Air Base. By noon we were on the shuttle bus to Ramstein. Stayed at the Ramstein Inn ($25 a night), across from the terminal. The next morning we and one other passenger took a C-9 to Souda Bay, Crete.

The Souda Bay base is very small, one street about 1/4 mile long. There are no quarters on base. At the "End Zone," a dining, entertainment and MWR-type facility, we rented a Fiat for $38 a day from KYR Travel and were told to stay at the Tower Loucerna in nearby Chania (Tel and fax: 0821-42898). The hotel charges $54 a day plus $4 for breakfast. The rooms are nice, each having a balcony overlooking the town. Next door is a very good Italian restaurant.

On base retirees may use the NEX and even can buy gas coupons for the rental car. You fill up on base only. The coupons cost $0.25 a liter compared to nearly $1 a liter at a station.

We traveled the general area looking at the site of the movie Zorba the Greek on Stavros, several beautiful beaches and a monastery or two. We drove about 100 miles east to the site of the ruins of Knosses.

We hoped for a Saturday Space-A flight back to Ramstein, but when told it sometimes did not stop at Souda Bay, we elected to take a KC-135 to Moron Air Base, Spain. We thought we could get back to Germany easier by being on the continent. We had reservations at the American Arms Hotel in Weisbaden over Christmas. Arrived at Moron on December 20. There were no known flights to Germany, but we could have gone to Mildenhall. The weather was bad in Germany, ice storms and all, so we decided to take a KC-10 to Pope, NC, on December 22. It was to refuel two F-117's on the way back. Got to the runway and found one of the F-117's wouldn't start so back to the base.

Next day it was going to try again, but then we heard of a Navy C-9 going to Jacksonville a couple of hours after the KC-10 departed. You should not pass up a flight going in your direction in hopes of getting another, but we did. In this case it worked out as we got on the C-9 and flew to Jacksonville on the 23rd with refueling stops at Lajes and Bermuda. There were about 15 passengers and many empty seats.

Moron is a large base with nothing going on over the weekend. There are only 50 permanent people stationed there. We could not use the NEX but were able to stay in the Hotel Frontera on base ($24 per night) and eat in the dining hall. There was a fitness center open and a club with bar and pool tables open some of the time. We were able to go into Seville one day.

Moron has no passenger terminal and a very casual approach to Space-A passengers. We didn't fill out any forms, and no one checked our passports or ID cards. Very unusual.

We arrived at Craig NAS near Jacksonville and got a ride to a motel with a fellow passenger. Then the next day rented a car in Jacksonville and were able to be home by

Christmas. We lost our return LTU ticket as it was non-refundable, but we got across the Atlantic anyway at no cost.

>Sincerely yours,
>Stanley K. Ink
>Major USAF (Ret)
>N. Ft Myers, FL

A FAR EAST JOURNEY BY SPACE-A

Dear Ann and Roy,
   We have subscribed to your **R&R Space-A Report**® for several years and have benefited from your advice and your books on our Space-A journeys. We had an interesting trip to the Far East in February flying on a variety of military planes and staying in military billeting. It was really exciting to have visited such places as Tokyo, Singapore, Okinawa, Hong Kong and Seoul as well as Hawaii in such a short time.
   January 28 we flew United to San Francisco from Moline, Il. We took the shuttle to Travis, 72 miles, $45 for the two of us. Our only delay was in leaving Travis due to repairs needed on a C-5. We had chosen to fly to Yokota (OKO), Japan, with a 3-hour refueling stop at Elmendorf AB, Alaska; so we left January 30, 73 seats available with 35 used (nine were Cat VI). Temperature at Elmendorf was 30 degrees with no wind after six inches of snowfall the previous night. Very beautiful and much warmer than the sub-zero temperature when we left our home in Illinois. For the 8-hour flight to Yokota we had plenty of room to stretch out and sleep. We arrived January 31 at 1730. Got a DV suite, $24.
   February 1 scheduled flight to Singapore was cancelled, so we decided to take the free shuttle to New Sanno Hotel, a 1-hour ride. Took a Sunshine tour of the city, $41 US pp. The shuttle leaves Kanto Lodge at Yokota daily at 0900 and 1300, return leaves New Sanno at 1330 and 2130. We used Yokota as our base as most flights go out from there. Kanto Lodge has a room for luggage storage, which is nice when you need to give up your room.
   Monday, February 3 call was at 0345 for DC-8 contract flight to Singapore. Twenty-two seats available, only 14 pax. Hot breakfast and cold snack served by flight attendant, n/c, also movies and magazines. Arrived at 1414 (an 8-hour flight) at Paya Lebar Airport and took a cab ($12,50S) to YMCA, Palmer Road. Rates here were the most reasonable: double with bath $66S ($47 US). It was very plain (no TV or radio) but clean and friendly. Would recommend the YMCA on Orchard Road ($88 US) for better location near shopping areas. We took a night tour ($45S) but would recommend the night Safari tour as Singapore has a neat zoo and bird park. Metro Rapid Transit (MRT) subway is fast and easy to use. MRT fares are $0.60. The SGP terminal was going to be closed for five days because of the Chinese New Year holiday, so we left February 5 (same DC-8 to Yokota).
   February 7 we boarded a C-141 to Kadena AB, Okinawa. We were nine pax, had reclining seats, box lunch for $2.75. The on-base shuttle has been discontinued, but it is rather easy to get a ride to billeting. Next day we took the WWII Battle Sites Tour, $14. It was nine hours with lunch at Seamen's Club and included the Japanese underground tunnels. This is an excellent tour sponsored by USO and is offered only two Saturdays a month. The Sunday brunch at Kadena Officers' Club was also excellent, $8.95. February 10 we boarded a DC-8 to Iwakuni AB and hoped to take the 45-minute train ride to

Hiroshima, but we found out it possibly could be three days before a flight would go back to Yokota, so we continued on the DC-8 to Yokota. February 11 we took the shuttle bus back to Tokyo and ventured to the Imperial Palace area by subway.

February 12 we appeared at the 0500 call for either Anderson AB, Guam, or Osan AB, Korea. The monitor showed an unscheduled flight to Hong Kong, 36 seats, only 12 filled. So we boarded the C-9 MEDEVAC to Hong Kong, refueling at Kadena. Saw a gorgeous view of Mt. Fugi! Two hours to Kadena, 2 1/2 hours to Hong Kong. We had to pay $22 per person airport tax and $13.50 departure tax since it is a commercial airport. Taxi to Mariners' Club, room for $803 HK ($105 US). Good location. Ate at YMCA, very reasonable, but rooms there were $158. Toured the city, $36.50 pp. Free Star Ferry to Hong Kong Island and walked to Fenwick Pier. Not too much there, but good prices, and Stanley Market with 70 shops had great prices! We enjoyed the night view of Hong Kong from the lovely promenade area of Kowloon. Taxis charge differently. We paid $12 US coming in and $5 returning to airport. No Space-A flights were scheduled back to Yokota or anywhere else in the area, so we took a commercial flight on Asiana Airlines to Seoul, Korea. Free shuttle to Dragon Hill Lodge at Yongsan, a beautiful place. No rooms available here so we rode the bus ($5) to Osan and got their last DV room for $32. Yongsan is a 10-minute walk to Itawaon, a good shopping area.

February 15 we took a C-135 flight from Osan to Yokota. We saw that a C-141 MEDEVAC was going to Hickam AB with 28 available seats. We made the call, so all seats filled. We had time for lunch at Yokota, checked our luggage and got ready for the 6 1/2-hour flight. An "R&R" in Hawaii and warmer weather sounded good to us at this point.

Because of President's weekend and Hawaiian Open, there were no cars or rooms available on Oahu, so we flew on Aloha Airlines to Hilo and got a cabin at Kilauea Military Camp (KMC) for three nights. Toured volcano area. Then we were able to get two nights at Hale Koa, two at Kaneohe and five at Hickam. Orville and Wilbur's restaurant at Hickam is an excellent place for breakfast. We even saw a nuclear submarine ride by! Our last evening we saw a beautiful rainbow "signaling" the end of a wonderful trip. Next day (February 27) we flew back to Travis on a C-141. It pays to have an early Julian date for a return trip to the mainland. Space-A travel can be a great adventure!

      Sincerely,
      B. Ben and Trudy Johnson
      LtCol USAF (Ret)
      Cambridge, IL

SPACE-A TO ISRAEL

Dear Ann and Roy,

My wife and I have just returned from a 10-day visit to Israel, 28 Feb 1995 to 11 March 1995. You may or may not have the following information:

1. There are almost daily flights from NAS Sigonella to Ben Gurion Airport, Tel Aviv, especially when US Navy ships are in the eastern Mediterranean.

2. Contact Laufer Aviation at Tel Aviv (Ben Gurion) for flights and pax information. The telephone number is 011-972-3-971-2018 (Laufer Aviation personnel are very helpful).

3. The two scheduled monthly flights (C-5) that originate from McGuire (WRI) are

handled by Kevin Meinhard (US Embassy employee). The telephone number is 03-935-8697 (he is very pleasant and very helpful).

This was our second Space-A trip; it was great. Your publications and newsletters have been excellent - full of good information. Keep up the good work and thanks!

Martin and Frances Katz
CDR USN (Ret)
Miami, FL

SPACE-A TIPS

Dear Ann,

We have subscribed to your report for quite a few years and my wife Dottie and I have obtained some very good information from your newsletter. It has saved us money on quite a few occasions. Also, we have signed up four or five new subscribers for the *R&R Space-A Report®* and have received extensions on our subscription. Thank you!

We have been traveling Space-A for 10 years and have visited over 20 different countries and Hawaii. We love traveling Space-A, and if I hit the lottery for the big one, I would still travel Space-A! We have never had a bad trip, and the people have been great. We have formed quite a few lasting friendships in the AMC terminals and on the airplanes.

Some random thoughts for new Space-A travelers:

1. Don't travel this way if you do not have plenty of time and are of a nervous disposition. There will be times when airplanes fill up way before your name is called and you may be stuck for days waiting for a ride.

2. Don't make your plans so firm that you cannot change them when another option comes along. Friends ask us where we are going on a trip and I reply, "We really are not sure, we are heading toward Europe, but you'll know for certain when you receive our post card."

3. We advise renting a car at the terminal as soon as you arrive at your destination. A car will let you see so much more of a country. You will not waste time waiting for a bus or a train. They will drop you in the center of a city where you will find more crime and higher hotel rates. We have found that inns and B&Bs on the outskirts are nicer and less expensive. If you rent a car at the terminal you can keep it until you are sure you are on a flight. If you don't get on you still have the car and can do day trips until your airship comes in. These car agents have places where you can drop the keys somewhere in the terminal. Another advantage of car rental is the trunk or "boot" to carry items for picnic lunches along the way. We usually buy a cheap styrofoam cooler so that we can have cold drinks along the way and when we get to our lodging. Many, many hotels and inns in Europe do not have ice! If they do have it, they will give you three or four cubes in a glass!

4. If you are going to visit a big city it may be better to park the car and take a tour. Be careful when parking in London. A parking ticket is $90! One rainy day we rode around London on the public buses for under a five spot.

5. We stayed at the Union Jack Club in London. The parking lot was full and we had to park in a public lot three blocks away for $35. We would have done better at a B&B.

6. If in Italy, don't overlook a side trip to Malta. Go after September as it is very hot in the summer. Great history and everyone speaks English! Ferries leave from Sicily and package deals can be had through travel agents on post. One will do better eating out

rather than in the English hotels.

7. There is a shortage of hotel rooms east of where the Iron Curtain used to be. Make reservations in advance! We were in Prague shortly after the curtain came down. There wasn't a room in the whole area. We went to the student tourist office and got a room in a private home for $12 for three nights.

8. If you land in Aviano, don't overlook Trieste and Udine. Two great cities that are overlooked by most tourists. Go through Maximilian's castle "Mirimar" when in Trieste. One of the great castles of Europe.

9. Call ahead for reservations at military bases. Some do and some don't take reservations. Every BEQ, BOQ and DV seem to have different policies! It's worth a phone call.

10. Hawaii has so many bases that one should be able to get a room in one of them. Hale Koa, Bellows and the Army rest area on the big island are all first class and will save a bundle.

11. Buy overseas 75 or 100 watt light bulbs. Many of the third world hotels use 25 watt bulbs even in three star hotels!

12. Travel light, eat the local food, meet the natives and have fun. It's later than you think!

Ann, these are a few random thoughts from our experiences on Space-A. We look forward to receiving your Space-A reports. I can tell that Roy is always looking for a new idea to publish. How about compiling all articles and information about a certain country from past issues and the latest terminal schedules in one report and sell each one as a package?

Enclosed find a copy of our cookbook, "Only the Best." Copies are available from me for $11.95 at this address: 285 Egremont Road, Sheffield, MA 01257.

Sincerely yours,
John J. Koneazny
Col USAR (Ret)
Sheffield, MA

EUROPE BY SPACE-A

Dear Ann and Roy,

My husband and I returned recently from a Space-A trip (Category 6-retirees) to Ramstein, Germany, a takeoff point for us to go to Munich's Oktoberfest and Prague. We waited almost four days at Dover in late September. We thought that families by late September would have completed their moves, but many wives and children were still traveling, at least this year. We also discovered that there were fewer flights than we remembered from previous years and more maintenance problems. Only a few C-5s were going and the C-141s, of course, did not hold as many people. At Ramstein a worker told us that the runways could not accommodate more than three C-5s (this may or may not be the case). But, as always, we enjoyed the good fellowship we had with the retirees who waited at Dover. Despite sitting up several nights, we greeted each day with anticipation wondering if we might that day win the lottery and get a seat on the plane!

On our return we did not wait at all. A Dover flight was cancelled early that morning as we sat watching many active military in their camouflaged uniforms and thick boots board flights for their special assignments in other countries. We decided to eat breakfast at the terminal and just as the eggs and toast were ready, a call went out reinstating the Dover flight. Since some folks had left, many with better dates than ours no doubt, we easily got called. We got on a C-141 piloted by a Mississippi Reserve Unit who were most pleasant (the bologna and cheese sandwiches in our lunch box could have been more tasty, but some additional room to stretch out more than made up for the food). One of my sandwiches was confiscated by the Customs inspector on arrival; I doubt that he ate it!

We do want to mention the marvelous tours that ITT offers at Ramstein AB. We took a 2-day tour to Prague and Karlsbad in a most comfortable, modern bus with large windows, a toilet in the middle of the bus and a guide by the name of Gail Lee Winfrey (it rhymes, he liked to point out). He had been leading tours for five or six years, and we hope he will still be doing it next year so we can take another one with him. Although 1-day tours are offered, the nine hours traveling each way plus the day of activities makes a long and exhausting day.

We do want to warn retirees, however, about the price of a room at Heidelberg's Patrick Henry Village. We foolishly did not ask the price when we arrived there because it was late at night after a long drive from Garmisch (yes, the General von Steuben and Patton Hotels are still thriving although we heard that in Berchtesgaden the General Walker Hotel had closed the end of September). We paid $70 for the room the next morning ($45 for my husband and $25 for me) and could scarcely believe our eyes and ears. After all, we had only paid $56 at the recreation hotels in Garmisch. The desk clerk told us the reason for the high price was that the hotel was not subsidized by the government. Anyway, we'll push on to the Ramstein area the next time where the rooms are just as attractive (we did share a bath but without any inconvenience) and the price is right.

O. Wayne and Grace I. Krumwiede
SMSgt USAF (Ret)
Falls Church, VA

SPACE-A TO ALASKA

Dear Ann and Roy,

We would like to thank you for the wonderful information in *Military Space-A Air Opportunities* and in *Military RV Camping & Rec Areas*. We saved lots of money and stayed at some delightful places this spring as we journeyed from Arizona to Alaska.

We left Tucson in the middle of May, which was a little late to avoid the summer rush. We had planned to drive all the way to Anchorage but decided to try to spend more time sightseeing and go Space-A from McChord near Tacoma. We stopped first at Pacific Beach Recreation Center a few hours southwest of Tacoma. The view there was lovely, and it is only a short walk to the beach. (We were surprised to get a room when we called mid-afternoon on the Thursday before the Memorial Day weekend because apparently most of the action there is on weekends and holidays.) We had failed to allow for the holiday weekend but were lucky enough to spend it at McChord Air Base in VIP lodging, a beautiful motel-like facility on park-like grounds surrounded by blossoming rhododendrons and azaleas. Unfortunately, we had spent too much time enjoying the seacoast and were unable to get a plane to Elmendorf although we watched and waited for a week. Apparently there is very little activity during a holiday and immediately after. There were two planes headed for Elmendorf, but one had only a few Category VI seats and another went from 20 to 0. Our wait made evaluation of most of the lodging and camping facilities possible. We give them all a rave review except for one noisy room above the parking lot. The service was friendly and caring.

Upon hearing that Travis had more traffic, we drove there and took an early flight that had 40 seats available. (We had to fill out a new travel request that put us at the bottom of the list, but there were seats for all who showed.) The next plane going on to Japan from Alaska was filled before they got to Category VI. We checked out the FAMCAMP at Travis. It is right inside the gate. We found a camp spot at 2300 but had difficulty getting the combination to open the bathroom doors. Long-term parking ($5 a week) was not as convenient as at McChord. It is a two-mile walk unless you can catch a shuttle (unlikely at 0400 when we left).

Our flight to Elmendorf was delayed because of "quiet time" in Anchorage, so we arrived late in the afternoon and quickly obtained lodging. Car rentals were available at the terminal. Although return was convenient, we avoided rough roads because of the condition of the car. We will check into other choices on our next trip.

During our sightseeing tour of Alaska, we stayed at Fort Greely near Delta Junction and at Fort Wainwright near Fairbanks. The lodging at Fort Wainwright was exceptionally attractive and about half the price of a single bed at Fort Greely ($22 + $7 for extra person). Still, the room at Fort Greely was cheap by Alaska standards, and we were happy to get it. A trip to Kodiak Island had to be postponed because we found it difficult to get enough information for convenient return (the ferry can be an option during most weeks). That gives us an excuse to go back!

Flying back to CONUS could have been a problem since they got only to Category III on the regularly scheduled Saturday flight (school was out); however, there was a midweek flight to Vandenberg AFB. They had sixty seats and about a dozen passengers. Fortunately six of us wanted to return to Travis. Vandenberg does not often get Space-A travelers and has few facilities and no ground transportation. We rented a van delivered from the nearby town of Lompoc. Our fellow travelers became friends by the end of the five-hour trip.

We used more Space-A facilities on this trip than we had expected, enjoyed them all and saved lots of money. Although our vacation was different than we had planned, we enjoyed it a lot.

       Sincerely,
       Duncan and Janice MacDonnell
       LtCol USAF (Ret)
       Tucson, AZ

LEMONS TO LEMONADE

Dear Ann & Roy,

If you are ever on a Space-A flight to or from Europe, this (North Star Inn, Thule Air Base) is the place to be stranded for a few days. The hospitality was beyond explanation: the treatment that we 43 passengers received was the best that we had received in my short life span. At the Top of the World we received top treatment (I'll get to that later in this report). I hope that by now you have received the information on the various air bases that I mailed to you yesterday. Referred to above is a delay we had at Thule on our way back, which was to be a three-hour layover, with fuel and cargo loading that turned into

76 - Military Space-A Air Basic Training

approximately two-and-a-half days of exceptional treatment.

Faxed out request 5 April to Dover, Ramstein and Rhein-Main. Arrived Dover at 1530 hours 6 May, was called for a 1630 flight, KC-10, to Lajes and Ramstein. Flight had a 24-hour layover in Lajes, so opted for the next one at 1730. It broke down and so did the 1830 one. They fixed the 1730 one with parts from the 1830 flight, so they said. Didn't lift off until 2130. Arrived Ramstein approximately 1215. No tours, opted to rent a car to drive to Berlin. This was a bad idea. First hour and 15 minutes traveled 19 km, West German autobahns are under repair and construction. Traffic tie-ups all around the major cities: 10, 15 and 20 km backups. Went to the route straight across via Nurnberg and then up through Hof. It seems they are not only repairing the roads, but they are moving some of them. Instead of getting to Berlin in five-and-a-half to six hours, well, seven-and-a-half hours later, we were in Hof for the night. Next morning crossed the East German border and the autobahn opened up into four lanes. Next two hours covered almost 300 km. Sixty km out of Berlin road turned rough, old autobahn, but was able to make good time. Still no place to park in Berlin. Turned in vehicle at Templehof, Hertz. What a big change in the terminal. At least two dozen airlines. Some you have never heard of. Shonefield is to be the big airport for Berlin, a lot of construction to complete it.

West Berlin is in a stagnated state. East is building and repairing. Latest tax in addition to the VAT tax is an 8% reunification tax, so 15+8=23% tax on everything. USA is moving 30 June 1997 to Mannheim, not enough retirees to keep it open. Checked with them for info on hotels for our reunion to be held in Berlin in 1999 (Berlin US Military Veterans Association). East Berlin hotels are the least expensive; however, if anyone is contemplating a visit to Berlin, BRING LOTS OF MONEY. Prices, with the taxes, are out of sight.

Truman Plaza has been leveled (looks like a sandy beach) to make way for new apartments. Both American schools - grade and high - are still empty. Military quarters are 95% empty waiting for the government employees to move from Bonn. Main HICOB building is still empty; main NCO Club and Officers' Club still vacant. These areas look like a ghost town.

The old Check Point Charlie building, enclosed by a fence by the old Outpost Theater, is becoming part of the Allied Military Museum that is suppose to open in Spring 1998. Stores are staying open a lot later than before, even on Saturdays. On the return from Berlin to the Zone, we opted for a tour bus as it was more relaxing and cheaper than car rental. Seventy-six DM to FRF each, while the trip up cost 88 DM gas, 99 DM overnight room in Hof and 80.5 DM car rental plus frustration of the delays. Gas is 1.69 DM per liter. Arrived FRF Rhein-Main. Place is clean. Gate guard doesn't know where the USAF base is. AP picked us up inside of base and took us to terminal. Empty, clean and plenty of seats. Didn't want to go to Philadelphia. Desk stated that they get everyone out on each flight.

Went to the PX which is a lot larger than your last R&R, #154, stated. Must have been writing about the one at the terminal. This one is part of the commissary building, shelves are very high with items and the local outlet from the hotel is now part of it.

Took the bus to Ramstein and arrived at 2210 (no flight until morning) stayed in VIP quarters across parking from terminal. Everything else was full including hotels off base.

Next morning checked flights and took first one at 0730 to Dover via Thule, Greenland. Three-hour layover in Thule extended into two-and-a-half days. Have never received such VIP treatment. The 43 passengers we had on the C-5 were treated like long lost sons and daughters. Very nice quarters with community toilets and washrooms,

Danish style. Mess hall was one of the best I have eaten in - all Danish cooks with Danish pastries. Took all of us on tour of the outside area, an old abandoned village, 1954, and in general saw a lot of ice, snow and pulverized rocks. We were highlighted on the USAF TV station as the C-5 stranded guests. Seemed odd to get up at 0200 and walk to the latrine and it is as bright as 1200. Parts for the C-5 arrived the night of the second day, but they forgot a pilot for the C-5. Part came up on a MEDEVAC going to Lajes, so since we were in an isolated post they put us all on it, including an IG team that just inspected the base, and the MEDEVAC took us to Dover. I don't think the medical personnel on the flight were happy about this, but at Thule when you are stranded, you must leave on the next available flight. (Once they went three weeks without a flight.) Arrived at Dover at 1758. Great trip and the unexpected delay was its highlight. A lot of people waiting at Ramstein, but only a few of them going to the states. Had three more flights to Dover the day we left. Seems like the drawdown has opened up more space for us Space-A travelers and the flights seem more frequent.

Sincerely,
Bob Matty
CSM USA (Ret)
Westminster, MD

SOME PLACES TO STAY IN THE USA

Dear Ann,

Practically every year since we've started receiving the *R&R Space-A Report*®, we've saved quite a bit of money plus enjoyed great vacations. From the west coast to east coast, Hawaii and Puerto Rico, we've stayed at many Army and Naval bases. In February 1996, we spent a week at the North Island Naval Air Station on Coronado Island. You really don't need a car. They have scheduled transportation - bus by day, and evenings you can call and a van will take you anywhere on base. At front gate you can pick up buses to San Diego. They are building a beautiful new building right next to the present Navy Lodge. We've also stayed at the guest house at Hunter Army Airfield in Savannah, Georgia, several times (be sure to ask for senior discount). A 2-bedroom apartment (we had guests with us) costs $38; 1-bedroom about $28. Our best deal yet was during this Christmas holiday. We spent four days with out daughter and her husband at the Naval Trailers near Old Town, Key West. While everyone else was paying from $200 up daily, we paid $55 for a 2-bedroom, living room, kitchen, and bathroom. Not fancy but adequate. We got a $3 discount for Old Town Trolley Tour from ITT office on Sigsbee Island. We have also stayed at the Navy Lodge there, very nice, also $55. The best place to start the Trolley Tour is at Key West Welcome Center on Roosevelt Blvd. We parked our car there (free) got off at Molloy Square. We did all our sightseeing in Old Town and back to car at 1800. Really a great deal as it is very difficult to find parking in Old Town and quite expensive. We could fill pages with all the places we've stayed in the past 15 years. Your book *Temporary Military Lodging Around the World* is our travel bible - We never leave home without it when we travel. It's wonderful how you update it - gets better each time. Also the 800 number is a great money and time saver.

Keep up the good work Ann, RJ and Roy - you sure do a super job of keeping us informed. We look forward to getting each issue. Every time we read it we get busy planning another trip. Our very best wishes to you.

Sincerely,
Lydia and John P. Myer
COL USA (Ret)
Boynton Beach, FL

BRIDE LOVES SPACE-A

Dear Ann and Roy,

Since the end of 1996, I had been telling my new bride, Sandy, that we were going to take a trip Space-A. Since we had recently married, Sandy had to obtain a passport before we could go anywhere. Finally, in January 1997 she received her passport. We were set to go.

Prior to this, I had flown to Yokota and Osan via Travis a couple of times. Also made a trip to Ohio and Washington DC with the Arizona (AZ) Air National Guard on KC-135's. I had kept up with the new sign-up regulations and had kept up-to-date with your publications. Where in the world would I take my new bride on her first AMC flight?

In February 1997, I found out the AZ Air Guard was going to RAF Mildenhall and would be on the ground for approximately 24-30 hours. Even though we had to compete for seats on the return flight, I felt confident we would have no problems on the return.

Sandy was excited! I explained to her about the type of aircraft we would be flying on and the probable seating arrangements ("jump seats"). She was game. About a week before departure, we were informed that the probability of getting on the flight was excellent. Sandy was happy and getting anxious! Departure was to be the following Tuesday, a week away. I had already faxed or E-mailed my requests for sign-up for the return flight to Mildenhall, Rota, Frankfurt, Naples and Howard AFB. Why Howard AFB? There is a flight from Howard to San Antonio. San Antonio is closer to Phoenix than the east coast. The cost to return to Phoenix, should we have to pay for it, would be less from San Antonio than Dover or Charleston.

The Friday before our departure, just for the heck of it, I telephoned the AMC counter at LAX to inquire about the AMC charter flight to Yokota and Osan. I was informed that show was 2300 hours on Sunday with a departure at 0200 on Monday. At that time, I was also informed that the plane, a 747, had in excess of 100 empty seats.

Sandy and I would have to fly to LAX at our own expense to take the 747 to Osan or Yokota. I also knew it would be less costly to return to Phoenix from Travis or LAX. So, I said, "Japan and Korea, here we come!" I then faxed requests for sign-up to Osan and Yokota.

We flew commercial to LAX. When we arrived at the AMC counter at approximately 2200 hours on Sunday, we were immediately manifested and paid our $6 each for airport tax. Cheap airfare to Japan!

Bad news! The flight was going to depart at 0630 vice 0200 due to weather on its inbound flight. At that time, I inquired as to the availability of seating in the first class or business sections. I figured as a retired Master Chief (E-9) it never hurts to ask. I was told I would be notified at the gate prior to boarding. Sandy and I had to show at the gate no later than 0500.

Now what to do for six hours? We caught a shuttle to a nearby hotel and slept until 0400 hours. Money well spent! Four-and-a-half hours of comfortable sleep allowed us to start the trip off somewhat rested.

Back to LAX. Upon arrival at the gate, the civilian AMC employee notified Sandy and me that we would be accommodated in business. Tower Airlines did not have first-class, only business class. As it turned out, business class equated to first-class seating on smaller airlines. The service and food were the same as coach, but as you well know the seating is the big difference.

Boarding was at 0615 hours and lift off shortly thereafter. After 11-and-a-half hours in the air, we arrived at Yokota AB, Japan. The flight and service on Tower Air was excellent. There were enough seats in coach that most of the passengers had an empty seat between them. In some cases, passengers had three seats to themselves. Everyone seemed to enjoy the flight.

Being Sandy's first Space-A flight, she immediately became spoiled. I told her that this was the ideal Space-A flight!

We spent the night at billeting at Yokota. Quarters were great! It had been three years since I had been to Yokota. AAFES cabs were no longer running. They had been replaced by Air Force buses which ran every 30 minutes. The bad thing is they did not start running until 0500. If you had a show time prior to 0530, the walk from billeting to the AMC terminal is a fair distance.

After checking the outbound flights to Korea for the next 72 hours, I concluded our best bet was to continue on to Osan. Show time was 0430 the next morning. No bus! Now my bride gets to enjoy the taste of the good life ... a mile or so walk to the AMC terminal at 0400! Was she ever "happy!"

The 2 1/2 hour flight was on a C-9 MEDEVAC. Sandy expected a cargo plane. As on all the previous AMC flights I have been on, the crew was professional and most helpful. Wonderful flight. Wife was delighted!

Upon arrival at Osan, I verified our status on the Space-A list. I found that our fax had been received, and we were listed. We contacted billeting. A C-141 had broken down and the crew and passengers had first priority on the available rooms. The billeting personnel told us to be patient but promised nothing, which is the only thing they could do. Being patient paid off. Chiefs' quarters were available for one night only. We were set!

The following day, we caught the contracted bus running between Osan and the Army base in Seoul. Upon arrival we proceeded to Dragon Hill Lodge. An earlier call to the Dragon Hill informed me there were no vacancies. Never give up. Upon arrival there was a cancellation for the night. Nothing else for the following two days. We left our baggage with the bell man and proceeded to the tailor shop at the Dragon Hill. Sandy was measured for two suits and some skirts and I for a suit. After lunch, we checked into our room. After getting settled, I called the reservation office at the Dragon Hill and found out two additional nights had become available. Three nights at the Dragon Hill without reservations! Never take no for an answer.

That evening and for the following days, we were tourists in Seoul. Although I had been there many times before, on this trip I had someone to share the sights with. We went to the two major outdoor markets, rode the subway and while on foot, got lost and were guided to our destination by a Korean lady who just happened to be going our way. The people were friendly and the city was beautiful.

On our final day in Seoul, our suits were ready to go. Sandy decided to order another suit and have it mailed to our home. We felt safe in doing this because the tailor was located in the Dragon Hill Lodge and had to be reputable. We were right! The suit arrived in about three weeks.

We checked out of the Dragon Hill and were off to Osan for our return flight. The AMC charter was to depart the following day. We hoped we could get on the flight. We overnighted in a civilian hotel outside Osan AB since billeting was not available. The hotel was small, clean and unlike hotels in the USA. Sandy was looking for a Hojo's or Holiday Inn but had to settle for this quaint establishment!

The next day we showed for the flight. It had not arrived and had been delayed for whatever reason. The flight was to proceed to LAX via Kadena AB and Yokota AB. The plane was full with passengers going to Kadena and Yokota and 11 passengers who wanted to go to LAX. We were guaranteed seats to Yokota. I inquired as to why we could not be manifested through to LAX. The answer was that Kadena controlled the seats and had not released anything for Osan's use. So what does one do? Go with the flow. After all, we are flying Space-A. This is all part of the fun. "Be patient" is the motto of those who fly Space-A. So we were!

We were off again. Coach section with three seats to ourselves on a Tower Airlines 747 on our way to Yokota with a stop at Kadena. Bad news! Because the flight was late arriving and departing Osan, we would have to remain overnight at Kadena. Tokyo had quiet hours and we could not arrive at Yokota before they went into effect.

At Kadena, customs was cleared, quarters procured, pizza eaten and the day came to an end. The only means of travel on the base at night or early in the morning was via civilian cabs. Although the cab meters were in yen, we were told the charge was in dollars. It made no difference; it beat walking. For those not familiar with Kadena, it is spread out. Without a car, one has to rely on the cabs.

The next morning Sandy and I arrived about 30 minutes before show for our flight. At that time, I inquired about through seats to LAX. I was informed by the NCOIC at the AMC terminal that Kadena had released 10 through seats for Osan's use to LAX. I informed the NCOIC that Osan had told passengers that no seats had been released. The NCOIC checked the computer and found the 10 seats unused. He asked us to be patient. He had to find out if any of the other passengers on the plane with a higher status than us wanted to go to LAX. In the end, all 11 of us who wanted to go to LAX were manifested thanks to the AMC NCOIC.

Sandy and I proceeded to check in our bags and pay our $12.50 each departure tax. Still cheap fare to get back home! I once again asked my favorite question, "Can a retired E-9 and his spouse get seating in business class?" I was told, "no problem!" I was happy, Sandy was delighted and we were on our way home. Next stop, Yokota AB.

All passengers had to disembark at Yokota for refueling. During this time, Sandy and I had to clear customs since we were departing Japan. One of the security police who escorted passengers to the Japanese customs office said he would take our passports over, and we would not have to physically make the trip. How lucky!

After a couple of hours, we were in the air again. This time, we were on our way home. Sandy and I enjoyed this trip and are looking forward to future Space-A flights. We both know that we were fortunate to have flown on a chartered 747 and a MEDEVAC flight. The truth is that we both know that future flights may be less comfortable, and we may incur longer waits. Whatever may follow will be another adventure ... an adventure with low costs while flying on probably the safest airline in the USA ... the planes of the Air Mobility Command (AMC)!

Military Space-A Air Basic Training - 81

In August we will be traveling to Minneapolis and hope to utilize billeting at the Air Guard Base adjacent to the airport. In September we will be vacationing in NYC and hope to procure billeting at Staten Island or Ft. Hamilton. In either case, your publications have assisted in our travel via AMC and in locating billeting as we travel.

We are anxiously awaiting the new edition of *Temporary Military Lodging Around the World*. Thank you for your very useful publications.

Sincerely,
Sandy & Manuel Rios
Avondale, AZ

ANOTHER SPACE-A FIRST TIMER!

Dear Ann and Roy,

In September, my wife and I made our first attempt at Space-A travel. We chose to go to Frankfurt on the Philadelphia R&R flight, but they never even called all the Cat 3's. Many other retirees were in the same boat and some of us went to McGuire, while others went to Dover. We went to McGuire and finally got to Naples via Norfolk, Rota and Sigonella. The trip might have been a disaster except for the companionship of others in the same boat and the willingness of the active forces to help us when we ended up on their doorstep at 2230 with no place to stay. Our return trip was much the same as we hoped to leave from Aviano, but that plane was full except for a few seats to Lajes. As we had more days on our Eur-Rail pass, we spent a day traveling south to Naples by train and got an unscheduled C-5 to Dover and then a rent-a-car to McGuire for our car. No matter what misfortune overtook us, there was company in other retirees suffering the same and the active forces did all possible to minimize any inconveniences. The terminal crews, for the most part, went the extra mile to check all possible flights and routes. Also, the experienced Space-A travelers were of immense help and we did learn to be flexible.

In late January, we drove to Florida and spent six days at Shades of Green™ on Walt Disney World® Resort. What a treat! The facility was unbelievably good and the staff was extremely accommodating. It seemed as if it was still a Disney property and all were still Disney employees as if they fit the Disney mold perfectly. One can't even complain about the food as it was good and reasonable. We are now making plans to join our children and grandchildren for a trip there in the fall or next spring. One daughter is a DoD employee at Aberdeen, so we'll have plenty of sponsors. This is one of the greatest deals ever experienced. I have stayed in the Contemporary and other Disney properties, so I know what they charge.

Yours very truly,
Donald L. Stegner
CAPT USNR (Ret)
Baltimore, MD

Ed's Note: A ha! The employees were so good you thought they must be Disney employees! Nope, they work for the Shades of Green AFRC, and we know they will be delighted with your comments.

SPACE-A TO THE ORIENT

Dear Roy and Ann,
   My wife Shelly and I just returned from our trip from Hickam AFB, Hawaii, to Misawa, Japan, and back. We have several Military Living Publications that came in handy for our trip including *US Forces Travel Guide to Overseas US Military Installations, Temporary Military Lodging Around the World* and *Military Space-A Air Opportunities Air Route Map*. We used the two books to look up phone numbers of the AMC terminals and billeting and make reservations for lodging and faxing my leave papers to get a better Julian date for Space-A role call. Here is our trip report.

Friday 6 June: Signed up for commercial contracted Air Transport International (ATI) DC-8 flight from Hickam AFB to Guam and Yokota, Japan. Due to a mechanical problem with the main cargo door, the flight was delayed one night. Since this was a commercial flight that the Air Force has contracted out to ATI, all the passengers with boarding passes were given free limo ride to the Outrigger Malia in Waikiki with free lodging and meal passes. We could have gone back to our house on NCTAM's Navy Base in Wahiawa, 15 miles from Hickam, but we wanted the free limo ride and night at the hotel. The Outrigger Malia is one of the nicest and most inexpensive hotels in Waikiki, centrally located behind the International Market Place; but it was especially affordable to us since we stayed there for free Friday night.

Saturday 7 June: Departed Hickam in DC-8 at 1350. Stopped in Guam to refuel then on to Yokota, Japan. Since it was a contract flight, we got to eat free hot meals with a choice of BBQ/Yakichobi chicken or pasta delivered by Kristi, our flight attendant. We also got to watch "Independence Day" and another movie about a lady disc jockey whose boyfriend didn't know what she really looked like. After a five-hour flight we landed in Guam on Sunday 8 June at 1715 - crossed the international date line. When we got to Guam to refuel, we took off an hour earlier than planned to Yokota. We were behind schedule and needed to get to Yokota before 2200 when the noise curfew for airplanes landing at Yokota went into effect. We got to Yokota about 2130 and took a shower in the AMC terminal. Then we called billeting/Kanto Lodge and got a room for a few hours of sleep.

Monday 9 June: We got up at three in the morning and checked out of billeting and walked back to the AMC terminal. It was cold and drizzling. There was only one person on duty at the checkout desk at billeting. He offered to give us a ride, but we would have to wait for an hour before someone could take his place behind the desk so we walked it. Lucky for us we left most of our luggage in a locker at the AMC terminal. We got to the AMC terminal for an 0500 role call for a C-130 going to Misawa, Japan. We got on the flight and arrived in Misawa at 0830. We met our sponsor in Misawa. He got off work to take us on a tour of the base and out in town. Then we went to the Base Exchange and got a rental car: $227.45 for seven days. There was a medical rodeo on Misawa over the weekend and a lot of people checked out of the Misawa Inn Monday morning, so we had to wait until 1030 to check in to give the housekeepers time to clean our room.

Tuesday 17 June: Departed Misawa in commercial contracted L-100 at 0700. The L-100 is a modified C-130 with airline seats and flight attendants. We got steak to eat on the way to Kunsan, Korea, for free. We refueled and took off from Kunsan to Yokota and got a look at the Patriot Missiles aimed up north towards North Korea. On the way to Yokota we told the flight attendant we'd like to see Mount Fuji, so the pilot flew closer for us to get a good picture with our video camera. There were only three people on the flight from Kunsan to Yokota since everyone else got off to take a bus to Osan and go shopping. About 1500 we landed in Yokota. Tuesday night we stayed at Kanto Lodge on base for $17. Due to a lot of people on EML Category II leave, we were not able to get a flight out of Yokota directly to Hickam.

Wednesday 18 June: We tried to get a room at billeting on base, but it was full so we went to the Morikawa Hotel outside the gate by the AMC terminal to the right behind the 7-Eleven. A lady at the AMC who was also trying to get a flight out with her kids gave us a ride to the Morikawa since it was raining. I didn't know for sure where the Morikawa Hotel was so I asked the lady to stop at the 7-Eleven so I could ask for directions. The lady behind the cash register didn't speak English, so she asked another Japanese lady to help me. The other lady took me outside and showed me the road behind the 7-Eleven and told me the Morikawa was there. We stayed the night at the Morikawa for $137.46 - ouch!

Thursday 19 June: We got up at 0300 for an 0400 role call and an 0700 departure. It was a C-5 to Travis, but at least we made it out of Yokota. It was good to get out of Yokota too because Typhoon Opal was due to arrive the next day and all flights, even commercial, were cancelled. It was a nine-hour flight, but we crossed the international date line. We got to Travis around 0800 and tried to get out on a flight to Hickam. There were a lot of people wanting to go to Hickam. Flights had been cancelled or rerouted because of the typhoon in Japan and some people had been waiting at Travis for a week or more. We waited at the terminal for two role calls, but we didn't have an early enough Julian date - 167. We took a taxi to the E-Z 8 Hotel in Fairfield. The taxi was $14.25 there and $13.50 coming back later that night for the 0145 role call of a DC-8 with 33 seats to Hickam. The EZ 8 Hotel was $37.45. We got up at 2330 to check out and take a taxi back to the AMC terminal.

Friday 20 June: We should have stayed at the Townhouse Inn. They are $56 a night, but they have a free shuttle van that takes you to and from the AMC terminal in Travis. We missed the DC-8 to Hickam since our Julian date was 167. Later we signed up for a C-5 to Hickam, and we make it out on the C-5 to Hickam. We got back to Hickam around 2000, walked from the temporary AMC terminal to the long-term parking lot across from the AMC terminal that is being renovated and drove home. The wheeled cart for our luggage came in handy several times during our trip. I was glad we brought it. We would have had to go commercial for about $500 from San Francisco if we hadn't made the flight because we were tired of waiting around in AMC terminals and not getting out. We picked a busy time of year to fly AMC. It would not have been so bad if we had been on EML Category II leave, but they only get that in overseas duty stations and only twice a year.

Hope this trip report will help out other people trying to fly AMC. Space-A is a good benefit for being in the military if you use it wisely.

            Dan and Shelly Wedeking
            CTI1 USN
            Wahiawa, HI

SPACE-A TO HAWAII

Dear Ann and Roy,

We just got back to Hawaii from our three-week vacation to Quitman, Arkansas. We saved about $720 by flying Space-A from Hickam AFB, Hawaii, to Travis AFB, California, and then taking a van to San Francisco International Airport and flying commercial the rest of the way. It is relatively easy to catch Space-A flights from Hickam to Travis and back as they usually have several flights a day.

We traveled on an Air Force KC-10 from Hickam to Travis. We left from Hickam on Tuesday, 29 August 1995 and returned from Travis on a C-141 on Wednesday, 20 September 1995. The Space-A planes are comfortable and the crews treat their passengers well. The only hard part about flying Space-A is getting up early enough to catch a flight before everyone gets up and gets on the flight before you.

Once we got to Travis, we called for a van from M&M Van Company; $40 for my wife, Shelly, and I to go to the Ramada Inn in San Francisco. With a military discount we stayed in a nice hotel for only $39 for one night. We took the free Ramada shuttle van to the airport the next morning to catch our $770 Delta free companion fare round-trip to Little Rock, Arkansas.

We originally planned to go in December for Christmas, but decided against it since the people at Hickam said that was a busy time of year and hard to get Space-A seats. There are flights out, but they are usually all full of people on environmental/moral leave from Japan, Guam, Australia and other remote outposts.

On the way back we flew into San Francisco Airport; stayed at the USO until the van driver picked us up and took us to the Motel 6 in Fairfield closest to Travis. We got up at four in the morning and caught a Yellow Cab taxi (422-5555) to the Travis AMC terminal for $16. We had signed up for a flight back to Hickam on 29 August. So when we stood in line for the role call on 20 September, we were the first on the list in the category of normal leave to get two of the 21 seats on the flight. There was one person ahead of us on EML leave from Guam.

So the moral of the story is to try to fly Space-A during the time of the year when they are not too busy, and you can get a flight out without too much trouble.

        Dan & Shelly Wedeking
        CTI1 USN
        Wahiawa, HI

MSGT & Mrs. D.R. Kirkwood fly a "Refrigerator" plane to visit their children in Alaska.

APPENDIX A: SPACE-A PASSENGER REGULATIONS

CHAPTER 6
SPACE-AVAILABLE TRAVEL

A. GENERAL POLICY

1. Definition and Scope. Space-available travel is the specific program of travel authorized by this Chapter allowing authorized passengers to occupy DoD aircraft seats which are surplus after all space-required passengers have been accommodated. Space-available travel is allowed on a non-mission interference basis only. DoD aircraft shall not be scheduled to accommodate space-available passengers. No (or negligible) additional funds shall be expended and no additional flying hours shall be scheduled to support this program. In order to maintain the equity and integrity of the space-available system, seats may not be reserved or "blocked" for use at en route stops along mission routes.

2. Purpose of the Space-Available Program. Space-available travel is a privilege (not an entitlement) which accrues to Uniformed Services members as an avenue of respite from the rigors of Uniformed Services duty. Retired Uniformed Services members are given the privilege in recognition of a career of such rigorous duty and because they are eligible for recall to active duty. The underlying criteria for extending the privilege to other categories of passengers is their support to the mission being performed by Uniformed Services members and to the enhancement of active duty Service members' quality of life.

3. Leave Status for Travel. Uniformed Services members on active duty must be in a leave or pass status to register for space-available travel, remain in a leave or pass status while awaiting travel, and be in a leave or pass status the entire period of travel. DoD civilian employees, when afforded space-available privileges listed in table 6-1, below, must be in a leave or non-duty (i.e., weekend or holiday) status to register for space-available travel. If in a non-duty status, leave must have been approved for the first normal working day following the non-duty period. A leave status must then be maintained while awaiting travel and for the entire period of travel. Those members in appellate leave status are not authorized space-available travel privileges.

4. In Conjunction with Space-Required Travel or to Restricted Tour Areas. Space-available travel may not be used instead of space-required travel, such as TDY, TAD and PCS travel, except emergency leave type travel (see Chapter 2, subsection A.4., above). Space-available travel may be used in conjunction with space-required travel as long as space-available travel does not substitute for any single leg for which the traveler has a space-required entitlement (except emergency leave type travel). For example, a Uniformed Services member may take leave with a TDY or TAD, as allowed by Service regulations, and may travel space-available while on leave. Travel from the PDS to the TDY or TAD location shall be space-required with the traveler in a duty status; any space-available travel from the TDY or TAD duty location shall return to the TDY or TAD location, with the traveler in a leave status; and the final leg shall be space-required from the TDY or TAD location to the PDS with the traveler in a duty status.

86 - Military Space-A Air Basic Training

APPENDIX A, continued

Dependents may not use space-available travel options in this Regulation to accompany their sponsor on space-required travel or to travel to or from a sponsor's restricted or all other (unaccompanied) tour locations.

5. Registers and Sign-Up Procedures

   a. Each base, installation or post from which space-available travel is accomplished shall maintain a single space-available register and all space-available passengers accepted for airlift from that location must have been selected from the register's roll. The maintenance of such a roster shall be the responsibility of the AMC passenger activity, where established. Where no AMC passenger activity is established, it shall be the responsibility of the base, installation, or post commander to designate the Agency responsible for maintaining the space-available roster.

   b. To compete for space-available travel, eligible personnel must sign up on the space-available roster in person and present all required documentation (see subsection A.6., below). The DoD Components and the USTRANSCOM may also accept sign-up information in writing from eligible space-available travelers (through mail, fax transmission, E-mail (approved change AMC 151556Z APR 96) where available). When adopted, the DoD Components and the USTRANSCOM shall provide detailed guidance outlining procedures for using "remote sign-up" services. Passengers shall declare their final destination when they sign up for space-available travel. The original date and time of sign-up shall be documented and stay with the traveler until his or her destination is reached. On reaching the destination, the traveler may again sign up for space-available travel to return to home station. Those registered are not required to accept any seat offered, and failure to accept an offered seat shall not jeopardize a passenger's position on the space-available register. All but Category VI passengers (see table 6-1, below) are automatically removed from the space-available register on expiration of leave, pass or after 60 days, whichever is sooner. Category VI passengers are removed from the list after 60 days. All space-available passengers dropped from the register may sign up again in their respective categories (see table 6-1, below) with a new date and time of sign-up.

   c. Eligible travelers who arrive at an air terminal seeking space-available transportation shall sign a document certifying compliance with the rules for eligibility and conditions of space-available travel, and be provided access to documentation showing the date and time their request for movement was entered onto the installation space-available roster.

   d. Reservations shall not be made for any space-available passenger. Travel opportunity shall be afforded on an equitable basis to officers, enlisted personnel, civilian employees, and their accompanying dependents without regard to rank or grade, military or civilian, or branch of Uniformed Service.

6. Required Documentation. Unique documentation required for specific types of individuals (e.g., Medal of Honor recipients) is cited in table 6-1, below, on a case-by-case

Military Space-A Air Basic Training - 87

APPENDIX A, continued

basis. Additionally, the following types of travelers shall present the documentation listed below to air terminal personnel, and shall have all the documentation in their possession during travel:

a. Active duty Uniformed Services Members (includes National Guard and Reserve members on active duty in excess of 30 days)

(1) DD Form 2 (Green) U.S. Armed Forces Identification Card (Active), or Form 2 NOAA (Green) Uniformed Services Identification and Privilege Card (Active), or PHS Form 1866-3 (Green) United States Public Health Service Identification Card (Active).

(2) A valid leave authorization or evidence of pass status as required by the Service concerned.

b. Retired Uniformed Services Members. DD Form 2 (Blue) U.S. Armed Forces Identification Card (Retired), or DD Form 2 (Blue) NOAA Uniformed Services Identification Card (Retired), or PHS Form 1866-3 (Blue) United States Public Health Service Identification Card (Retired).

c. National Guard and Reserve Members

(1) Authorized Reserve Component Members (National Guard and Reserve) of the Ready Reserve. and members of the Standby Reserve who are on the Active Status List; On presentation of the following valid:

(a) DD Form 2 (Red), "Armed Forces of the United States Identification Card (Reserve).

(b) DD Form 1853, "Authentication of Reserve Status for Travel Eligibility."

(2) Retired Reservists Entitled to Retired Pay at Age 60; On presentation of the following valid:

(a) DD Form 2 (Red).

b) A notice of retirement eligibility as described in DoD Directive 1200.15, (reference (kk)). If the automated DD Form 2 (Red) has been issued, the member is registered in his or her Service personnel system as a Reserve retiree entitled to retired pay at age 60, and a notice of retirement eligibility is not required.

(3) Retired Reservists Qualified for Retired Pay; Documentation, as prescribed in subsection A.6.b., above. For space-available travel eligibility, no distinction is made between members retired from the Reserves and members retired from active duty.

APPENDIX A, continued

(4) On Active Duty for 30 Days or Less; On presentation of the following valid:

(a) DD Form 2 (Red).

(b) Orders placing the Reservist on active duty.

(c) A valid leave authorization or evidence of pass status as required by the Service concerned.

(5) ROTC. Nuclear Power Officer Candidate (NUPOC). and Civil Engineer Corps (CEC) Members; When enrolled in an advanced ROTC, NUPOC, or CEC course or enrolled under the financial assistance program, on presentation of the following valid:

(a) DD Form 2 (Red).

(b) DD Form 1853.

d. Dependents of Uniformed Services Members. DD Form 1173, "United States Uniformed Services Identification and Privilege Card."

e. EML Travelers. Besides any documentation required by paragraphs A.6.a. through A.6.d., above, EML orders issued in accordance with Unified Command procedures (see paragraph B.4.a., below).

7. Categories of Travel and Priorities of Movement

a. Categories. There are six categories of space-available travel. Space-available travelers are placed in one of the six categories based on their status (e.g., active duty Uniformed Services member, and DoDDS teacher, etc.) and their situation (e.g., emergency leave, and ordinary leave, etc.). Once accepted for movement, a space-available passenger may not be "bumped" by another space-available passenger, regardless of category. See table 6-1, below, for a list of specific travelers and the category in which they fall.

b. Priority of Movement. The numerical order of space-available categories indicates the precedence of movement between categories; e.g., travelers in Category III move before travelers in Category IV. The order in which travelers are listed in a particular category in table 6-l, below, does not indicate priority of movement in that category. In each category, transportation is furnished on a first-in, first-out basis.

c. Changes to Movement Priorities. Wherever the issue may arise, the local installation commander may change the priority of movement of any space-available traveler for emergency or extreme humanitarian reasons when the facts provided fully support such an exception. The installation commander may delegate the authority to make such changes to no lower than the Chief of the Passenger Service Center or its

APPENDIX A, continued

equivalent when a movement priority is changed, the passenger shall be moved no higher than the bottom of the Category I space-available list. Where AMC units are tenants, the senior local AMC authority shall advise the installation commander of this authority and offer technical assistance, as needed.

8. Destinations and International Restrictions

   a. If authorized by this Chapter for a particular traveler's status and situation (see table 6-1, below), transportation may be between overseas stations, between CONUS stations, and between overseas and CONUS stations where adequate border clearance facilities exist or can be made readily available. Theater or international restrictions shall be observed and all requirements pertaining to passports, visas, foreign customs, and immunizations shall be met.

   b. Individuals traveling to or from the CONUS, and who are not otherwise eligible to travel space-available in the CONUS, may travel on any CONUS leg segment (i.e., on a flight with en route stops) when no change of aircraft or mission is involved.

9. Conditions of Travel. There is no guaranteed space for any traveler. The Department of Defense is not obligated to continue an individual's travel or return him or her to point of origin, or any other point. Travelers shall have sufficient personal funds to pay for commercial transportation to return to their residence or duty station if space-available transportation is not available. Space-available travel shall not be used for personal gain, for a business enterprise or outside employment, when theater or international restrictions prohibit such travel, or to establish a home overseas or in the CONUS (except for permissive TDY house hunting trips as authorized in table 6-1, below).

10. Dependent Travel. Except where specifically noted in this chapter, dependents may travel space-available only when accompanied by their sponsor.

B. EML TRAVEL

Except as noted, unfunded EML travel is subject to the space-available travel program rules and guidance outlined in this section A., above, and table 6-l, below. Funded EML travel is discussed in Chapter 2, sections B.l.e. B.3.a.(14).

1. Definition. EML is leave granted with an EML program, as prescribed in DoD Directive 1327.5 (reference (d)), established at an overseas installation where adverse environmental conditions require special arrangements for leave in more desirable places at periodic intervals.

2. Program Description. For a complete description of the EML program, see reference (d).

APPENDIX A, continued

    a. <u>EML Locations and Destinations</u>. Specified locations where adverse environmental conditions exist and at which EML is authorized, are called "EML locations." The Under Secretary of Defense (Personnel and Readiness) designates Funded EML (FEML) locations and relief destinations. Unified commanders designate locations under the unfunded EML program. Under the EML program, not more than two relief destinations shall be designated unless additional destinations are needed to provide a reasonable prospect of relief. The CONUS shall not be designated an "EML destination" except when such designation is necessary to provide a realistic opportunity for relief.

    b. <u>Priority, Timing, and Frequency</u>. Passengers traveling space-available under the EML program are given a higher priority than those traveling on ordinary leave (see table 6-1, below). The timing and the frequency of EML is limited by DoD Directive 1327.5 (reference (d)). Transportation officials are not responsible for monitoring this timing and frequency, but rather are responsive to EML documentation issued by the commanders concerned.

   3. <u>Responsibilities</u>. Unified commanders shall ensure that administrative controls are in place to ensure that all eligible travelers are able to participate in the EML space-available travel program on a fair and equitable basis. The unified commanders concerned shall forward two copies of each implementing directive, and of any modifications to such directive, to The Department of the Army (DAPE-MBB-C), the Commandant of the U.S. Marine Corps (LFT), the Chief of Naval Operations (N4l), HQ USAF/LGTT, NOAA Corps (NC), and the USTRANSCOM (TCJ3/J4).

   4. <u>Policy and Procedures</u>

    a. Unified command procedures shall include the issuance of a separate set of EML orders each time an individual is approved for EML.

    b. Unfunded EML travelers may travel in Category II status (See table 6-1, below) to only one EML destination for each set of EML orders. This does not preclude several approved EML destinations being included in a single set of EML orders as long as procedures are in effect to ensure that the individual is provided Category II status only for travel to and from the first authorized EML destination actually reached. Subsequent space-available travel; e.g., from the EML destination to a third location and return, or from the third location to another EML location, may only be provided in Category III status (table 6-1, below).

    c. When traveling under EML orders, dependents who are 18-years of age or older may travel unaccompanied by their sponsor. Dependents who are under 18-years of age traveling under EML orders must be accompanied by an EML eligible parent or legal guardian who is traveling in an EML status.

Military Space-A Air Basic Training - 91

APPENDIX A, *continued*

C. ELIGIBILITY

The travelers listed in table 6-1, below, are eligible to travel space-available in the categories and over the geographical segments cited, subject to any limitations cited in table 6-1, below, under "Traveler's Status and Situation," or elsewhere in this Regulation.

ELIGIBLE SPACE-AVAILABLE TRAVELERS, PRIORITIES, AND APPROVED GEOGRAPHICAL TRAVEL SEGMENTS

This table lists travelers who are eligible to travel on DoD aircraft according to the space-available program outlined in paragraphs A. and B., above. "Item" is a sequential numbering and is for reference purposes only. "Cat" is the category of travel as explained in section A.7.a, above. These are used to determine priority of movement as explained in section A.7.b., above. "Traveler's Status and Situation" lists specific travelers and conditions under which space-available travel may be authorized. The approved geographical travel segments, i.e. origin and destination combinations, are C-C (CONUS to CONUS), O-O (overseas to overseas), C-O (CONUS to overseas) and O-C (overseas to CONUS) (reference section A.8.). A "yes" in the column headed by one of these abbreviations indicates that travel is authorized in that particular geographical travel segment for the particular type traveler cited in that item number, and subject to any limitations cited. Lack of a "yes" indicates travel is not authorized in that particular geographical travel segment.

* **refers to P 210939Z OCT 95, from HQ AMC SCOTT AFB IL//DOJ// to AIG 8521, dated 20 October 1995, regarding: change 1 to DoD 4515.13-R, Air Transportation Eligibility.**

Table 6-1. Eligible space-available travelers, priorities, and approved geographical travel segments.

Item	Category	Traveler's Status and Situation	C-C	O-O	C-O and O-C
1		**Category I - Emergency Leave Unfunded Travel**			
2		Transportation by the most expeditious routing only for bona fide immediate family emergencies, as determined by DoD Directive 1327.5 (reference (d)) and Service regulations, for the following travelers:			
3	I	Uniformed Services members with emergency status indicated in leave orders (for space-required option see Chapter 2, sections B.1.L and B.1.b., above.	yes	yes	

92 - Military Space-A Air Basic Training
APPENDIX A, continued

Item	Category	Traveler's Status and Situation	C-C	O-O	C-O and O-C
4	I	*continued* Civilians, U.S. citizens, stationed overseas, employees of: (1) Uniformed Services; or (2) NAF activities and whose travel from the CONUS, Alaska or Hawaii was incident to a PCS assignment at NAF expense (for space-required option see Chapter 2, sections B.2.a. and B.4.a., above.		yes	yes
5	I	Dependents of members of the Uniformed Services, command-sponsored, accompanied or unaccompanied (for space-required option see Chapter 2, sections B.3.a(1), B.3.a(2), and B.3.a.(4), above).		yes	yes
5A*	I	Dependents of members of the Uniformed Services when accompanied by their sponsor.	*yes*		
6	I	Dependents of members of the Uniformed Services, noncommand-sponsored, residing overseas with the sponsor, one-way only to emergency destination (for space-required option see Chapter 2, sections.3.b.(1) and B.3.b.(2), above).		yes	C-O no O-C yes
7	I	Dependents, command-sponsored, of: (1) U.S. citizen civilian employees of the Uniformed Services stationed overseas;(2) U.S. citizen civilian employees of the DoD stationed overseas and paid from NAF; or (3) American Red Cross full-time, paid personnel, serving		yes	yes

Military Space-A Air Basic Training - 93

APPENDIX A, continued

Item	Category	Traveler's Status and Situation	C-C	O-O	C-O and O-C
7	I	*continued* with a DoD component overseas (for space-required option see Chapter 2, section B.3.a. 2 above).			
8	I	Professional Scout leaders, and American Red Cross full-time, paid personnel, serving with a DoD component overseas (for space-required option see Chapter 2 section B.6., above).		yes	yes
9		**Category II - EML**			
10	II	Sponsors in an EML status and their dependents traveling with them, also in an EML status. "Sponsors" includes: (1) Uniformed Services members. (2) U.S. citizen civilian employees of the Armed Forces who are eligible for Government-funded transportation to the United States at tour completion (including NAF employees). (3) American Red Cross full-time, paid personnel on duty with a DoD component overseas. (4) USO professional staff personnel on duty with the Uniformed Services. (5) DoDDS teachers during the school year and for Employer-approved training during recess periods.		yes	yes
11		**Category III - Ordinary Leave, Close Blood or Affinitive Relatives, House Hunting Permissive TDY, Medal of Honor Holders and Others**			
12	III	Uniformed Services members in a leave or pass status other than			

APPENDIX A, continued

Item	Category	Traveler's Status and Situation	C-C	O-O	C-O and O-C
12	III	*continued* leave (use Category I) or excess appellate leave, for which space-available travel is not authorized. This includes members of the Reserve components on active duty, in a leave or pass status.	yes	yes	yes
13	III	Dependents of a member of the Uniformed Services accompanied by their sponsor in a leave status other than emergency leave (use Category I) or excess appellate leave, for which space-available travel is not authorized.		yes	yes
14	III	Close blood or affinitive relatives who are permanent members of the household and dependent upon a Military Service member, a DoD civilian employee, or American Red Cross employee serving with a DoD component overseas, when the sponsor is authorized transportation of dependents at Government expense. Travel must be with the sponsor's, or his or her dependent's, PCS move.			yes
15	III	Dependent spouses of military personnel officially reported in a missing status under 37 U.S.C. 551 (reference (11)), and accompanying dependent children and parents, when traveling for humanitarian reasons and on approval on a case-by-case basis by the Head	yes	yes	yes

Military Space-A Air Basic Training - 95

APPENDIX A, continued

Item	Category	Traveler's Status and Situation	C-C	O-O	C-O and O-C
15	III	*continued* of the Service concerned (Chief of Staff of the Army, the Chief of Naval Operations, the Chief of Staff of the Air Force, and the Commandant of the Marine Corps) or their designated representative. Travelers shall present an approval document from the Service concerned.			
16	III	Uniformed Services members traveling under permissive TDY orders for house hunting incident to a pending PCS.	yes	yes	yes
17*	III	Uniformed Services members traveling under permissive TDY orders for house hunting incident to a pending PCS and one accompanying dependent.	*yes*	yes	yes
18	III	Medal of Honor recipients. Except for active duty, traveler shall present a copy of the Medal of Honor award certificate.	yes	yes	yes
19	III	Dependents of Medal of Honor recipients when accompanied by their sponsor.		yes	yes
20	III	Command-sponsored dependents of Uniformed Services members accompanying their sponsor on approved circuitous travel. Commanders authorized to publish circuitous travel orders for members under current policy of their Uniformed Service, where extenuating circumstances prevail, may approve requests for space-available travel of their dependents within and between overseas areas and the CONUS,		yes	yes

APPENDIX A, continued

Item	Category	Traveler's Status and Situation	C-C	O-O	C-O and O-C
20	III	*continued* incident to approved circuitous travel of the member. (For space-required option see Chapter 2, section B.3.a.(7), above).			
21	III	Cadets and midshipmen of the U.S. Service academies, and foreign cadets and midshipmen attending U.S. Service academies, in a leave status. Foreign cadets' and midshipmen's native countries must be identified in the leave authorization.	yes		yes
22	III	Civilian U.S. Armed Forces patients who have recovered after treatment in medical facilities and their accompanying nonmedical attendants. Travel is permitted by the most expeditious routing to return the recovered patient and nonmedical attendant to the overseas post of assignment (During the death or extended hospitalization of the patient, the nonmedical attendant retains the space-available travel authority to return to the patient's overseas post of assignment).		yes	C-O yes O-C no
23	III	Foreign exchange service members on permanent duty with the Department of Defense, when in a leave status.	yes	yes	yes
24	III	Dependents of foreign exchange service members on			

APPENDIX A, continued

Item	Category	Traveler's Status and Situation	C-C	O-O	C-O and O-C
24	III	*continued* permanent duty with the Department of Defense, when accompanying their sponsor.		yes	yes
25		**Category IV - Unaccompanied Dependents on EML and DoDDS Teachers on EML During Summer**			
26	IV	Dependents traveling under the EML Program, unaccompanied by their sponsor, traveling under subsection B.4.c., above ("Sponsor" as defined in item 10, above).		yes	yes
27	IV	DoDDS teachers or dependents (accompanied or unaccompanied) traveling under the EML Program during the summer break.		yes	yes
28		**Category V - Permissive TDY (Non-house hunting), Foreign Military, Students, Dependents & Others**			
29	V	Military personnel traveling on permissive TDY orders other than for house hunting.	yes	yes	yes
30	V	Dependents (children) who are college students attending in residence an overseas branch of an American (U.S.) university located in the same overseas area in which they reside, command sponsored, stationed overseas with their sponsor who is: (1) A member of the Uniformed Services; (2) A U.S. citizen civilian employee of the Department of Defense (paid from either appropriated funds or		yes	

98 - Military Space-A Air Basic Training

APPENDIX A, continued

Item	Category	Traveler's Status and Situation	C-C	O-O	C-O and O-C
30	V	*continued* NAF); or (3) An American Red Cross full-time, paid employee serving with the Department of Defense. Unaccompanied travel is permitted from the overseas military passenger terminal nearest their sponsor's permanent duty station to the overseas military passenger terminal nearest the university, and to return during school breaks. Students must present written authorization from an approving authority and only one round-trip each year is authorized. Unused trips may not be accumulated from school year to school year.			
31	V	Dependents, command-sponsored, stationed overseas with their sponsor who is: (1) A member of the Uniformed Services; (2) A U.S. citizen civilian employee of the Department of Defense (paid from either appropriated funds or NAF); or (3) An American Red Cross full-time, paid employee serving with the Department of Defense. Unaccompanied travel is permitted to and from the nearest overseas military academy testing site to take scheduled entrance examinations for entry into any of the US service academies.		yes	
32	V	Dependents of active duty US military personnel stationed overseas who, at the time of PCS, were not entitled to			

Military Space-A Air Basic Training - 99

APPENDIX A, continued

Item	Category	Traveler's Status and Situation	C-C	O-O	C-O and O-C
32	V	*continued* transportation at government expense. Travel is to accompany or join their sponsor at his or her duty station. Travel may be unaccompanied and is limited to travel from the APOE in the CONUS, Alaska, or Hawaii to the overseas APOD serving the sponsor's duty station. Before travel, approval of the overseas major commander is required. (For space-required option see Chapter 2, section B.3.(8), above).			C-O yes O-C no
33	V	Noncommand-sponsored dependents, acquired in an overseas area during a military member's current tour of assigned duty, not otherwise entitled to transportation at government expense. Travel must be with the member's PCS, may be unaccompanied, and is limited to travel from the overseas APOE to the APOD in the CONUS, Alaska, or Hawaii. Member's PCS orders are required for travel. Command regulations pertaining to the acquisition of dependents must have been followed. (For space-required option see Chapter 2, section B.3.b. (2) above).			C-O no O-C yes
34	V	Unaccompanied spouses of Uniformed Services members stationed in overseas areas in response to written requests from school officials for personal consultation on matters about the needs of family members attending school at an overseas		yes	

100 - Military Space-A Air Basic Training

APPENDIX A, continued

Item	Category	Traveler's Status and Situation	C-C	O-O	C-O and O-C
34	V	*continued* location away from the Uniformed Services member's PDS.			
34A*	V	Command-sponsored dependents of Uniformed Services members who are stationed overseas. Travel restrictions may apply to certain overseas destinations as determined by the appropriate unified commander. Documentation signed by the sponsor's commander verifying command sponsorship shall be present to air terminal personnel and shall be in the dependent's possession during travel. This documentation is valid for one round-trip from sponsor's PCS duty location. Dependents under 18 years of age must be accompanied by an eligible parent or legal guardian.		*yes*	*yes*
35		**Category VI - Retired, Dependents, Reserve, ROTC, NUPOC, and CEC**			
36	VI	Retired Uniformed Services members	yes	yes	yes
37	VI	Dependents of retired Uniformed Services members, when accompanying their sponsor.		yes	yes
38	VI	Dependents, command-sponsored, stationed overseas with their sponsor who is: (1) A member of the Uniformed Services; (2) A U.S. citizen civilian employee of the Department of Defense (paid from either appropriated funds or			

Military Space-A Air Basic Training - 101

APPENDIX A, continued

Item	Category	Traveler's Status and Situation	C-C	O-O	C-O and O-C
38	VI	*continued* NAF); or (3) An American Red Cross full-time, paid employee serving with the Department of Defense. Unaccompanied travel is permitted to the U.S. for enlisting in one of the Armed Forces when local enlistment in the overseas area is not authorized. If an applicant for Military Service is rejected, return travel to the overseas area may be provided under this eligibility.		yes	yes
39	VI	Authorized Reserve component members and authorized Reserve component members entitled to retired pay at age 60, traveling in the CONUS and directly between the CONUS and Alaska, Hawaii, Puerto Rico, the U.S. Virgin Islands, Guam, and American Samoa (Guam and American Samoa travelers may transit Hawaii or Alaska); or traveling within Alaska, Hawaii, Puerto Rico or the U.S. Virgin Islands.	yes		
40	VI	NUPOC, CEC, and ROTC students of the Army, Navy, or Air Force, receiving financial assistance or enrolled in advanced training, in uniform, during authorized absences from the school. Travel is authorized within and between the CONUS, Alaska, Hawaii, and the U.S. territories.	yes		

102 - Military Space-A Air Basic Training

APPENDIX A, continued

ADDITIONAL SPACE-A INFORMATION FROM CHAPTER 1

C. USE OF MILITARY AIRCRAFT, INELIGIBLE TRAFFIC, AND RESTRICTIONS

1. Commanders' Responsibility. The commanders at all levels shall exercise prudent judgment to ensure that only authorized traffic is transported and that they do not misuse the authority delegated to them by this Regulation. The commanders and other officials responding to requests for transportation not specifically authorized by this Regulation shall make no commitments concerning prospective travelers or cargo until they receive all required approvals.

2. Ineligible Traffic Procedures

   a. When an order or authorization for movement of traffic (passenger or cargo) which is neither authorized by this Regulation nor approved according to the procedures in this Regulation is presented, transportation shall be denied. The station making the determination shall document the case and forward it through channels to USTRANSCOM TCJ3/J4-LP, 508 SCOTT DRIVE, SCOTT AFB IL 62225-5357 for necessary action.

   b. Any traffic transported by DoD aircraft which is ineligible, even though documentation may have been issued, is liable for reimbursement at the non-U.S. Government rate tariff according to APR 76-28 (reference (f)) for all transportation furnished. If any passenger or cargo is challenged for eligibility or authority, every effort shall be made to provide assistance short of delaying a scheduled aircraft.

3. Restrictions on Use of Unit or Operational Support Aircraft. Unless requested and authorized under DoD Directive 4500.43 (reference (t)), unit aircraft shall not be utilized to transport DoD passengers and cargo. Similarly, the use of unit or operational support airlift aircraft to provide PCS transportation for DoD members or their dependents is not authorized.

4. Pregnant and Post Partum Mothers and Newborn Infants

   a. Pregnant women up to the 34th week of gestation may be accepted for air transportation unless medically inadvisable.

   b. Women who are 6 weeks, or more, post partum and infants at least 6 weeks old may be accepted for air transportation unless medically inadvisable. Infants under 6 weeks old and women who are less than 6 weeks post partum may be accepted if considered medically sound and so certified in writing by a responsible medical officer or civilian physician.

5. Unaccompanied Minors. Restrictions on travel by unaccompanied minors vary with types of travel (see Chapters 2, 5, 6, and 7).

6. Passengers on "Non-Transport-Type" Aircraft. Aircraft not designed or normally configured for passenger (non-aircrew personnel) carrying capability, such as, but not limited to, fighter aircraft, are not to be used for passenger travel. This does not restrict use of these type aircraft for orientation flights, as prescribed in Chapter 4 below.

7. Disabled Passenger. Every effort shall be made to transport passengers with disabilities who are otherwise eligible to travel. Passenger service personnel and crew members shall provide assistance in loading, seating, and unloading the disabled passenger. Travel may be disapproved by the chief of the passenger travel section or the aircraft commander if there is an unacceptable risk to the safety of the disabled passenger, other passengers or the crew, or if operational necessity or equipment or manpower limitations preclude accepting disabled passengers. Such disapprovals shall be rare. In such cases, air terminal personnel must ensure that the passenger understands why air transport is not possible on the mission in question. When a disabled passenger is denied transportation for the above reasons, and when his or her sponsor or dependent, who is otherwise eligible to travel, accompanies the disabled passenger to assist in his or her needs, travel shall be approved if such assistance will eliminate the reasons for denying travel.

D. BAGGAGE

1. Timeliness. Baggage must arrive at the APOE either with the traveler or sufficiently in advance to permit the owner to document and offer it for movement as "accompanied baggage."

2. Allowances

   a. Normal Free Checkable Baggage Allowance. Duty and space-available passengers are authorized two pieces of checked baggage and one carry-on piece. Checked baggage may not exceed 62 linear inches (length plus width plus height) or 70 pounds for each piece. Carry-on baggage must fit under the seat and may not exceed 45 linear inches (length plus width plus height). For duty passengers only, a duffel bag, sea bag, B-4 bag, flyer's kit bag, or diver's traveling bag, any of which exceeds 62 linear inches, may be substituted for one of the 62 linear inch items.

   b. Excess Baggage Allowance. When authorized by service regulations or directives, an excess baggage allowance may be included in an individual's orders. Excess baggage shall be stated in terms of number of pieces, not by weight. Use the formula of 70 pounds for each piece and round to the next highest whole piece to determine the number of pieces necessary. For example, if 100-pounds excess is needed, then two pieces of excess baggage are authorized. Excess baggage is not authorized for space-available passengers.

   c. Unauthorized Excess Baggage. Baggage which exceeds the normal baggage allowance without proper authorization may be accepted for shipment at the discretion of air terminal representatives. Passengers owning such baggage will be charged the

APPENDIX A, continued

appropriate excess baggage fee. Air terminal representatives are authorized to refuse to accept baggage in excess of that authorized. Disposition of unauthorized baggage not accepted for shipment shall be the personal responsibility of the owner. Shipment may be made at personal expense through postal facilities or commercial transportation companies. If shipment is otherwise authorized to be made at government expense, arrangements for forwarding may be made with the APOE transportation office.

   d. Patients. Patients are limited to two pieces of baggage not to exceed 70 pounds each.

   e. Baggage Allowance Restriction. To maximize seat availability, terminal personnel may further restrict passenger baggage allowances when air transportation services are provided by an activity not financed through the DBOF-T.

   f. Other Modes. This Regulation limits only the baggage that may be carried by passengers traveling on DoD aircraft. It does not restrict or increase the baggage allowance that may be prescribed by other directives for shipment by other modes.

   3. Firearms and Ammunition. Unloaded personal firearms and small arms ammunition may be carried as checked baggage within the authorized weight allowance as long as they are in compliance with the laws and regulations of the United States, foreign governments, the Department of Defense, and the Military Departments. The Military Departments shall establish procedures which require the passenger to identify the items to passenger service personnel or their equivalent at the time of processing for flight and which ensure that the items are in checked baggage, or otherwise adequately secured, so as to be inaccessible to passengers while they are aboard the aircraft.

E. DRESS. CONDUCT. AND STANDARD OF SERVICE

   1. Dress. The wearing of the uniform on DoD aircraft by members of the Uniformed Services on active duty, members of the Reserve components not on active duty, and authorized foreign military personnel shall be governed by the directives of the Service concerned and by DoD 4500.54-6, "Foreign Clearance Guide" (reference (u)). When civilian clothing is worn, it shall be in good taste and not in conflict with accepted attire in the overseas country of departure, transit, or destination.

   2. Conduct. Under no circumstances shall a passenger be accepted for transportation or be permitted to board an aircraft if he or she is unruly, under the influence of alcohol or narcotic, may create a hazard to the safety of the aircraft or passengers, or is a disruptive influence.

   3. Standard of Service. The DoD components shall establish and maintain standards of appearance, conduct, and service for flight and ground personnel who come in contact with customers of the airlift system which shall ensure professional, courteous, and responsive service.

F. ANIMALS

1. Seeing Eye Dogs

a. Transportation of a dog properly trained to lead the blind, and officially identified by a bona fide organization which trains or registers such dogs, is authorized without charge when accompanying its blind owner who is otherwise authorized transportation under this Regulation.

b. The dog must be properly harnessed to lead a blind person, muzzled to safeguard other passengers and crew members, remain at the blind person's feet, and not create a safety hazard to others by being in the aisle. The dog shall be permitted to accompany the owner in the cabin, but may not occupy a seat or be in the galley area. Sanitation must be maintained at all times.

c. Transportation of Seeing Eye dogs shall be subject to country quarantine procedures. When it is necessary to detain the animal pending determination of its admissibility, the owner shall provide detention facilities satisfactory to the cognizant quarantine officer. The owner shall bear the expense of such detention, including necessary examinations and vaccinations, and other expenses incurred due to the dog's accompanying the owner.

2. Pets. Passengers traveling under PCS orders may be allowed to ship their pets at their own personal expense. For this privilege, pets are defined as "dogs and cats only," and are limited to two for each family. Requests to deviate from this policy, i.e., number, type, or weight of pets, will be submitted through Service Headquarters to AMC for consideration.

a. Owner Responsibilities. The owner of the pet(s) is responsible for the preparation and care of the animal and for all documentation, immunization, and border clearance requirements including quarantine. The owner shall provide a pet shipment container approved by the International Air Transport Association of sufficient size to allow the animal to stand up, turn around, and lie down with normal posture and body movements.

b. Aircraft Operator Responsibility. The DoD component operating the aircraft shall ascertain that the means and facilities exist at origin and destination to permit the owner to accomplish his or her responsibilities before accepting the animal for shipment. The operator of the aircraft shall establish procedures to ensure that the pets accepted for movement are stowed in areas heated and pressurized adequately to sustain health and comfort according to accepted commercial industry practice.

3. Other Animals. There is no restriction on shipping other animals aboard DoD aircraft for official purposes if they meet all criteria for shipment of official cargo established by this Regulation. Animals shall be housed, caged, and shipped in a humane fashion consistent with law and industry standards.

106 - Military Space-A Air Basic Training

APPENDIX A, continued

G. FORMS

    1. DD Form 1381. "Air Transportation Agreement." Before travel aboard aircraft operated by an activity not financed through DBOF-T, the DD Form 1381 shall be executed by the non-DoD personnel specified in Chapters 2, 3, 4,5, 8, and 10, below, when their flight originates in a foreign country. NATO member national personnel traveling in the performance of official duties are exempt from this requirement. The completed DD Form 1381 shall be attached to the passenger manifest and filed at the point of origin. Sponsors will execute DD Form 1381 for minor dependents or individuals incapable of signing for themselves.

    2. DD Form 1839. "Baggage Identification." All checked and carry-on baggage shall be identified with required data clearly annotated on the DD Form 1839. When the DD Form is unavailable, substitute tags, such as those used in the commercial aviation industry, may be used.

    3. DD Form 1853. "Authentication of Reserve Status for Travel Eligibility." Members of the Reserve components traveling under the provisions of Chapter 6, below, shall have a completed DD Form 1853 in their possession at all times.

    4. Boy Scouts of America. "Parent/Guardian Consent Form for Aviation Flights." Explorer Scouts participating in an orientation flight under the provisions of Chapter 4, below, shall present a completed Parent/Guardian Consent Form for Aviation Flights before the flight.

    5. Supply of Forms. DD Forms 1381, 1839, and 1853 shall be made available to users by forms management officers of the DoD components. To ensure availability to users, forms management officers are encouraged to permit local reproduction of these forms. The Parent/Guardian Consent Form for Aviation Flights shall be obtained from the individual's Scout Troop.

AUTHOR'S NOTE: This Appendix (chapter 6, SPACE AVAILABLE TRAVEL, of DoD 4515.13-R and related) contains references to other related documents which are independent of DoD 4515.13-R and other chapters in DoD 4515.13-R **all of which are not published here because of space limitations.** In most cases, this documentation amplifies, provides background information and further explains chapter 6 of DoD 4515.13-R. Although not completely essential to the understanding of the Space Available Travel directive, persons wishing to view the entire DoD 4515.13-R and related documents may do so upon request and presentation of appropriate entitlement identification at military space-A departure locations and Uniformed Services Personnel Offices. The following chapter 6, SPACE AVAILABLE TRAVEL and part of chapter 1, DoD 4515.13-R was released to Military Living Publications by the Office of The Under Secretary of Defense, Jan 1995.

APPENDIX A, continued

SPACE-A EXPANDS FOR ACTIVE DUTY FAMILY MEMBERS

The following unclassified message, P 210939Z OCT 95, from HQ AMC SCOTT AFB IL//DOJ// to AIG 8521, dated 20 October 1995, regarding: change 1 to DoD 4515.13-R, Air Transportation Eligibility.

"1. The following changes to DoD 4515.13-R are effective immediately: changes appear on pages 6-7, 6-9, and 6-11. New page changes will be sent to all locations on requirement for this regulation through normal distribution channels. In the interim, use this message as authorization to execute movement for all eligible passengers under this change.

A. Page 6-7 add: Item 5A CAT I. Dependents of members of the uniformed services when accompanied by their sponsor. (CONUS to CONUS) Yes.

B. Page 6-9 add: Item 17 CAT III. Uniformed services members traveling under permissive TDY orders for house hunting incident to a pending PCS and one accompanying dependent. (CONUS to CONUS) Yes; (OVERSEAS to OVERSEAS) Yes; (CONUS to OVERSEAS) and (OVERSEAS to CONUS) Yes.

C. Page 6-11 add: Item 34A CAT V. Command-sponsored dependents of uniformed services members who are stationed overseas. Travel restrictions may apply to certain overseas destinations as determined by the appropriate unified commander. Documentation signed by the sponsor's commander verifying command sponsorship shall be presented to air terminal personnel and shall be in the dependent's possession during travel. This documentation is valid for one round-trip from sponsor's PCS duty location. Dependents under 18 years of age must be accompanied by an eligible parent or legal guardian. (OVERSEAS to OVERSEAS) Yes; (CONUS to OVERSEAS) and (OVERSEAS to CONUS) Yes.

2. These changes are effective immediately."

:-) Tootie, a military dependent dog, invites you and your pets to visit her on the world-wide web.
Tootie Talks gives military pets a chance to voice their concerns about travel, fun, quarantines & more!

Visit her at:
http://www.militaryliving.com
E-mail: TootieDog@aol.com

PET TRAVEL

"I can't fly Space-A because only those on PCS can take a pet. **BUT** - I'll keep you informed on Pet Travel News!"

APPENDIX B: PROCEDURES FOR REMOTE SPACE-A TRAVEL SIGN-UP AND ONE-TIME SIGN-UP (USE AMC FORM 140, FEB 95 APPENDIX D)

The Assistant Secretary of Defense (OSDUSD-TP), gave approval to USCINCTRANS on 30 March 1994 to implement remote sign-up for Space-available (Space-A) travel and sought service headquarters planned implementation instructions/guidelines. **The following (summarized) procedures for this initiative became effective 1 July 1994.**

1. ACTIVE DUTY MEMBERS OF THE SEVEN UNIFORMED SERVICES:

A. Fax a copy of the applicable service leave (or pass) (**OF Form 988, DA Form 31, NAVCOMP 3065 and NAVMC 3) and other service leave (or pass) forms from USCG, USPH and NOAA or use AMC Form 140, Feb 95 (Appendix D).**

B. A statement that required border clearance documents are current, i.e., I.D. cards for sponsor and eligible dependents (family members); passports for sponsor (if required) and dependents (family members); visas for sponsor and dependents (family members) and immunizations (PHS-731, I. International Certificates of Vaccination and II. Personal Health History), as required for all travelers.

C. A list of five desired country destinations (5th may be "ALL" to take advantage of opportune airlift).

D. The fax should be sent on the effective date of leave (or pass): **Therefore, the fax header will establish the basis for date/time of sign-up.**

E. Members will remain on the Space-A travel register for a period of 60 days or upon expiration of leave (or pass), whichever is sooner. As an option the Services (USA, USN, USMC, USCG, USAF, USPH, NOAA) may designate a central point of contact to assist members by answering basic questions and ensuring information is correct to minimize delayed sign-up. (NOTE: none have been so designated.)

F. Mail (United States Postal Service) and Courier (Base/Installation official distribution) entries will be permitted. The Air Mobility Command (AMC) has indicated that commercial courier/delivery services such as United Parcel Service (UPS), Federal Express (FEDEX), and E-mail on the worldwide web (where available) are acceptable media for filing your application for Space-A air travel. Upon receipt, the service leave (or pass) form can then be stamped with the current date/time (please keep in mind that mail on military installations goes through distribution channels and may take longer than normal mail). NOTE: Active duty members on pass may utilize this enhancement. Fax a request indicating desired destination, name, rank and inclusive dates of pass.

2. ACTIVE STATUS MEMBERS OF THE RESERVE COMPONENTS:

A. Fax a current copy of their DD Form 1853, **"Authentication of Reserve Status For Travel Eligibility" and use AMC Form 140, Feb 95.**

Military Space-A Air Basic Training - 109

APPENDIX B, continued

B. A statement that border clearance documents are current, if applicable for United States Possessions.

C. A list of five desired destinations (no foreign country destinations; 5th destination may be "ALL" to take advantage of opportune airlift).

D. Active Status members will remain on the Space-A register for a period of 60 days. NOTE: Active Status members of the Reserve components may only register for travel to/from the CONUS and Alaska, Hawaii, Puerto Rico, the US Virgin Islands, American Samoa and Guam. **Dependents (family members) of an Active Status Reservist do not have a Space-Available travel eligibility.**

E. Mail and Courier entries will be permitted. Upon receipt the DD Form 1853 can then be stamped with the current date/time (please keep in mind, mail on military installations goes through distribution channels and may take longer than normal mail).

3. ELIGIBLE RETIRED MEMBERS OF THE SEVEN UNIFORMED SERVICES:

A. Fax a request to the desired aerial port(s) (station) of departure giving five desired destinations (5th destination may be "ALL" to take advantage of opportune airlift). **The fax data/time header will be the basis for the date/time of Space-A travel sign-up, or use AMC Form 140, Feb 95.**

B. Retirees may remain on the Space-A travel register for a period of 60 days.

C. Mail, E-mail and Courier entries will be permitted. Upon receipt the request can be stamped with the current date/time (please keep in mind that mail on military bases goes through distribution channels and may take longer than normal mail).

4. MEMBERS OF THE RESERVE COMPONENTS (GREY AREA RETIREES) WHO HAVE RECEIVED NOTIFICATION OF RETIREMENT ELIGIBILITY BUT HAVE NOT YET REACHED AGE 60:

A. These members are limited to the same travel destinations as Active Status Reserve Members. **Dependents (family members) of these Reservists do not have a Space-Available travel eligibility. Use AMC Form 140, Feb 95.**

5. Appendix C has a list of AMC Terminals (Stations) having the best capability of providing Space-A travel. Units listed in USAF, AMCP 76-4 will also provide remote Space-A travel sign-up. The Services (other than USAF/AMC, USA, USN, USMC, USCG and other USAF) are requested to augment this listing with their Base/Installation manifesting agencies capable of providing this service. **NOTE: Remote Space-A travel sign-up is the sole responsibility of each member unless a (Uniformed) Service designates a single Point of Contact (POC) for a specific installation. Uniformed Services have not designated single POCs.**

APPENDIX B, continued

6. Please note that **worldwide Space-A sign-up in person and at self-service counters remains available at Services terminals and stations which operate Space-A registers.** Times available for registration in person are based on local operating hours.

ONE-TIME SIGN-UP FOR SPACE-AVAILABLE PASSENGERS

Passengers traveling Space-A on military and contract charter aircraft **now can retain their initial date/time (Julian date) of sign-up when traveling through more than one destination/station (traveling in the same general direction, i.e., East to West, North to South) to reach their final destination.** The new procedure is the result of a recommendation made by the US Air Force's, Air Mobility Command (AMC) and approved by the Assistant Under Secretary of Defense.

In the past, travelers received a new sign-up date at each stop on their way to their final destination, which caused some to say that those stationed or living at or in the vicinity of the en route location had an unfair advantage. **Under the new rules, passengers still are required to sign up at all en route stops, but they keep their date and time of sign-up from their originating location.** For example a passenger who originates his/her travel at Incirlik AB (ADA), TU to Rhein-Main AB (FRF), GE, and plans to continue straight through to CONUS, will get priority over people starting their flights at Rhein-Main AB, GE.

The process is not automatic. **Passengers must still sign up at all stops to continue their Space-A flights and retain their original sign-up date.** However, passengers receive an "in transit" stamp on their travel order or boarding pass indicating date, time and location where they entered the system. This stamp identifies en route travelers to terminal personnel and gives the travelers priority on subsequent flights.

*Ed's Note: Message from HQ AMC Scott AFB, FL//DOJP//, R 51515Z Aug 96-- paragraph 1-D "One-time Space-Available sign-up. We continue to receive inquiries on this subject. Apparently, some passenger terminals have procedures to honor other terminals' date/time of sign-up for passengers who do not arrive in-transit on DoD aircraft. This is a misapplication of the one-time sign-up rules. Unless arriving your station via DoD aircraft, passengers desiring Space-Available transportation must sign up with a new date/time of sign-up in person or use established remote means, i.e,. fax or E-mail. **We are exploring future implementation of a one-time/round-trip Space-A sign-up. We will be soliciting your input in the near future. Until then, all passenger terminals must consistently follow current guidance.**"*

There are restrictions. **Passengers traveling (hopping) by Space-A air through terminals/bases for extended visits will lose their transient status.** For example, if the above passenger gets to Rhein-Main, AB, GE and takes six days of leave/pass/vacation there, he/she will get a new date and time for his next Space-A flight.

APPENDIX C: SPACE-A AIR TRAVEL REMOTE SIGN-UP

The following is a list of Air Mobility Command Terminals/Stations providing Space-A Travel and their fax numbers for Remote Space-A Travel. **NOTE:** Fax numbers are constructed for dialing from the North American touch tone dial code system. Please pause where there are dashes located in number groups.

LI/ICAO	Terminal/Stations	Fax Number
ASP/YBAS	Alice Springs Apt, Australia	011-61-89-530-382
AKT/LCRA	Akrotiri RAFB, Cyprus	011-357-2-465944
UAM/PGUA	Andersen AFB, Guam	(671) 366-3984
ADW/KADW	Andrews AFB, MD	(301) 981-4241
NJA/RJTA	Atsugi NAF, Japan	011-81-3117-64-3149
AVB/LIPA	Aviano AB, Italy	011-39-434-66-7722/7066
BAH/OBBI	Bahrain IAP, Bahrain	011-973-727-360
TLV/LLBG	Ben Gurion IAP, Israel	011-972-3-972-1989
CAI/HECA	Cairo IAP, Egypt	011-20-2-279-1290
NAP/LIRN	Capodichino Apt (Naples), Italy	011-39-81-568-5259/5499
CHS/KCHS	Charleston AFB, SC	(803) 566-3060/5808
CHS/KCHS	Charleston IAP, SC	(803) 566-3845
CHC/NZCH	Christchurch IAP, New Zealand	011-64-3-358-1458
IGL/LTBL	Cigli TAFB, Turkey	011-90-232-441-7044
BKK/VTBD	Don Muang Apt, Thailand	011-66-2-287-1027
DOV/KDOV	Dover AFB, DE	(302) 677-2953
EIL/PAEI	Eielson AFB, AK	(907) 377-2287/1862
EDF/PAED	Elmendorf AFB, AK	(907) 552-3996
SKA/KSKA	Fairchild AFB, WA	(509) 247-4909
RDR/KRDR	Grand Forks, ND	(701) 747-6540
HIK/PHIK	Hickam AFB, HI	(808) 448-1503
HOW/MPHO	Howard AFB, Panama	011-507-284-3848
ADA/LTAG	Incirlik Apt (Adana), Turkey	011-90-322-316-3420
IWA/RJOI	Iwakuni MCAS, Japan	011-81-6117-53-3301
DNA/RODN	Kadena AB, Japan	011-81-611-734-4221
KEF/BIKF	Keflavik Apt, Iceland	011-354-425-4649
KUZ/RKJK	Kunsan AB, Korea (Republic of)	011-82-654-470-7550
LGS/LPLA	Lajes Field AB (Azores), Portugal	011-351-95-540-100 ext 25110
LAX/KLAX	Los Angeles IAP, CA	(310) 363-2790
TCM/KTCM	McChord AFB, WA	(206) 984-5659
IAB/KIAB	McConnell AFB, KS	(316) 652-4957
WRI/KWRI	McGuire AFB, NJ	(609) 724-4621
MHZ/EGUN	RAF Mildenhall, United Kingdom	011-44-1-638-54-2250
MSJ/RJSM	Misawa AB, Japan	011-81-3117-62-6141
OZP/LEMO	Moron AB, Spain	011-34-55-84-8008
NGU/KNGU	Norfolk NAS, VA	(757) 444-7501
OSN/RKSO	Osan AB, Korea (Republic of)	011-82-333-661-4897
PPG/NTSU	Pago Pago IAP, American Samoa	011-684-699-9991
COF/KCOF	Patrick AFB, FL	(407) 494-7991
SGP/WSAP	RSAF Paya Lebar, Singapore	011-65-382-3614

112 - Military Space-A Air Basic Training

APPENDIX C, continued

LI/ICAO	Terminal/Stations	Fax Number
PHL/KPHL	Philadelphia IAP, PA	(215) 897-5627
RMS/ETAR	Ramstein AB, Germany	011-49-6371-47-2364
FRF/EDAF	Rhein-Main AB, Germany	011-49-69-699-6309
RCM/YSRI	Richmond RAAFB, Australia	011-61-45-88-5366
NRR/TJNR	Roosevelt Roads NAS, Puerto Rico	(787) 865-4208/5542
RTA/LERT	Rota NAS, Spain	011-34-56-82-2968
BLV/KBLV	Scott AFB, IL	(618) 256-1946
SIZ/LICZ	Sigonella Apt, Italy	011-39-95-783-6729/1547
SOC/LGSA	Souda Bay NSA/AF, Greece	011-30-821-66200-1525
SUU/KSUU	Travis AFB, CA	(707) 424-2048
UMR/YPWR	Woomera AS, Australia	011-61-86-739-439
OKO/RJTY	Yokota AB, Japan	011-81-425-52-2511 ext 59768

An All-New Edition

Are you taking advantage of military morale, welfare, and recreation-type lodging? Most of it is located on military RV, camping and recreation areas.

If not, you are missing out on true value, the beauty of the great outdoors and military camaraderie.

As you can see in a couple of the features in this issue on military RV, camping and recreation areas, you don't have to sleep in a pup tent to enjoy this type of lodging! You don't even have to have an RV, tent or camping gear.

More good news - your patronage helps keep these morale-boosters self-supporting! Military Living is proud to help them flourish!

Military Living's RV, Camping & Rec Areas Around the World has 223 listings. Each one has details on what's available for those with RVs, pop-up campers, or for the "get down on the ground" old-fashioned tent campers.

If a facility has cottages, A-frames, yurts, log cabins, or motels, that info is also given.

Number of units, electrical connections and more are supplied. Descriptions are given for each location with appropriate phone numbers and addresses for reservations.

You and your family can have a lot of fun with this book! Look for it at your favorite military Exchange and $ave! If not available, call 703-237-0203 for credit card orders.

Military Space-A Air Basic Training - 113

APPENDIX D: SPACE AVAILABLE TRAVEL REQUEST (AMC FORM 140, Feb 95)

This is the "Space Available Travel Request" you or the lead traveler in your group will be required to complete when you apply for Space-A air travel.

SPACE AVAILABLE TRAVEL REQUEST *This form is affected by the Privacy Act of 1974 - See below.*	INSERT HERE

This information is required for space available travel registration. Upon completion, place the upper right corner of this form and the back of your leave form into the Date/Time validator. Be sure to deposit one copy of this request into the box; retain carbon copy for the Space Available roll call. Space-A sign-up is good for a 60-day period, or when your leave expires, whichever comes first. For facsimile (fax) requests, telefax header will establish date and time of sign-up.

PLEASE PRINT CLEARLY

1. NAME (*Last, First, MI*)

2. RANK, GRADE	3. SSN	4. SEATS REQUIRED

5. TRAVEL STATUS (*Type of leave*)

	FOR OVERSEAS TRAVEL:
CATEGORY I - Civ or Mil Dependent on Emergency Leave	Border Clearance Document Current?
CATEGORY II - Environmental Morale Leave (EML)	
CATEGORY III - Active Duty on Ordinary Leave / House Hunting	☐ YES ☐ NO
CATEGORY IV - (EML) Unaccompanied Dependents	
CATEGORY V - Permissive TDY or TAD / Student Travel	(See note on reverse)
CATEGORY VI - Retired Military / Reserves	

6. SERVICE:	ARMY	NAVY	AF	MARINES	OTHER

7. DATE LEAVE BEGINS (*Active Duty Only*)	8. DATE LEAVE ENDS (*If extended, you must notify us before this date*)

9. COUNTRY CHOICES (*List up to 5, one choice may be all*)

10. LIST NAMES OF DEPENDENTS TRAVELING AND TYPE OF PASSPORT (*US or Foreign*)

11. I CERTIFY THAT I AM ON LEAVE OR PASS STATUS AT THE TIME I REGISTER FOR SPACE AVAILABLE TRAVEL AND WILL REMAIN IN SUCH STATUS WHEN AWAITING AND/OR HAVE BEEN ACCEPTED FOR SPACE AVAILABLE TRAVEL. IF ACCOMPANIED BY DEPENDENTS, I FURTHER CERTIFY THAT MY TRAVEL IS NOT IN CONJUNCTION WITH TDY/TAD AND THAT I AM NOT USING SPACE AVAILABLE TRAVEL TO TRANSPORT MY DEPENDENTS TO OR FROM MY RESTRICTED DUTY STATION OR ALL OTHER (UNACCOMPANIED) TOUR LOCATION STATIONS. I CERTIFY THAT MY REQUEST FOR AND ACCEPTANCE OF TRANSPORTATION VIA DOD OWNED OR CONTROLLED AIRCRAFT IS NOT FOR PERSONAL GAIN NOR FOR, OR IN CONNECTION WITH BUSINESS OF ANY NATURE AND THAT THIS TRIP WILL NOT RESULT IN ANY FORM OF RENUMERATION TO MYSELF OR TO MY FAMILY. I UNDERSTAND VIOLATION OF ANY OF THE ABOVE COULD RESULT IN BILLING AND OR PUNITIVE ACTION.

12. DATE	13. SIGNATURE

PRIVACY ACT STATEMENT

AUTHORITY 10 USC. 8013; EO 9397, 22 November 1943.
PRINCIPAL PURPOSE: To apply for air travel. SSN is needed for positive ID.
ROUTINE USE(S): Records from this system of records may be disclosed for any of the blanket routine uses published by the Air Force.
DISCLOSURE IS VOLUNTARY: Failure to provide the information may result in member not being accepted for travel on military aircraft. Disclosure of SSN is voluntary.

AMC FORM 140, FEB 95 (*EF*) (*PerFORM PRO*)	AMC COPY

APPENDIX E: INTERNATIONAL CIVIL AVIATION ORGANIZATION (ICAO) LOCATION IDENTIFIERS AND FEDERAL AVIATION ADMINISTRATION (FAA) LOCATION IDENTIFIERS (LI) CONVERSION TABLES

The location identifiers (LIs) used in this book are the Federal Aviation Administration coordinated three letter LIs for the United States, its possessions and Canada. Foreign country LIs have been coordinated by the Department of Defense. An LI represents the name/location of an airport/air base. They are considered permanent (changes are made for air safety only) and cannot be transferred. The original LI remains in effect even if it becomes necessary to change the name of a given facility.

The International Civil Aviation Organization (ICAO) has established an international location indicator which is a four letter code used in international telecommunications. If the ICAO is shown on the departure board or other displays, look under the encode for the ICAO listed alphabetically to find the three letter Location Identifier (LI), the local standard time (LST) and the clear text name and location of the airport. If the LI is shown on the departure board or other display, look under the decode for the LI listed alphabetically to find the four letter ICAO, LST and the clear text name and location of the airport.

The ICAO/LIs listed below are primarily used to identify military stations/locations around the world. Some of the stations listed may not be active at all times, and all worldwide stations may not be listed. Local standard time (LST) gives the difference in LST from Greenwich Mean Time (GMT).

ENCODE (ICAO vs LI)

ICAO	LI	LST	STATION/NAME	LOCATION
AGGH	HIR	+11:00	HENDERSON IAP	HONIARA,SI
BGSF	SFJ	-03:00	*SONDRESTROM AB	SONDRESTROM, GL (DN)
BGTL	THU	-04:00	THULE AB	THULE, GL (DN)
BIKF	KEF	+00:00	KEFLAVIK APT	KEFLAVIK, IC
CYAW	YAW	-04:00	HALIFAX SHEARWATER	HALIFAX (NS), CN
CYFB	YFB	+00:00	FROBISHER BAY	FROBISHER BAY, CN
CYQX	YQX	-03:30	GANDER IAP	NEWFOUNDLAND, CN
CYYR	YYR	-04:00	*GOOSE BAY AB	GOOSE BAY NFLD, CN
CYYT	YYT	-03:30	ST JOHNS APT	ST JOHNS NFLD, CN
DIAP		+00:00	ABIDJAN/ PORT BOUET	ABIDJAN/ PORT BOUET
DNMM		+00:00	LAGOS/ MURTALA	LAGOS/ MURTALA
DRRN	NIM	+01:00	NAIMEY IAP	NIAMEY, NG
EBBR	BRU	+01:00	BRUSSELS NATL	BRUSSELS, BE
EDAF	FRF	+01:00	RHEIN-MAIN AB	FRANKFURT, GE
EDAS	SEX	+01:00	SEMBACH AB (RUNWAY CLOSED)	SEMBACH, GE
EDDF	FRA	+01:00	FRANKFURT MAIN IAP	FRANKFURT, GE
EDDH	HAM	+01:00	HAMBURG APT	HAMBURG, GE
EDDN	NUE	+01:00	NURNBERG APT	NURNBERG, GE
EDDS	STR	+01:00	STUTTGART APT	STUTTGART, GE
EDFH	HHN	+01:00	*HAHN AB	HAHN, GE
EDIH	DIH	+01:00	HOHENFELS AAF	HOHENFELS, GE
EDNN	NRV	+01:00	*NORVENICH GAFB	NORVENICH, GE
EDNO	OBG	+01:00	*OLDENBURG GAFB	OLDENBURG, GE

Military Space-A Air Basic Training - 115

APPENDIX E, continued

ICAO	LI	LST	STATION/NAME	LOCATION
EDSD	LPH	+01:00	*LEIPHEIM GAFB	LEIPHEIM, GE
EDSF	FEL	+01:00	FURSTENFELD-BRUCK AAF	FURSTENFELD-BRUCK, GE
EGKK		+00:00	LONDON/ GATWICK	LONDON, UK
EGPK	PIK	+00:00	*PRESTWICK APT	PRESTWICK, SCOTLAND(UK)
EGSS	STN	+00:00	STANSTED APT	STANSTED, UK
EGUL	LKH	+00:00	RAF LAKENHEATH	SUFFOLK, UK
EGUN	MHZ	+00:00	RAF MILDENHALL	SUFFOLK, UK
EGUP	FKH	+00:00	*RAF SCULTHORPE	SUFFOLK, UK
EGVG	WOB	+00:00	*RAF WOODBRIDGE	SUFFOLK, UK
EGVJ	BWY	+00:00	*RAF BENTWATERS	SUFFOLK, UK
EGWZ	AYH	+00:00	RAF ALCONBURY	SUFFOLK, UK
EHSB	SSS	+01:00	*SOESTERBERG RNLAFB	UTRECHT, NT
EINN	SNN	+00:00	*SHANNON APT	LIMERICK, IR
ENFB	OSL	+01:00	OSLO FORNEBU	OSLO, NO
ETAR	RMS	+01:00	RAMSTEIN AB	LANDSTUHL, GE
ETFT	THF	+01:00	*TEMPELHOF CENTRAL APT/AIR STATION	BERLN, GE
ETNA	LHN	+01:00	AHLHORN GAFB	ALHORN, GE
ETNN	NRV	+01:00	*NORVENICH GAFB	NORVENICH, GE
ETSI	IDT	+01:00	*INGOLSTADT	INGOLSTADT, GE
FAJS	JNB	+02:00	*JAN SMUTS APT	JOHANNESBURG, SF
FGSL		+00:00	MALABO	MALABO, GUINEA
FHAW	ASI	+00:00	ASCENSION AUX AF	GEORGETOWN ASC, UK
FJDG	NKW	+00:00	DIEGO GARCIA ATOLL	CHAGOS IS, IO
FTTJ	NDJ	+01:00	N'DJAMENA IAP	N'DJAMENA, CD
FZAA	FIH	+01:00	KINSHASA NDJILI APT	KINSHASA, ZA
GFLL	KAI	+00:00	FREETOWN	FREETOWN, LUNGI
GLMR	ROB	+00:00	MONROVIA/ SPRIGGS PAYNE	MONROVIA, LI
GLRB	ROB	+00:00	*MONROVIA ROBERTS IAP	MONROVIA, LI
GOOY	DKR	+03:00	DAKAR YOFF	DAKAR, SE
HCMI	BBE	+03:00	BERBERA	BERBERA, SM
HCMM	MGQ	+03:00	MOGADISHU IAP	MOGADISHU, SM
HECA	CAI	+02:00	CAIRO IAP	CAIRO, EG
HECW	CAI	+02:00	CAIRO WEST	CAIRO, EG
HFFF	JBD	+02:00	DJIBOUTI/ AMBOULI	DJIBOUTI/ AMBOULI
HKMO	MBA	+00:00	MOMBASA	MOMBASA, KE
HKNA	NBO	+03:00	JOMO KENYATTA IAP	NAIROBI, KE
HSSP	PZU	+02:00	PORT SUDAN APT	PORT SUDAN, SU
HSSS	KRT	+02:00	KHARTOUM APT	KHARTOUM SU
KADW	ADW	-05:00	ANDREWS AFB	CAMP SPRINGS, MD
KAEX	AEX	-06:00	ENGLAND AFB	ALEXANDRIA, LA
KATL	ATL	-05:00	THE WILLIAM B. HARTSFIELD ATLANTA IAP	ATLANTA, GA
KBAB	BAB	-08:00	BEALE AFB	BEALE AFB, CA
KBAD	BAD	-06:00	BARKSDALE AFB	SHREVEPORT, LA
KBDL	BDL	-05:00	BRADLEY IAP	WINDSOR LOCKS, CT
KBGR	BGR	-05:00	BANGOR IAP	BANGOR, ME
KBIF	BIF	-06:00	BIGGS AAF	FORT BLISS, TX
KBIX	BIX	-06:00	KEESLER AFB	BILOXI, MS
KBLV	BLV	-06:00	SCOTT AFB	BELLEVILLE, IL
KBNA	BNA	-06:00	NASHVILLE METRO APT	NASHVILLE, TN
KCEF	CEF	-05:00	WESTOVER ARB	CHICOPEE, MA
KCHS	CHS	-05:00	CHARLESTON AFB/ IAP	CHARLESTON, SC
KCLT	CLT	-05:00	CHARLOTTE/ DOUGLAS IAP	CHARLOTTE, NC

116 - Military Space-A Air Basic Training

APPENDIX E, continued

ICAO	LI	LST	STATION/NAME	LOCATION
KCOF	COF	-05:00	PATRICK AFB	COCOA BEACH, FL
KCOS	COS	-07:00	CITY OF COLORADO SPRINGS	COLORADO SPRINGS, CO
KCRW	CRW	-05:00	YEAGER/ CHARLESTON APT	CHARLESTON, WV
KCYS	CYS	-07:00	CHEYENNE MUNI APT	CHEYENNE, WY
KDAY	DAY	-06:00	JAMES M. COX-DAYTON IAP	DAYTON, OH
KDFW	DFW	-06:00	DALLAS/FORT WORTH REG	DALLAS/ FORT WORTH, TX
KDOV	DOV	-05:00	DOVER AFB	DOVER, DE
KDYS	DYS	-06:00	DYESS AFB	ABILENE, TX
KELP	ABQ	-06:00	EL PASO IAP	EL PASO, TX
KFFO	FFO	-06:00	WRIGHT-PATTERSON AFB	WRIGHT-PATTERSON AFB, OH
KFLL	FLL	-05:00	FT LAUDERDALE INTL	FT LAUDERDALE, FL
KFOE	FOE	-06:00	FORBES FIELD	FORBES FIELD, KS
KGFA	GFA	-07:00	MALMSTROM AFB	MALMSTROM AFB, MT
KGRK	GRK	-06:00	ROBERT GRAY AAF	KILLEEN, TX
KGSB	GSB	-05:00	SEYMOUR JOHNSON AFB	GOLDSBORO, NC
KIAB	IAB	-06:00	MCCONNELL AFB	McCONNELL AFB, KS
KILG	ILG	-05:00	GREATER WILMINGTON	WILMINGTON, DE
KIND	IND	-06:00	INDIANAPOLIS IAP	INDIANAPOLIS, IN
KJAN	JAN	-06:00	THOMPSON FIELD	JACKSON, MS
KJFK	JFK	-05:00	JOHN F KENNEDY IAP	NEW YORK, NY
KLAW	LAW	-06:00	LAWTON MUNICIPLE	LAWTON, OK
KLAX	LAX	-08:00	LOS ANGELES IAP	LOS ANGELES, CA
KLCK	LCK	-06:00	RICKENBACKER AFB	RICKENBACKER AFB, OH
KLFI	LFI	-05:00	LANGLEY AFB	HAMPTON, VA
KLIZ	LIZ	-05:00	LORING AFB	LORING, ME
KLRF	LRF	-06:00	LITTLE ROCK AFB	JACKSONVILLE, AR
KLSF	LSF	-05:00	LAWSON FIELD	FORT BENNING, GA
KLTS	LTS	-06:00	ALTUS AFB	ALTUS, OK
KMDT	MDT	-05:00	OLMSTED FIELD	MIDDLETOWN, PA
KMEM	MEM	-06:00	MEMPHIS IAP	MEMPHIS, TN
KMFD	MFD	-05:00	MANSFIELD LAHM MUNICIPAL APT	MANSFIELD, OH
KMIA	MIA	-05:00	MIAMI IAP	MIAMI, FL
KMKE	GMF	-06:00	GENERAL MITCHELL FIELD	MILWAUKEE, WI
KMRB	MRB	-05:00	EAST WV REGIONAL APT	MARTINSBURG, WV
KMSP	MSP	-06:00	MPLS-ST PAUL IAP	MINNEAPOLIS, MN
KMTN	MTN	-05:00	GLEN L. MARTIN STATE APT	BALTIMORE, MD
KNBE	NBE	-06:00	HENSLEY FIELD NAS	DALLAS, TX
KNGU	NGU	-05:00	NORFOLK NAS	NORFOLK, VA
KNIP	NIP	-05:00	JACKSONVILLE NAS	JACKSONVILLE, FL
KNQA	NQA	-06:00	MEMPHIS NAS	MEMPHIS, TN
KNZC	NZC	-05:00	CECIL FIELD NAS	CECIL FIELD NAS, FL
KOAK	OAK	-08:00	METRO OAKLAND IAP	OAKLAND, CA
KOKC	OKC	-06:00	WILL ROGERS WLD APT	OKLAHOMA CITY, OK
KORF	ORF	-05:00	NORFOLK IAP	NORFOLK, VA
KPBG	PBG	-05:00	PLATTSBURGH IAP	PLATTSBURGH, NY
KPHL	PHL	-05:00	PHILADELPHIA IAP	PHILADELPHIA, PA
KPIT	PIT	-05:00	GREATER PITTSBURGH IAP	CORAPOLIS, PA
KPOB	POB	-05:00	POPE AFB	FAYETTEVILLE, NC
KPVD	PVD	-05:00	THEO FRAN GREEN ST	PROVIDENCE, RI

Military Space-A Air Basic Training - 117

APPENDIX E, continued

ICAO	LI	LST	STATION/NAME	LOCATION
KRDR	RDR	-07:00	GRAND FORKS AFB	GRAND FORKS AFB, ND
KRIV	RIV	-08:00	MARCH ARB	RIVERSIDE, CA
KRME	RME	-05:00	*GRIFFISS AFB	ROME, NY
KSAV	SAV	-05:00	SAVANNAH IAP	SAVANNAH, GA
KSBD	SBD	-08:00	NORTON AFB	SAN BERNARDINO, CA
KSCH	SCH	-05:00	SCHENECTADY CO APT	SCHENECTADY, NY
KSDF	SDF	-06:00	STANDIFORD FIELD	LOUISVILLE, KY
KSFO	SFO	-08:00	SAN FRANCISCO IAP	SAN FRANCISCO, CA
KSHV	SHV	-06:00	SHREVEPORT REG	SHREVEPORT, LA
KSKA	SKA	-08:00	FAIRCHILD AFB	FAIRCHILD AFB, WA
KSKF	SKF	-06:00	KELLY AFB	SAN ANTONIO, TX
KSTJ	STJ	-06:00	ROSECRANS MEM APT	ST JOSEPH, MO
KSTL	STL	-06:00	*LAMBERT-ST LOUIS IAP	ST LOUIS, MO
KSUU	SUU	-08:00	TRAVIS AFB	FAIRFIELD, CA
KSVN	SVN	-05:00	HUNTER AAF	SAVANNAH, GA
KSWF	SWF	-05:00	STEWART IAP/ANGB	NEWBURGH, NY
KTCM	TCM	-08:00	MCCHORD AFB	TACOMA, WA
KTIK	TIK	-06:00	TINKER AFB	OKLAHOMA CITY, OK
KTPA	TPA	-05:00	TAMPA INTL APT	TAMPA, FL
KVNY	VNY	-08:00	VAN NUYS APT	VAN NUYS, CA
KWRI	WRI	-05:00	MCGUIRE AFB	WRIGHTSTOWN, NJ
KXMR	XMR	-05:00	CAPE CANAVERAL AI	COCOA BEACH, FL
LATI	TIA	+02:00	TIRANA CITY	TIRANA CITY
LCLK	LCA	+02:00	*LARNACA RAFB	LARNACA, CY
LCRA	AKT	+02:00	AKROTIRI RAFB	AKROTIRI, CY
LDZA	ZAG	+02:00	ZAGREB	ZAGREB, YU
LEMH	MAH	+01:00	*MENORCA APT	MAHON, SP
LEMO	OZP	+02:00	MORON AB	MORON AFB, SP
LERT	RTA	+01:00	ROTA NAS	ROTA, SP
LESJ	PMI	+01:00	*PALMA DE MALLORCA APT	ALEARIC IS, SP
LETO	TOJ	+01:00	TORREJON DE ARDOZ AB	MADRID, SP
LEZA	ZAZ	+02:00	*ZARAGOZA AB	SANJURJO, SP
LFPO	ORY	+02:00	PARIS/ORLY	PARIS, FR
LGAT	ATH	+02:00	*ATHINAI APT	ATHENS, GR
LGIR	VWH	+02:00	*IRAKLION APT	IRAKLION (CR), GR
LGRX	GRX	+02:00	ARAXOS GAFB	ARAXOS, GR
LGSA	SOC	+02:00	SOUDA BAY NSA	KHANIA (CR), GR
LGTS	SKG	+02:00	*THESSALONIKI APT	THESSALONIKI, GR
LIBR	BDS	+01:00	BRINDISI/CASALE APT	CAMPO CASALE, IT
LICR	REG	+01:00	*REGGIO CALABRIA ITAF	TITO MENNITI, IT
LICZ	SIZ	+01:00	SIGONELLA APT	GERBINI (SICILY), IT
LIED	DCU	+01:00	*DECIMOMANNU ITAB	DECIMOMANNU, IT
LIEO	OLB	+01:00	OLBIA/ COSTA ESMERALDA	OLBIA, IT
LIPA	AVB	+01:00	AVIANO AB	AVIANO, IT
LIPT	VCE	+01:00	VICENZA APT	VICENZA, IT
LIPX	VRN	+01:00	VILLAFRANCA APT	VERONA, IT
LIPZ	VEN	+01:00	VENEZIA/TESSERA APT	VENICE, IT
LIRF	FCO	+02:00	ROMA/FIUMICINO	ROME, IT
LIRN	NAP	+01:00	CAPODICHINO APT	NAPLES, IT
LIRP	PSA	+01:00	*PISA APT	PISA, IT
LLBG	TLV	+02:00	BEN GURION IAP	TEL AVIV, IS
LPAR	ALA	+00:00	ALVERCA APT	ALVERCA, PO
LPLA	LGS	+00:00	LAJES FIELD AB	LAJES (AZORES IS), PO
LTAC	ESB	+02:00	ESENBOGA APT	ANKARA, TU
LTAG	ADA	+02:00	INCIRLIK APT	ADANA, TU
LTAT	EHC	+02:00	*ERHAC TUAF	MALATYA, TU
LTBA	YES	+02:00	ATATURK/YESILKOY IAP	ISTANBUL, TU

118 - Military Space-A Air Basic Training

APPENDIX E, continued

ICAO	LI	LST	STATION/NAME	LOCATION
LTBF	BZI	+02:00	*BALIKESIR APT	BALIKESIR, TU
LTBI	ESK	+02:00	*ESKISEHIR TUAF	ESKISEHIR, TU
LTBL	IGL	+02:00	CIGLI TAFB	IZMIR, TU
LTCC	DIY	+02:00	*DIYARBAKIR APT	DIYARBAKIR, TU
LTCE	ERZ	+02:00	*EAZURUM APT	ERZURUM, TU
LTSI	SIO	+02:00	*SINOP AAF	SINOP, TU
MDSI	SDQ	-04:00	SAN ISIDRO AB	SANTO DOMINGO, DR
MGGT	GUA	-06:00	LA AURORA APT	GUATEMALA CITY, GT
MHLC	LCE	-06:00	GOLOSON IAP	LA CEIBA, HO
MHLM	SAP	-06:00	LA MESA IAP	LA MESA, HO
MHSC	PLA	-06:00	SOTO CANO AB	COMAYAGUA, HO
MHTG	TGU	-06:00	TONCONTIN IAP	TEGUCIGALPA, HO
MKJP	KIN	-05:00	NORMAN MANLEY IAP	KINGSTON, JM
MKJT	GDT	-05:00	GRAND TURK AUX FIELD	GRAND TURK IS, UK
MMCZ	CZM	-06:00	COZUMEL INTL	COZUMEL, MX
MMUN	CUN	-06:00	CANCUN INTL	CANCUN, MX
MNMG	MGA	-06:00	AUGUSTO C SANDINO IAP	MANAGUA, NI
MPHO	HOW	-05:00	HOWARD AFB	BALBOA, PN
MPTO	PTY	-05:00	TOCUMEN/TORRIJOS IAP	PANAMA CITY, PN
MROC	OCO	-06:00	SANTAMARIA IAP	SAN JOSE, CS
MSSS	SAL	-06:00	ILOPANGO IAP	SAN SALVADOR, ES
MTPP	PAP	-05:00	HAITI IAP	PORT-AU-PRINCE, HA
MUGM	GAO	-05:00	GUANTANAMO BAY NAS	GUANTANAMO, CU
MWCR		-05:00	OWEN ROBERTS IAP	CAYMEN IS
MYGM	GBI	-05:00	GRAND BAHAMA AUX AF	GRAND BAHAMA, BH
MZBZ	BZE	-06:00	BELIZE IAP	BELIZE CITY, BZ
NSTU	PPG	-11:00	PAGO PAGO IAP	PAGO PAGO, AS
NZCH	CHC	+12:00	CHRISTCHURCH IAP	CHRISTCHURCH, NZ
OBBI	BAH	+03:00	BAHRAIN IAP	MUHARRAQ, BA
OEDR	DHA	+03:00	DHAHRAN IAP	DHAHRAN, SA
OEJB		+03:00	JUBAIL	JUBAIL, SA
OEJD	JED	+03:00	JIDDAH IAP	JIDDAH, SA
OEJF	KFJ	+03:00	KING FAISAL NB	JIDDAH, SA
OEJN	JDW	+03:00	KING ABDUL AZIZ IAP	JIDDAH, SA
OEKJ		+00:00	AL KHARJ	AL KHARJ, AE
OEKK		+03:00	KING KAHLID MILIT	KING KHALID MILIT, SA
OEKM	KAL	+03:00	KHAMIS MUSHAIT AB	ABHA, SA
OERY	RUH	+03:00	RIYADH IAP	RIYADH, SA
OETB	TUU	+03:00	KING FAISAL AB	TABUK, SA
OETF	TIF	+03:00	TAIF APT	TAIF, SA
OJAF	AMM	+02:00	KING ABDULLAH AB	AMMAN, JR
OKBK	KWI	+03:00	KUWAIT IAP	KUWAIT CITY, KW
OMAM	MAM	+03:00	AL DHAFRA	ABU DHABI, AE
OMDB	DBI	+03:00	DUBAI IAP	AL KHARJ, AE
OMFJ	FUJ	+03:00	AL FUJAIRAH	FUJAIRAH, AE
OOMA	MSH	+04:00	MASIRAH OAFB	MASIRAH, OM
OOMS	SBE	+04:00	SEEB IAP	MUSCAT, OM
OOTH	TTH	+04:00	THUMRAIT OAFB	MIDWAY, OM
PACD	CDB	-09:00	COLD BAY APT	COLD BAY, AK
PACZ	CZF	-09:00	CAPE ROMANZOF AFS	CAPE ROMANZOF, AK
PADK	ADK	-10:00	*ADAK ISLAND NS	ADAK, AK
PAED	EDF	-09:00	ELMENDORF AFB	ANCHORAGE, AK
PAEH	EHM	-09:00	CAPE NEWENHAM AFS	CAPE NEWENHAM, AK
PAEI	EIL	-09:00	EIELSON AFB	FAIRBANKS, AK
PAFA	FAI	-09:00	FAIRBANKS IAP	FAIRBANKS, AK
PAFY	FYU	-09:00	FORT YUKON APT	FORT YUKON, AK
PAGA	GAL	-09:00	GALENA APT	GALENA, AK
PAHT	AHT	-09:00	AMCHITKA ISL APT	AMCHITKA, AK

Military Space-A Air Basic Training - 119

APPENDIX E, continued

ICAO	LI	LST	STATION/NAME	LOCATION
PAIM	UTO	-09:00	INDIAN MOUNTAIN AFS	UTOPIA CREEK, AK
PAKN	AKN	-09:00	KING SALMON APT	KING SALMON, AK
PALU	LUR	-09:00	CAPE LISBURNE AFS	CAPE LISBURNE, AK
PANC	ANC	-09:00	ANCHORAGE IAP	ANCHORAGE, AK
PAOT	OTZ	-09:00	RALPH WIEN MEMORIAL	KOTZEBUE, AK
PASV	SVW	-09:00	SPARREVOHN AFS	SPARREVOHN, AK
PASY	SYA	-10:00	EARECKSON AFS	SHEMYA, AK
PATC	TNC	-09:00	TIN CITY AFS	TIN CITY, AK
PATL	TLJ	-09:00	TATALINA AFS	TATALINA, AK
PGSN	SPN	+10:00	SAIPAN IAP	MARIANA IS(SAIPAN), US
PGUA	UAM	+10:00	ANDERSEN AFB	GUAM MARIANAS, GU
PGUM	GUM	+10:00	*AGANA NAS	BREWER FIELD, GU
PHIK	HIK	-10:00	HICKAM AFB	HONOLULU, HI
PHNL	HNL	-10:00	HONOLULU IAP	HONOLULU, HI
PJON	JON	-10:00	JOHNSTON ATOLL AFB	JOHNSTON IS, JO
PKMA	ENT	+12:00	ENEWETAK AUX AF	MARSHALL IS, MI
PKWA	KWA	-12:00	BUCHOLZ AAF KMR	KWAJALEIN ATOLL, MI
PMDY	MDY	-11:00	MIDWAY NAF	MIDWAY IS, MW
PTKK	TKK	+10:00	TRUK IAP	MOEN IS SOU PAC, FM
PTPN	PNI	+11:00	PONAPE IAP	PONAPE, TTPI
PTRO	ROR	+09:00	BABELTHUAP	PALAU IS, RP
PTTK	KSA	+09:00	KOSRAE APT	KOSRAE, FM
PTYA	YAP	+10:00	YAP IAP	YAP CAROLINE IS, FM
PWAK	AWK	+12:00	WAKE ISLAND AFB	WAKE IS, WK
RJAM	MUS	+10:00	MINAMI TORISHIMA APT	MARCUS IS, JA
RJAW	IWO	+09:00	IWO JIMA AB	IWO JIMA IS, JA
RJCB	OBO	+09:00	OBIHIRO APT	HOKKAIDO, JA
RJCJ	CTS	+09:00	CHITOSE APT	SAPPORO, JA
RJCK	KUH	+09:00	KUSHIRO AB	KUSHIRO HOKKAIDO, JA
RJFF	FUK	+09:00	FUKUOKA/ ITAZUKE	KYUSHU IS, JA
RJOI	IWA	+09:00	IWAKUNI MCAS	HONSHU IS, JA
RJSM	MSJ	+09:00	MISAWA AB	HONSHU IS, JA
RJTA	NJA	+09:00	ATSUGI NAF	HONSHU IS, JA
RJTY	OKO	+09:00	YOKOTA AB	TOKYO, JA
RKJJ	KWJ	+09:00	*KWANG JU ROKAFB	KWANG JU, RK
RKJK	KUZ	+09:00	KUNSAN AB	KUNSAN, RK
RKPC	CJU	+09:00	CHEJU IAP	CHEJU DO IS, RK
RKPK	KHE	+09:00	*KIMHAE IAP	PUSAN, RK
RKSO	OSN	+09:00	OSAN AB	OSAN, RK
RKSS	SEL	+09:00	KIMPO IAP	SEOUL, RK
RKSW	HLV	+09:00	*SUWON ROKAFB	SUWON, RK
RKTN	TAE	+09:00	*TAEGU AB	TAEGU, RK
ROAH	OKA	+09:00	NAHA APT	OKINAWA IS, JA
RODN	DNA	+09:00	KADENA AB	OKINAWA, JA
RPLB	CUA	+08:00	*SUBIC BAY IAP	LUZON, RP
RPMM	MNL	+08:00	NINOY AQUINO IAP	MANILA, RP
RPWL	CGY	+09:00	CAGAYAN DE ORO APT	MINDANAO IS, RP
SADP	PAL	-03:00	EL PALOMAR AF LD	BUENOS AIRES, AG
SAEZ	BUE	-03:00	EZEIZA APT	BUENOS AIRES, AG
SBBR	BSB	-03:00	BRASILIA APT	BRASILIA, BR
SBGL	RIO	-03:00	RIO DE JANEIRO IAP	RIO DE JANEIRO, BR
SBRF		-03:00	GUARARAPES APT	RECIFE, BR
SCEL	SCL	-04:00	ARTURO MERINOBENITEZ	SANTIAGO, CH
SEQU	UIO	-05:00	MARISCAL SUCRE APT	QUITO, EC
SGAS	ASU	-04:00	PRES STROESSNER APT	ASUNCION, PG
SKBO	BOG	-05:00	EL DORADO IAP	BOGOTA, CL
SKCG	CTG	-05:00	CRESPO APT	CARTAGENA, CL
SLLP	LPB	-04:00	JF KENNEDY IAP	LA PAZ, BO
SMZY	PBM	-03:00	ZANDERY APT	PARAMARIBO, SR

120 - Military Space-A Air Basic Training

APPENDIX E, continued

ICAO	LI	LST	STATION/NAME	LOCATION
SPIM	LIM	-05:00	JORGE CHAVEZ IAP	LIMA, PE
SUMU	MVD	-03:00	CARRASCO IAP	MONTEVIDEO, UG
SVBL	ELR	-04:00	EL LIBERATADOR AB	NEGRO, VE
SVMI	MIQ	-04:00	SIMON BOLIVAR IAP	CARACAS, VE
SYTM	GEO	-03:00	TIMEHRI IAP	GEORGETOWN, GY
TAPA	SJH	-04:00	V C BIRD IAP	ST JOHNS, AN
TBPB	BGI	-04:00	GRANTLEY ADAMS IAP	BRIDGETOWN, BB
TISX	STX	-04;00	ALEX HAMILTON APT	ST CROIX, VI
TJNR	NRR	-04:00	ROOSEVELT ROADS NAS	ROOSEVELT ROADS, PR
TXKF	BOA	-04:00	*BERMUDA NAS	HAMILTON, BM
VLVT		+06:00	VIEN TIANE	VIEN TIANE, LO
VTBD	BKK	+07:00	DON MUANG APT	BANGKOK, TH
VTBU	VBU	+07:00	U-TAPAO RTN	BAN U-TAPAO, TH
VVNB	VNB	+07:00	HANOI/NOIBA	HANOI, VIET NAM
WIIH	DJK	+07:00	HALIN PERDANAKUSUMA	JAKART, IE
WMKK	MKK	+08:00.	KUALA LUMPUR IAP	SUBANG, MA
WSAP	SGP	+08:00	RSAF PAYA LEBAR	SINGAPORE, SG
WSSS	SIN	+08:00	SINGAPORE CHANGI	SINGAPORE CHANGI
YBAS	ASP	+09:30	ALICE SPRINGS	ALICE SPRINGS, AU
YPAD	ADL	+09:30	ADELAIDE APT	WEST TORRENS, AU
YPDN		+09:30	DARWIN IAP	DARWIN, AU
YPLM	LEA	+08:00	*LEARMONTH RAAFB	EXMOUTH GULF, AU
YPWR	UMR	+09:30	WOOMERA AS	WOOMERA, AU
YSRI	RCM	+10:00	RICHMOND RAAFB	RICHMOND, AU
YSSY	SYD	+10:00	SIDNEY IAP	SIDNEY IAP, AU

DECODE (LI vs ICAO)

LI	ICAO	LST	NAME	LOCATION
	DIAP	+00:00	ABIDJAN/ PORT BOUET	ABIDJAN/ PORT BOUET
	DNMM	+00:00	LAGOS/ MURTALA	LAGOS/ MURTALA
	EGKK	+00:00	LONDON/GATWICK	LONDON, UK
	FGSL	+00:00	MALABO	MALAB, GUINEA
	MWCR	-05:00	OWEN ROBERTS IAP	CAYMEN IS
	OEJB	+03:00	JUBAIL	JUBAIL, SA
	OEKJ	+03:00	AL KHARJ	AL KHARJ, AE
	OEKK	+03:00	KING KAHLID MILIT	KING KAHLID MILIT, SA
	SBRF	+03:00	GUARARAPES APT	RECIFE, BR
	VLVT	+06:00	VIEN TIANE	VIEN TIANE, LO
	YPDN	+09:30	DARWIN IAP	DARWIN, AU
ABQ	KELP	-06:00	EL PASO IAP	EL PASO, TX
ADA	LTAG	+02:00	INCIRLIK APT	ADANA, TU
ADK	PADK	-10:00	*ADAK ISLAND NS	ADAK, AK
ADL	YPAD	+09:30	ADELAIDE APT	WEST TORRENS, AU
ADW	KADW	-05:00	ANDREWS AFB	CAMP SPRINGS, MD
AEX	KAEX	-06:00	ENGLAND AFB	ALEXANDRIA, LA
AHT	PAHT	-09:00	AMCHITKA ISL APT	AMCHITKA, AK
AKN	PAKN	-09:00	KING SALMON APT	KING SALMON, AK
AKT	LCRA	+02:00	AKROTIRI RAFB	AKROTIRI, CY
ALA	LPAR	+00:00	ALVERCA APT	ALVERCA, PO
AMM	OJAF	+02:00	KING ABDULLAH AB	AMMAN, JR
ANC	PANC	-09:00	ANCHORAGE IAP	ANCHORAGE, AK
ASI	FHAW	+00:00	ASCENSION AUX AF	GEORGETOWN ASC, UK
ASP	YBAS	+09:30	ALICE SPRINGS RAAFB	ALICE SPRINGS, AU

Military Space-A Air Basic Training - 121

APPENDIX E, continued

ICAO	LI	LST	STATION/NAME	LOCATION
ASU	SGAS	-04:00	PRES STROESSNER APT	ASUNCION, PG
ATH	LGAT	+02:00	*ATHINAI APT	ATHENS, GR
ATL	KATL	-05:00	ATLANTA IAP	ATLANTA, GA
AVB	LIPA	+01:00	AVIANO AB	AVIANO, IT
AWK	PWAK	+12:00	WAKE ISLAND AFB	WAKE IS, WK
AYH	EGWZ	+00:00	RAF ALCONBURY	SUFFOLK, UK
BAB	KBAB	-08:00	BEALE AFB	BEALE AFB, CA
BAD	KBAD	-06:00	BARKSDALE AFB	SHREVEPORT, LA
BAH	OBBI	+03:00	BAHRAIN IAP	MUHARRAQ, BA
BBE	HCMI	+03:00.	BERBERA	BERBERA, SM
BDL	KBDL	-05:00	BRADLEY IAP	WINDSOR LOCKS, CT
BDS	LIBR	+01:00	BRINDISI/CASALE APT	CAMPO CASALE, IT
BGI	TBPB	-04:00	GRANTLEY ADAMS IAP	BRIDGETOWN, BB
BGR	KBGR	-05:00	BANGOR IAP	BANGOR, ME
BIF	KBIF	-06:00	BIGGS AAF	FORT BLISS, TX
BIX	KBIX	-06:00	KEESLER AFB	BILOXI, MS
BKK	VTBD	+07:00	DON MUANG APT	BANGKOK, TH
BLV	KBLV	-06:00	SCOTT AFB	BELLEVILLE, IL
BNA	KBNA	-06:00	NASHVILLE METRO APT	NASHVILLE, TN
BOA	TXKF	-04:00	*BERMUDA NAS	HAMLTON, BM
BOG	SKBO	-05:00	EL DORADO IAP	BOGOTA, CL
BRU	EBBR	+01:00	BRUSSELS NATL	BRUSSELS, BE
BSB	SBBR	-03:00	BRASILIA APT	BRASILIA, BR
BUE	SAEZ	-03:00	EZEIZA APT	BUENOS AIRES, AG
BWY	EGVJ	+00:00	*RAF BENTWATERS	SUFFOLK, UK
BZE	MZBZ	-06:00	BELIZE IAP	BELIZE CITY, BZ
BZI	LTBF	+02:00	*BALIKESIR APT	BALIKESIR, TU
CAI	HECA	+02:00	CAIRO IAP	CAIRO, EG
CAI	HECW	+02:00	CAIRO WEST	CAIRO, EG
CDB	PACD	-09:00	COLD BAY APT	COLD BAY, AK
CEF	KCEF	-05:00	WESTOVER ARB	CHICOPEE, MA
CGY	RPWL	+09:00	CAGAYAN DE ORO APT	MINDANAO IS, RP
CHC	NZCH	+12:00	CHRISTCHURCH IAP	CHRISTCHURCH, NZ
CHS	KCHS	-05:00	CHARLESTON AFB/IAP	CHARLESTON, SC
CJU	RKPC	+09:00	CHEJU IAP	CHEJU DO IS, RK
CLT	KCLT	-05:00	CHARLOTTE/DOUGLAS IAP	CHARLOTTE, NC
COF	KCOF	-05:00	PATRICK AFB	COCOA BEACH, FL
COS	KCOS	-07:00	CITY OF COLORADO SPRINGS	COLORADO SPRINGS, CO
CRW	KCRW	-05:00	YEAGER/CHARLESTON APT	CHARLESTON, WV
CTG	SKCG	-05:00	CRESPO APT	CARTAGENA, CL
CTS	RJCJ	+09:00	CHITOSE APT	SAPPORO, JA
CUA	RPLB	+08:00	*SUBIC BAY IAP	LUZON, RP
CUN	MMUN	-06:00	CANCUN INTL	CANCUN, MX
CYS	KCYS	-07:00	CHEYENNE MUNI APT	CHEYENNE, WY
CZF	PACZ	-09:00	CAPE ROMANZOF AFS	CAPE ROMANZOF, AK
CZM	MMCZ	-06:00	COZUMEL INTL	COZUMEL, MX
DAY	KDAY	-06:00	JAMES M COX-DAYTON IAP	DAYTON, OH
DBI	OMDB	+03:00	DUBAI IAP	AL KHARJ, AE
DCU	LIED	+01:00	*DECIMOMANNU ITAB	DECIMOMANNU, IT
DFW	KDFW	-06:00	DALLAS/FORT WORTH REG	DALLAS/FORT WORTH, TX
DHA	OEDR	+03:00	DHAHRAN IAP	DHAHRAN, SA
DIH	EDIH	+01:00	HOHENFELS AAF	HOHENFELS, GE
DIY	LTCC	+02:00	DIYARBAKIR APT	DIYARBAKIR, TU
DJK	WIIH	+07:00	HALIN PERDANAKUSUMA	JAKARTA, IE

122 - Military Space-A Air Basic Training

APPENDIX E, continued

ICAO	LI	LST	STATION/NAME	LOCATION
DKR	GOOY	+03:00	DAKAR YOFF	DAKAR, SE
DNA	RODN	+09:00	KADENA AB	OKINAWA, JA
DOV	KDOV	-05:00	DOVER AFB	DOVER, DE
DYS	KDYS	-06:00	DYESS AFB	ABILENE, TX
EDF	PAED	-09:00	ELMENDORF AFB	ANCHORAGE, AK
EHC	LTAT	+02:00	*EHRAC TUAF	MALATYA, TU
EHM	PAEH	-09:00	CAPE NEWENHAM AFS	CAPE NEWENHAM, AK
EIL	PAEI	-09:00	EIELSON AFB	FAIRBANKS, AK
ELR	SVBL	-04:00	EL LIBERATADOR AB	NEGRO, VE
ENT	PKMA	+12:00	ENEWETAK AUX AF	MARSHALL IS, MI
ERZ	LTCE	+02:00	*ERZURUM APT	ERZURUM, TU
ESB	LTAC	+02:00	*ESENBOGA APT	ANKARA, TU
ESK	LTBI	+02:00	*ESKISEHIR TUAF	ESKISEHIR, TU
FAI	PAFA	-09:00	FAIRBANKS IAP	FAIRBANKS, AK
FCO	LIRF	+02:00	ROMA/FIUMICINO	ROME, IT
FEL	EDSF	+01:00	FURSTENFELD-BRUCK AAF	FURSTENFELD-BRUCK, GE
FFO	KFFO	-06:00	WRIGHT-PATTERSON AFB	WRIGHT-PATTERSON AFB, OH
FIH	FZAA	+01:00	KINSHASA NDJILI APT	KINSHASA, ZA
FKH	EGUP	+00:00	*RAF SCULTHORPE	SUFFOLK, UK
FLL	KFLL	-05:00	FT LAUDERDALE INTL	FT LAUDERDALE, FL
FOE	KFOE	-06:00	FORBES FIELD	FORBES FIELD, KS
FRA	EDDF	+01:00	FRANKFURT MAIN IAP	FRANKFURT, GE
FRF	EDAF	+01:00	RHEIN-MAIN AB	FRANKFURT, GE
FUJ	OMFJ	+03:00	AL FUJAYRAH IAP	FUJAYRAH, AE
FUK	RJFF	+09:00	FUKUOKA/ITAZUKE	KYUSHU IS, JA
FYU	PAFY	-09:00	FORT YUKON APT	FORT YUKON, AK
GAL	PAGA	-09:00	GALENA APT	GALENA, AK
GAO	MUGM	-05:00	GUANTANAMO BAY NAS	GUANTANAMO, CU
GBI	MYGM	-05:00	GRAND BAHAMA AUX AF	GRAND BAHAMA, BH
GDT	MKJT	-05:00	GRAND TURK AUX FIELD	GRAND TURK IS, UK
GEO	SYTM	-03:00	TIMEHRI IAP	GEORGETOWN, GY
GFA	KGFA	-07:00	MALMSTROM AFB	MALMSTROM AFB, MT
GMF	KMKE	-06:00	GENERAL MITCHELL FIELD	MILWAUKEE, WI
GRK	KGRK	-06:00	ROBERT GRAY AAF	KILLEEN, TX
GRX	LGRX	+02:00	ARAXOS GAFB	ARAXOS, GR
GSB	KGSB	-05:00	SEYMOUR JOHNSON AFB	GOLDSBORO, NC
GUA	MGGT	-06:00	LA AURORA APT	GUATEMALA CITY, GT
GUM	PGUM	+10:00	*AGANA NAS	BREWER FIELD, GU
HAM	EDDH	+01:00	HAMBURG APT	HAMBURG, GE
HHN	EDFH	+01:00	*HAHN AB	HAHN, GE
HIK	PHIK	-10:00	HICKAM AFB	HONOLULU, HI
HIR	AGGH	+11:00	HENDERSON IAP	HONIARA, SI
HLV	RKSW	+09:00	*SUWON ROKAFB	SUWON, RK
HNL	PHNL	-10:00	HONOLULU IAP	HONOLULU, HI
HOW	MPHO	-05:00	HOWARD AFB	BALBOA, PN
HRT	KHRT	-06:00	HURLBURT FIELD	MARY ESTHER, FL
IAB	KIAB	-06:00	MCCONNELL AFB	McCONNELL AFB, KS
IDT	ETSI	+01:00	*INGOLSTADT AB	INGOLSTADT, GE
IGL	LTBL	+02:00	CIGLI TAFB	IZMIR, TU
ILG	KILG	-05:00	GREATER WILMINGTON	WILMINGTON, DE
IND	KIND	-06:00	INDIANAPOLIS IAP	INDIANAPOLIS, IN
IWA	RJOI	+09:00	IWAKUNI MCAS	HONSHU IS, JA
IWO	RJAW	+09:00	IWO JIMA AB	IWO JIMA IS, JA
JAN	KJAN	-06:00	THOMPSON FIELD	JACKSON, MS
JBD	HFFF	+02:00	DJBOUTI/ AMBOULI	DJBOUTI/ AMBOULI

Military Space-A Air Basic Training - 123

APPENDIX E, continued

ICAO	LI	LST	STATION/NAME	LOCATION
JDW	OEJN	+03:00	KING ABDUL AZIZ IAP	JIDDAH, SA
JED	OEJD	+03:00	JIDDAH IAP	JIDDAH, SA
JFK	KJFK	-05:00	JOHN F. KENNEDY IAP	NEW YORK, NY
JNB	FAJS	+02:00	*JAN SMUTS APT	JOHANNESBURG, SF
JON	PJON	-10:00	JOHNSTON ATOLL AFB	JOHNSTON IS, JO
KAI	GFLL	+00:00	FREETOWN	FREETOWN, LUNGI
KAL	OEKM	+03:00	KHAMIS MUSHAIT AB	ABHA, SA
KEF	BIKF	+00:00	KEFLAVIK APT	KEFLAVIK, IC
KFJ	OEJF	+03:00	KING FAISAL NB	JIDDAH, SA
KHE	RKPK	+09:00	*KIMHAE IAP	PUSAN, RK
KIN	MKJP	-05:00	NORMAN MANLEY IAP	KINGSTON, JM
KRT	HSSS	+02:00	KHARTOUM APT	KHARTOUM, SU
KSA	PTTK	+09:00	KOSRAE APT	KOSRAE, FM
KUH	RJCK	+09:00	KUSHIRO AB	KUSHIRO HOKKAIDO, JA
KUZ	RKJK	+09:00	KUNSAN AB	KUNSAN, RK
KWA	PKWA	-12:00	BUCHOLZ AAF KMR	KWAJALEIN ATOLL, MI
KWI	OKBK	+03:00	KUWAIT IAP	KUWAIT CITY, KW
KWJ	RKJJ	+09:00	*KWANG JU ROKAFB	KWANG JU, RK
LAW	KLAW	-06:00	LAWTON MUNICIPLE	LAWTON, OK
LAX	KLAX	-08:00	LOS ANGELES IAP	LOS ANGELES, CA
LCA	LCLK	+02:00	*LARNACA RAFB	LARNACA, CY
LCE	MHLC	-06:00	GOLOSON IAP	LA CEIBA, HO
LCK	KLCK	-06:00	RICKENBACKER AFB	RICKENBACKER AFB, OH
LEA	YPLM	+08:00	*LEARMONTH RAAFB	EXMOUTH GULF, AU
LFI	KLFI	-05:00	LANGLEY AFB	HAMPTON, VA
LGS	LPLA	+00:00	LAJES FIELD AB	LAJES (AZORES IS), PO
LHN	ETNA	+01:00	*AHLHORN GAFB	AHLHORN, GE
LIM	SPIM	-05:00	JORGE CHAVEZ IAP	LIMA, PE
LIZ	KLIZ	-05:00	LORING AFB	LORING, ME
LKH	EGUL	+00:00	RAF LAKENHEATH	SUFFOLK, UK
LPB	SLLP	-04:00	JF KENNEDY IAP	LA PAZ, BO
LPH	EDSD	+01:00	*LEIPHEIM GAFB	LEIPHEIM, GE
LRF	KLRF	-06:00	LITTLE ROCK AFB	JACKSONVILLE, AR
LSF	KLSF	-05:00	LAWSON FIELD	FORT BENNING, GA
LTS	KLTS	-06:00	ALTUS AFB	ALTUS, OK
LUR	PALU	-09:00	CAPE LISBURNE AFS	CAPE LISBURNE, AK
MAH	LEMH	+01:00	*MENORCA APT	MAHON, SP
MAM	OMAM	+03:00	AL DHAFRA	ABU DHABI, AE
MBA	HKMO	+00:00	MOMBASA	MOMBASA, KE
MDT	KMDT	-05:00	OLMSTED FIELD	MIDDLETOWN, PA
MDY	PMDY	-11:00	MIDWAY NAF	MIDWAY IS, MW
MEM	KMEM	-06:00	MEMPHIS IAP	MEMPHIS, TN
MFD	KMFD	-05:00	MANSFIELD LAHM MUNICIPAL APT	MANSFIELD, OH
MGA	MNMG	-06:00	AUGUSTO C. SANDINO IAP	MANAGUA, NI
MGQ	HCMM	+03:00	MOGADISHU IAP	MOGADISHU, SM
MHZ	EGUN	+00:00	RAF MILDENHALL	SUFFOLK, UK
MIA	KMIA	-05:00	MIAMI IAP	MIAMI, FL
MIQ	SVMI	-04:00	SIMON BOLIVAR IAP	CARACAS, VE
MKK	WMKK	+08:00	KUALA LUMPUR IAP	SUBANG, MA
MNL	RPMM	+08:00	NONOY AQUINO IAP	MANILA, RP
MRB	KMRB	-05:00	EAST WV REGIONAL APT	MARTINSBURG, WV
MSH	OOMA	+04:00	MASIRAH OAFB	MASIRAH, OM
MSJ	RJSM	+09:00	MISAWA AB	HONSHU IS, JA
MSP	KMSP	-06:00	MPLS-ST PAUL IAP	MINNEAPOUS, MN
MTN	KMTN	-05:00	GLEN L. MARTIN STATE APT	BALTIMORE, MD
MUS	RJAM	+10:00	MINAMI TORISHIMA APT	MARCUS IS, JA
MVD	SUMU	-03:00	CARRASCO IAP	MONTEVIDEO, UG

124 - Military Space-A Air Basic Training

APPENDIX E, continued

ICAO	LI	LST	STATION/NAME	LOCATION
NAP	LIRN	+01:00	CAPODICHINO APT	NAPLES, IT
NBE	KNBE	-06:00	HENSLEY FIELD NAS	DALLAS, TX
NBO	HKNA	+03:00	JOMO KENYATTA IAP	NAIROBI, KE
NDJ	FTTJ	+01:00	N'DJAMENA IAP	N'DJAMENA, CD
NGU	KNGU	-05:00	NORFOLK NAS	NORFOLK, VA
NIM	DRRN	+01:00	NIAMEY IAP	NIAMEY, NG
NIP	KNIP	-05:00	JACKSONVILLE NAS	JACKSONVILLE, FL
NJA	RJTA	+09:00	ATSUGI NAF	HONSHU IS, JA
NKW	FJDG	+00:00	DIEGO GARCIA ATOLL	CHAGOS IS, IO
NQA	KNQA	-06:00	MEMPHIS NAS	MEMPHIS, TN
NRR	TJNR	-04:00	ROOSEVELT ROADS NAS	ROOSEVELT ROADS, PR
NRV	ETNN	+01:00	*NORVENICH GAFB	NORVENICH, GE
NUE	EDDN	+01:00	NURNBERG APT	NURNBERG, GE
NZC	KNZC	-05:00	CECIL FIELD NAS	CECIL FIELD NAS, FL
OAK	KOAK	-08:00	METRO OAKLAND IAP	OAKLAND, CA
OBG	EDNO	+01:00	*OLDENBURG GAFB	OLDENBURG, GE
OBO	RJCB	+09:00	OBHIRO APT	HOKKAIDO, JA
OCO	MROC	-06:00	SANTAMARIA IAP	SAN JOSE, CS
OKA	ROAH	+09:00	NAHA APT	OKINAWA IS, JA
OKC	KOKC	-06:00	WILL ROGERS WLD APT	OKLAHOMA CITY, OK
OKO	RJTY	+09:00	YOKOTA AB	TOKYO, JA
OLB	LIEO	+01:00	OLBIA/COSTA ESMERALDA	OLBIA, IT
ORF	KORF	-05:00	NORFOLK IAP	NORFOLK, VA
ORY	LFPO	+02:00	PARIS/ORLY	PARIS, FR
OSL	ENFB	+01:00	OSLO FORNEBU	OSLO, NO
OSN	RKSO	+09:00	OSAN AB	OSAN, RK
OTZ	PAOT	-09:00	RALPH WEIN MEMORIAL	KOTZEBUE, AK
OZP	LEMO	+02:00	MORON AB	MORON, SP
PAL	SADP	-03:00	EL PALOMAR AF LD	BUENOS AIRES, AG
PAP	MTPP	-05:00	HAITI IAP	PORT-AU-PRINCE, HA
PBG	KPBG	-05:00	PLATTSBURGH IAP	PLATTSBURGH, NY
PBM	SMZY	-03:00	ZANDEREY APT	PARAMARIBO, SR
PHL	KPHL	-05:00	PHILADELPHIA IAP	PHILADELPHIA, PA
PIK	EGPK	+00:00	*PRESTWICK APT	PRESTWICK (SCOTL), UK
PIT	KPIT	-05:00	GREATER PITTSBURGH IAP	CORAPOLIS, PA
PLA	MHSC	-06:00	SOTO CANO AB	COMAYAGUA, HO
PMI	LESJ	+01:00	*PALMA DE MALLORCA APT	ALEARIC IS, SP
PNI	PTPN	+11:00	PONAPE IAP	PONAPE, TTPI
POB	KPOB	-05:00	POPE AFB	FAYETTEVILLE, NC
PPG	NSTU	-11:00	PAGO PAGO IAP	PAGO PAGO, AS
PSA	LIRP	+01:00	*PISA APT	PISA, IT
PTY	MPTO	-05:00	TOCUMEN/TORRIJOS IAP	PANAMA CITY, PN
PVD	KPVD	-05:00	THEO FRAN GREEN ST	PROVIDENCE, RI
PZU	HSSP	+02:00	PORT SUDAN APT	PORT SUDAN, SU
RCM	YSRI	+10:00	RICHMOND RAAFB	RICHMOND, AU
RDR	KRDR	-07:00	GRAND FORKS AFB	GRAND FORKS AFB, ND
REG	LICR	+01:00	*REGGIO CALABRIA ITAF	TITO MENNITI, IT
RIO	SBGL	-03:00	RIO DE JANEIRO IAP	RIO DE JANEIRO, BR
RIV	KRIV	-08:00	MARCH ARB	RIVERSIDE, CA
RME	KRME	-05:00	*GRIFFISS AFB	ROME, NY
RMS	ETAR	+01:00	RAMSTEIN AB	LANDSTUHL, GE
ROB	GLMR	+00:00	MONROVIA/ SPRIGGS PAYNE	MONROVIA, LI
ROB	GLRB	+00:00	*MONROVIA ROBERTS IAP	MONROVIA, LI
ROR	PTRO	+09:00	BABELTHUAP	PALAU IS, RP
RTA	LERT	+01:00	ROTA NAS	ROTA, SP

Military Space-A Air Basic Training - 125

APPENDIX E, continued

ICAO	LI	LST	STATION/NAME	LOCATION
RUH	OERY	+03:00	RIYADH IAP	RIYADH, SA
SAL	MSSS	-06:00	ILOPANGO IAP	SAN SALVADOR, ES
SAP	MHLM	-06:00	LA MESA IAP	LA MESA, HO
SAV	KSAV	-05:00	SAVANNAH IAP	SAVANNAH, GA
SBE	OOMS	+04:00	SEEB IAP	MUSCAT, OM
SBD	KSBD	-08:00	NORTON AFB	SAN BERNARDINO, CA
SCH	KSCH	-05:00	SCHENECTADY CO APT	SCHENECTADY, NY
SCL	SCEL	-04:00	ARTURO MERINOBENITEZ	SANTIAGO, CH
SDF	KSDF	-06:00	STANFORD FIELD	LOUISVILLE, KY
SDQ	MDSI	-04:00	SAN ISIDRO AB	SANTO DOMINGO, DR
SEL	RKSS	+09:00	KIMPO IAP	SEOUL, RK
SEX	EDAS	+01:00	SEMBACH AB (RUNWAY CLOSED)	SEMBACH, GE
SFJ	BGSF	-03:00	*SONDRESTROM AB	SONDRESTROM GL(DN)
SFO	KSFO	-08:00	SAN FRANCISCO IAP	SAN FRANCISCO, CA
SGP	WSAP	+08:00	RSAF PAYA LEBAR	SINGAPORE, SG
SHV	KSHV	-06:00	SHREVEPORT REG	SHREVEPORT, LA
SIN	WSSS	+08:00	SINGAPORE CHANGI	SINGAPORE CHANGI
SIO	LTSI	+02:00	SINOP AAF	SINOP, TU
SIZ	LICZ	+01:00	SIGONELLA APT	GERBINI (SICILY), IT
SJH	TAPA	-04:00	V C BIRD IAP	ST JOHNS, AN
SKA	KSKA	-08:00	FAIRCHILD AFB	FAIRCHILD AFB, WA
SKF	KSKF	-06:00	KELLY AFB	SAN ANTONIO, TX
SKG	LGTS	+02:00	*THESSALONIKI APT	THESSALONIKI, GR
SNN	EINN	+00:00	*SHANNON APT	LIMERICK, IR
SOC	LGSA	+02:00	SOUDA BAY NSA	KHANIA (CR), GR
SPN	PGSN	+10:00	SAIPAN IAP	MARIANA IS(SAIPAN), US
SSS	EHSB	+01:00	*SOESTERBERG RNLAFB	UTRECHT, NT
STJ	KSTJ	-06:00	ROSECRANS MEM APT	ST JOSEPH, MO
STL	KSTL	-06:00	*LAMBERT-ST LOUIS IAP	ST LOUIS, MO
STN	EGSS	+00:00	STANSTED APT	STANSTED, UK
STR	EDDS	+01:00	STUTTGART APT	STUTTGART, GE
STX	TISX	-04:00	ALEX HAMILTON APT	ST CROIX, VI
SUU	KSUU	-08:00	TRAVIS AFB	FAIRFIELD, CA
SVN	KSVN	-05:00	HUNTER AAF	SAVANNAH, GA
SVW	PASV	-09:00	SPARREVOHN AFS	SPARREVOHN, AK
SWF	KSWF	-05:00	STEWART IAP/ANGB	NEWBURGH, NY
SYA	PASY	-10:00	EARECKSON AFS	SHEMYA, AK
SYD	YSSY	+10:00	SYDNEY IAP	SYDNEY, AU
TAE	RKTN	+09:00	*TAEGU AB	TAEGU, RK
TCM	KTCM	-08:00	MCCHORD AFB	TACOMA, WA
TGU	MHTG	-06:00	TONCONTIN IAP	TEGUCIGALPA, HO
THF	ETFT	+01:00	*TEMPLEHOF CENTRAL APT/ AIR STATION	BERLIN, GE
THU	BGTL	-04:00	THULE AB	THULE, GL(DN)
TIA	LATI	+02:00	TIRANA CITY	TIRANA CITY
TIF	OETF	+03:00	TAIF APT	TAIF, SA
TIK	KTIK	-06:00	TINKER AFB	OKLAHOMA CITY, OK
TKK	PTKK	+10:00	TRUK APT	MOEN IS SOU PAC, FM
TLJ	PATL	-09:00	TATALINA AFS	TATALINA, AK
TLV	LLBG	+02:00	BEN GURION IAP	TEL AVIV, IS
TNC	PATC	-09:00	TIN CITY AFS	TIN CITY, AK
TOJ	LETO	+01:00	TORREJON DE ARDOZ AB	MADRID, SP
TPA	KTPA	-05:00	TAMPA INTL APT	TAMPA, FL
TTH	OOTH	+04:00	THUMRAIT OAFB	MIDWAY, OM
TUU	OETB	+03:00	KING FAISAL AB	TABUK, SA
UAM	PGUA	+10:00	ANDERSEN AFB	GUAM MARIANAS, GU
UIO	SEQU	-05:00	MARISCAL SUCRE APT	QUITO, EC
UMR	YPWR	+09:30	WOOMERA AS	WOOMERA, AU

APPENDIX E, continued

ICAO	LI	LST	STATION/NAME	LOCATION
UTO	PAIM	-09:00	INDIAN MOUNTAIN AFS	UTOPIA CREEK, AK
VBU	VTBU	+07:00	U-TOPAO RTN	BAN U-TOPAO, TH
VCE	LIPT	+01:00	VICENZA APT	VICENZA, IT
VEN	LIPZ	+01:00	VENEZIA/TESSERA APT	VENICE, IT
VNB	VVNB	+07:00	HANOI/NOIBA	HANOI, VN
VNY	KVNY	-08:00	VAN NUYS APT	VAN NUYS, CA
VRN	LIPX	+01:00	VILLAFRANCA APT	VERONA, IT
VWH	LGIR	+02:00	*IRAKLION AS	IRAKLION (CR), GR
WOB	EGVG	+00:00	*RAF WOODBRIDGE	SUFFOLK, UK
WRI	KWRI	-05:00	MCGUIRE AFB	WRIGHTSTOWN, NJ
XMR	KXMR	-05:00	CAPE CANAVERAL AI	COCOA BEACH, FL
YAP	PTYA	+10:00	YAP IAP	YAP CAROLINE IS, FM
YAW	CYAW	-04:00	HALIFAX SHEARWATER	HALIFAX (NS), CN
YES	LTBA	+02:00	ATATURK/YESILKOY IAP	ISTANBUL, TU
YFB	CYFB	+00:00	FROBISHER BAY	FROBISHER BAY, CN
YQX	CYQX	-03:30	GANDER IAP	NEWFOUNDLAND, ON
YYR	CYYR	-04:00	*GOOSE BAY AB	GOOSE BAY NFLD, CN
YYT	CYYT	-03:30	ST JOHNS APT	ST JOHNS, CN
ZAG	LDZA	+02:00	ZAGREB	ZAGREB, YU
ZAZ	LEZA	+02:00	*ZARAGOZA AB	SANJURJO, SP

* US PORTION CLOSED

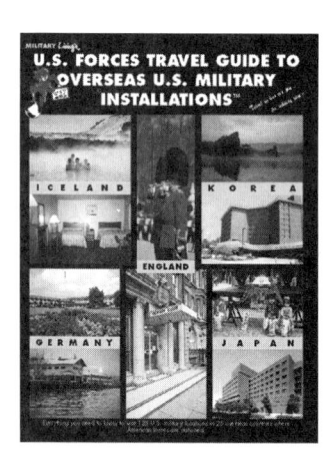

U.S. Forces Travel Guide to Overseas U.S. Military Installations

Save time, money & heartache!
Take me with you overseas!

APPENDIX F: JULIAN DATE CALENDARS AND MILITARY (24-HOUR) CLOCK

Julian Date Calendar: The following tables will be used to convert the Gregorian (official United States Commerce Calendar) calendar dates to a three numerical digit Julian Date. The first Julian Date Calendar table is a perpetual calendar for all years except leap years. The second Julian Date Calendar table is a perpetual calendar for leap years only, such as 1996, 2000, 2004, etc.

How to use the Julian Date Calendars: The calendars are constructed in a matrix with the days of the month in the left hand column from 1-31. The months are displayed in rows from left to right starting with January and continuing through each month to December on the extreme right.

If you made an application for Space-A travel on 15 April 1997 (a non-leap year), then read down the date column to 15 and across to the right to April where you find the number 105 or the 105th day in the Julian Date Calendar. If this were a leap year, i.e., 15 April 2000, check the number-it would be the 106th day. Please try to convert some sample dates (birthdays, holidays, etc.) until you are comfortable using this system.

The entire Julian Date is constructed using the last two digits of the calendar year, i.e., 1997 is 97, 105 for 15 April. The last four digits of the Julian Date are taken from the **twenty-four hour clock,** frequently **known as the military clock,** or time where the hour is a period of time equal to one twenty-fourth of a mean solar or civil day and equivalent to sixty minutes. The Julian Day is divided into a series of twenty-four hours from midnight to midnight. See the table below.

Conventional Clock	Military Clock	Conventional Clock	Military Clock
12 am (midnight)	2400 hours	1 pm	1300 hours
1 am	0100 hours	2 pm	1400 hours
2 am	0200 hours	3 pm	1500 hours
3 am	0300 hours	4 pm	1600 hours
4 am	0400 hours	5 pm	1700 hours
5 am	0500 hours	6 pm	1800 hours
6 am	0600 hours	7 pm	1900 hours
7 am	0700 hours	8 pm	2000 hours
8 am	0800 hours	9 pm	2100 hours
9 am	0900 hours	10 pm	2200 hours
10 am	1000 hours	11 pm	2300 hours
11 am	1100 hours		

So, if you apply for Space-A air travel at 2:45pm on April 15, 1997, your complete Julian Date and time would be 97 105 1445 or the year 1997, 105th Day, 14th hour and 45th minute.

128 - Military Space-A Air Basic Training

APPENDIX F, continued

MILITARY (24-HOUR) CLOCK

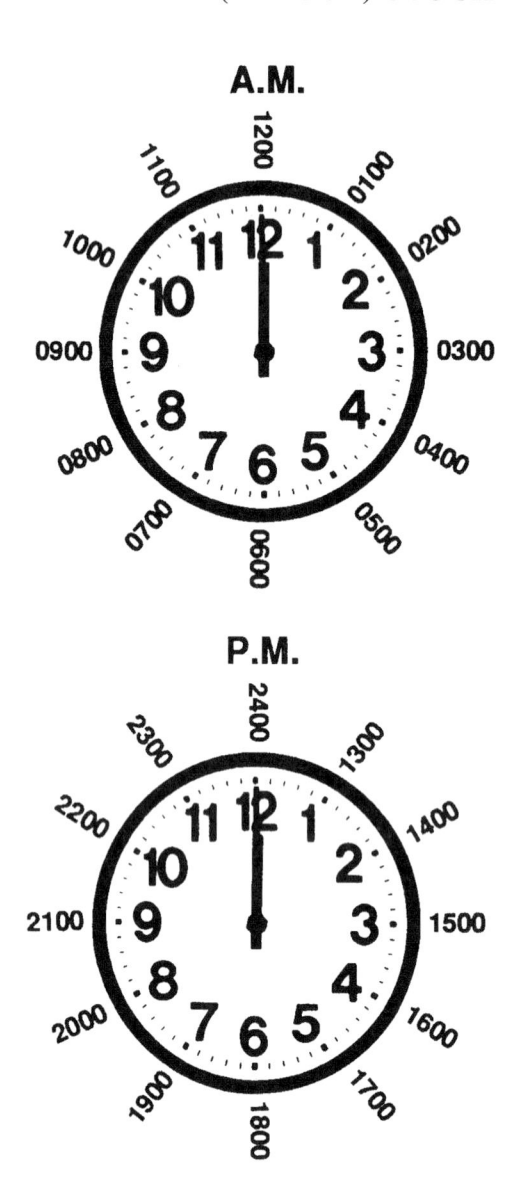

A.M.

P.M.

APPENDIX F, continued

JULIAN DATE CALENDAR (NON-LEAP YEAR)

DAY	JAN	FEB	MAR	APR	MAY	JUN	JUL	AUG	SEP	OCT	NOV	DEC
1	001	032	060	091	121	152	182	213	244	274	305	335
2	002	033	061	092	122	153	183	214	245	275	306	336
3	003	034	062	093	123	154	184	215	246	276	307	337
4	004	035	063	094	124	155	185	216	247	277	308	338
5	005	036	064	095	125	156	186	217	248	278	309	339
6	006	037	065	096	126	157	187	218	249	279	310	340
7	007	038	066	097	127	158	188	219	250	280	311	341
8	008	039	067	098	128	159	189	220	251	281	312	342
9	009	040	068	099	129	160	190	221	252	282	313	343
10	010	041	069	100	130	161	191	222	253	283	314	344
11	011	042	070	101	131	162	192	223	254	284	315	345
12	012	043	071	102	132	163	193	224	255	285	316	346
13	013	044	072	103	133	164	194	225	256	286	317	347
14	014	045	073	104	134	165	195	226	257	287	318	348
15	015	046	074	105	135	166	196	227	258	288	319	349
16	016	047	075	106	136	167	197	228	259	289	320	350

APPENDIX F, continued

JULIAN DATE CALENDAR (NON-LEAP YEAR), continued

DAY	JAN	FEB	MAR	APR	MAY	JUN	JUL	AUG	SEP	OCT	NOV	DEC
17	017	048	076	107	137	168	198	229	260	290	321	351
18	018	049	077	108	138	169	199	230	261	291	322	352
19	019	050	078	109	139	170	200	231	262	292	323	353
20	020	051	079	110	140	171	201	232	263	293	324	354
21	021	052	080	111	141	172	202	233	264	294	325	355
22	022	053	081	112	142	173	203	234	265	295	326	356
23	023	054	082	113	143	174	204	235	266	296	327	357
24	024	055	083	114	144	175	205	236	267	297	328	358
25	025	056	084	115	145	176	206	237	268	298	329	359
26	026	057	085	116	146	177	207	238	269	299	330	360
27	027	058	086	117	147	178	208	239	270	300	331	361
28	028	059	087	118	148	179	209	240	271	301	332	362
29	029		088	119	149	180	210	241	272	302	333	363
30	030		089	120	150	181	211	242	273	303	334	364
31	031		090		151		212	243		304		365

Military Space-A Air Basic Training - 131

APPENDIX F, continued

JULIAN DATE CALENDAR (LEAP YEAR)

DAY	JAN	FEB	MAR	APR	MAY	JUN	JUL	AUG	SEP	OCT	NOV	DEC
01	001	032	061	092	122	153	183	214	245	275	306	336
02	002	033	062	093	123	154	184	215	246	276	307	337
03	003	034	063	094	124	155	185	216	247	277	308	338
04	004	035	064	095	125	156	186	217	248	278	309	339
05	005	036	065	096	126	157	187	218	249	279	310	340
06	006	037	066	097	127	158	188	219	250	280	311	341
07	007	038	067	098	128	159	189	220	251	281	312	342
08	008	039	068	099	129	160	190	221	252	282	313	343
09	009	040	069	100	130	161	191	222	253	283	314	344
10	010	041	070	101	131	162	192	223	254	284	315	345
11	011	042	071	102	132	163	193	224	255	285	316	346
12	012	043	072	103	133	164	194	225	256	286	317	347
13	013	044	073	104	134	165	195	226	257	287	318	348
14	014	045	074	105	135	166	196	227	258	288	319	349
15	015	046	075	106	136	167	197	228	259	289	320	350
16	016	047	076	107	137	168	198	229	260	290	321	351

APPENDIX F, continued

JULIAN DATE CALENDAR (LEAP YEAR), continued

DAY	JAN	FEB	MAR	APR	MAY	JUN	JUL	AUG	SEP	OCT	NOV	DEC
17	017	048	077	108	138	169	199	230	261	291	322	352
18	018	049	078	109	139	170	200	231	262	292	323	353
19	019	050	079	110	140	171	201	232	263	293	324	354
20	020	051	080	111	141	172	202	233	264	294	325	355
21	021	052	081	112	142	173	203	234	265	295	326	356
22	022	053	082	113	143	174	204	235	266	296	327	357
23	023	054	083	114	144	175	205	236	267	297	328	358
24	024	055	084	115	145	176	206	237	268	298	329	359
25	025	056	085	116	146	177	207	238	269	299	330	360
26	026	057	086	117	147	178	208	239	270	300	331	361
27	027	058	087	118	148	179	209	240	271	301	332	362
28	028	059	088	119	149	180	210	241	272	302	333	363
29	029	060	089	120	150	181	211	242	273	303	334	364
30	030		090	121	151	182	212	243	274	304	335	365
31	031		091		152		213	244		305		366

APPENDIX G: STANDARD TIME CONVERSION TABLE

The world is divided into 24 time zones or areas. The zero time zone is known as Greenwich Mean Time (GMT), which is physically located at Greenwich, England (UK), on the Meridian of Greenwich. Other areas in this time zone are Iceland, Ascension Islands, England and Scotland. The following table shows major areas and their respective time zones in plus (+) and minus (-) hours from GMT time. Across the top row of the table each area (zone) to the right of GMT is a plus (+), meaning an hour ahead. Each zone to the left of GMT is a minus (-), meaning an hour behind. The columns down the page are simply the next 24 hours from the base line at the top. For example, if you are in Germany, Italy or Spain (GMT +1), the local time is 0800 hours and you wish to know the time in San Francisco, CA, USA, you read down the GMT +1 column to 0800 hours and left to GMT -8 (Pacific Time USA, San Francisco, CA, USA) where it is 2300 hours the previous day. Practice with these tables until you are proficient.

NOTE: This chart is for planning purposes only, as local times may vary due to local conditions, such as daylight savings time, etc. For exact local times, consult the DoD Foreign Clearance Guide, DoT Flight Information Publication or Commercial Air Almanacs.

When You Reach Your Destination ... Where Will You Stay?

Temporary Military Lodging Around the World

Bigger than ever! More than 425 listings of places you can stay for less on U.S. military installations using temporary military lodging (TML). These in-depth TML listings give you an idea of what the lodging is like, recent renovations, cost, location, phone info, whether or not TML has cooking or laundry facilities, what niceties are available and much much more. Includes the lodging of Army, Navy, Marine Corps, U.S. Air Force and U.S. Coast Guard. Guard and Reserve personnel are now eligible for most TML! Published late June 1997.

APPENDIX G, continued

STANDARD TIME CONVERSION TABLE

-12	-11	-10	-9	-8	-7	-6	-5	-4	-1	GMT	+1
0600	0700	0800	0900	1000	1100	1200	1300	1400	1700	1800	1900
0700	0800	0900	1000	1100	1200	1300	1400	1500	1800	1900	2000
0800	0900	1000	1100	1200	1300	1400	1500	1600	1900	2000	2100
0900	1000	1100	1200	1300	1400	1500	1600	1700	2000	2100	2200
1000	1100	1200	1300	1400	1500	1600	1700	1800	2100	2200	2300
1100	1200	1300	1400	1500	1600	1700	1800	1900	2200	2300	2400
1200	1300	1400	1500	1600	1700	1800	1900	2000	2300	2400	0100
1300	1400	1500	1600	1700	1800	1900	2000	2100	2400	0100	0200
1400	1500	1600	1700	1800	1900	2000	2100	2200	0100	0200	0300
1500	1600	1700	1800	1900	2000	2100	2200	2300	0200	0300	0400
1600	1700	1800	1900	2000	2100	2200	2300	2400	0300	0400	0500
1700	1800	1900	2000	2100	2200	2300	2400	0100	0400	0500	0600
1600	1900	2000	2100	2200	2300	2400	0100	0200	0500	0600	0700
1900	2000	2100	2200	2300	2400	0100	0200	0300	0600	0700	0800
2000	2100	2200	2300	2400	0100	0200	0300	0400	0700	0800	0900
2100	2200	2300	2400	0100	0200	0300	0400	0500	0800	0600	1000
2200	2300	2400	0100	0200	0300	0400	0500	0600	0900	1000	1100

APPENDIX G, continued

-12	-11	-10	-9	-8	-7	-6	-5	-4	-1	GMT	+1
2300	2400	0100	0200	0300	0400	0500	0600	0700	1000	1100	1200
2400	0100	0200	0300	0400	0500	0600	0700	0800	1100	1200	1300
0100	0200	0300	0400	0500	0600	0700	0800	0900	1200	1300	1400
0200	0300	0400	0500	0600	0700	0800	0900	1000	1300	1400	1500
0300	0400	0500	0600	0700	0800	0900	1000	1100	1400	1500	1600
0400	0500	0600	0700	0800	0900	1000	1100	1200	1500	1600	1700
0500	0600	0700	0800	0900	1000	1100	1200	1300	1600	1700	1800

Zone GMT -12: Kwajalein Atoll. -11: Midway Island, Pago Pago, Canton. -10: Hawaii, Eareckson. -9: Elmendorf. -8: US Pacific Time. -7: US Mountain Time. -6: US Central Time. -5: US Eastern Time, Panama, Cuba. -4: Bermuda, Puerto Rico, Greenland. -1: Azores. GMT: Iceland, Ascension Islands, England, Scotland. +1: Germany, Italy, Spain.

136 - Military Space-A Air Basic Training

APPENDIX G, continued

+2	+3	+6	+7	+8	+9	+9:30	+10	+12
2000	2100	2330	0100	0200	0300	0330	0400	0600
2100	2200	0030	0200	0300	0400	0430	0500	0700
2200	2300	0130	0300	0400	0500	0530	0600	0800
2300	2400	0230	0400	0500	0600	0630	0700	0900
2400	0100	0330	0500	0600	0700	0730	0800	1000
0100	0200	0430	0600	0700	0800	0830	0900	1100
0200	0300	0530	0700	0800	0900	0930	1000	1200
0300	0400	0630	0800	0900	1000	1030	1100	1300
0400	0500	0730	0900	1000	1100	1130	1200	1400
0500	0600	0830	1000	1100	1200	1230	1300	1500
0600	0700	0930	1100	1200	1300	1330	1400	1600
0700	0800	1030	1200	1300	1400	1430	1500	1700
0800	0900	1130	1300	1400	1500	1530	1600	1800
0900	1000	1230	1400	1500	1600	1630	1700	1900
1000	1100	1330	1500	1600	1700	1730	1800	2000
1100	1200	1430	1600	1700	1800	1830	1900	2100
1200	1300	1530	1700	1800	1900	1930	2000	2200
1300	1400	1630	1800	1900	2000	2030	2100	2300
1400	1500	1730	1900	2000	2100	2130	2200	2400
1500	1600	1830	2000	2100	2200	2230	2300	0100
1600	1700	1930	2100	2200	2300	2330	2400	0200
1700	1800	2030	2200	2300	2400	0030	0100	0300
1800	1900	2130	2300	2400	0100	0130	0200	0400
1900	2000	2230	2400	0100	0200	0230	0300	0500

Zone GMT +2: Greece, Egypt. +3: Dhahran, Turkey, Bahrain. +6: Diego Garcia. +7: Thailand. +8: Philippines, Taiwan: Okinawa JA, Korea. +9:30: Alice Springs AU, Woomera AU. +10: Guam, Richmond AU. +12: Wake Island, New Zealand.

APPENDIX H: AUTHENTICATION OF RESERVE STATUS FOR TRAVEL ELIGIBILITY (DD FORM 1853)

Active Duty Status Reserve Component members must present the form below, DD Form 1853, completed and signed by the Reserve organization commander within the previous 180 days when applying for Space-A air travel.

AUTHENTICATION OF RESERVE STATUS FOR TRAVEL ELIGIBILITY

PRIVACY ACT STATEMENT

AUTHORITY: 10 USC 8102, 44 USC. 3101 and EO 9397.
PRINCIPAL PURPOSE: Use of your SSN is necessary to positively identify you.
ROUTINE USE: Used by Reserve personnel for space available on DoD-owned or controlled aircraft.
DISCLOSURE IS VOLUNTARY: However, failure to disclose it will prevent you from traveling on a DoD-owned or controlled aircraft.

PART A. TO BE COMPLETED BY APPLICANT

1. DATE PREPARED (YYMMDD)

2. NAME (Last, First, MI)	3. PAY GRADE	4. BRANCH OF SERVICE	5. SSN

6. UNIT/COMMAND NAME	7. UNIT/COMMAND ADDRESS

I hereby certify that my space-available travel on military aircraft is not for personal gain, or in connection with business enterprise or employment, or to establish a home either overseas or in the United States.

8. SIGNATURE	9. DATE SIGNED (YYMMDD)

PART B. TO BE COMPLETED BY RESERVE ORGANIZATION COMMANDER

The Reservist named above is an active reserve component member and is eligible for space-available transportation on DoD-owned or controlled aircraft in accordance with DoD Regulation 4515.13-R, and is authorized to so travel from _____ to _____ (*Not to exceed 30 days*) 10. Date (YYMMDD) 11. Date (YYMMDD)

12. NAME (Last, First, MI)	13. PAY GRADE	14. SIGNATURE	15. DATE SIGNED (YYMMDD)

DD Form 1853, 84 APR   Previous editions are obsolete   *US Government Printing Office: 1984-460-983/23245

APPENDIX I: BOARDING PASS/TICKET RECEIPT (AMC FORM 148/2)

This or similar form will be used to record boarding, baggage, meals and other charges.

AMC-

FLIGHT CODE/DATE	
SEAT NO	
AGENT NUMBER	
CASH COLLECTED	
FROM	
TO	

BOARDING PASS/TICKET

AMC-

NAME (Last, First, Middle)	FLIGHT NO.	GATE	BOARDING TIME	SEAT NO.	TAX/INSP FEE
DESTINATION			DEPARTURE DATE	MEAL (Kind/Type/Quantity)	MEAL COST
VIA			BAG WGT/PIECES	EXCESS WEIGHT	BAGGAGE COST
ORIGIN			REMARKS		OTHER COSTS
CARRIER			REASON/DATE OF REFUND		TOTAL
AGENT	SIGNATURE		PASSENGER SIGNATURE		FINAL DEST

AMC FORM 148, JUN 96 — PREVIOUS EDITIONS ARE OBSOLETE

Military Space-A Air Basic Training - 139

APPENDIX J: BAGGAGE IDENTIFICATION
(DD FORM 1839, AMC FORM 20-ID, AND USAF FORM 94)

This baggage identification tag, and others, are used to identify checked and cabin luggage.

SUU

TRAVIS AFB, CALIFORNIA

MISSION NUMBER/DATE

FROM

0 0 0 0 0 0

Strap Check - Not a Claim Check

BAGGAGE IDENTIFICATION

NAME *(Last, First, M.I.)*

STREET ADDRESS *(Home or Unit/APO)*

CITY, STATE AND ZIP CODE

DD FORM 1839   USE PREVIOUS EDITION.
   80 SEP

FOLD HERE ➤ AND TUCK UNDER FLAP

PRINT NAME *(Last, First, Middle Initial)*   ADDRESS *(Unit/New Station)*

CITY/BASE   STATE

ZIP CODE   TELEPHONE NUMBER (COMMERCIAL/AUTOVON)
AMC FORM 20-ID, DEC 92

APPENDIX K: AIR PASSENGER COMMENTS (AMC FORM 253)

As a Space-A passenger you are encouraged to use this (or similar) form to report positive and negative information to managers of the system who are in a position to correct deficiencies and/or reward outstanding performance of duty. You may also be requested to participate in AMC Passengers Surveys from time to time (AMC form 22 APR 96). (Form size adjusted to fit on this page; actual size is larger.) *Please send a courtesy copy of your comments to: Military Living's R&R Space-A Report®, P.O. Box 2347, Falls Church, VA 22042-0347.*

AIR PASSENGER COMMENTS

Please provide a copy to terminal management by placing in the slot marked for Squadron/Port Operations Officer. Terminal addresses are listed on the reverse in case you desire to mail your comments to a terminal you have passed through. Your comments to Squadron/Port Operations Officers will let them take immediate action. If you feel we need to know about a particular item, send a copy of your comments to us:

HQ Air Mobility Command/DOJP
402 Scott Drive Unit 3A1
Scott AFB, IL 62225-5302

COMMENTS

To assist us, please provide the following information when applicable.

NAME (Last, First, M.I.) (Optional)	GRADE (Optional)	DUTY ADDRESS (Optional)	DUTY PHONE (Optional)

FLIGHT NUMBER	DEPARTING FROM	DESTINATION	DATE FORM PREPARED (Day, Month, Year)

AMC FORM 253, MAR 95 *(EF) (PerFORM PRO)*   PREVIOUS EDITION IS OBSOLETE

Military Space-A Air Basic Training - 141

APPENDIX L: INTERNATIONAL CERTIFICATES OF VACCINATION AND PERSONAL HEALTH HISTORY (PHS FORM 731)

This document provides for the recording of international certificates of vaccination and revaccination in both the English and French languages and the personal health history of international travelers. This document, with current health entries, is required as a Personnel Entrance Requirement for many foreign countries.

I. INTERNATIONAL CERTIFICATES OF VACCINATION

AS APPROVED BY

THE WORLD HEALTH ORGANIZATION

(EXCEPT FOR ADDRESS OF VACCINATOR)

CERTIFICATS INTERNATIONAUX DE VACCINATION APPROUVES PAR L'ORGANISATION MONDIALE DE LA SANTE

(SAUF L'ADRESSE DU VACCINATEUR)

II. PERSONAL HEALTH HISTORY

TRAVELERS NAME Nom du voyageur

ADDRESS (Number——Numéro)   (Street—Rue)
ADRESSE

(City—Ville)

(Country—Départment)   (State—État)

US DEPARTMENT OF HEALTH, EDUCATION, AND WELFARE
PUBLIC HEALTH SERVICE

READ INSTRUCTIONS CAREFULLY

PHS—731
Rev. 9-66

142 - Military Space-A Air Basic Training

APPENDIX L, continued

INTERNATIONAL CERTIFICATES OF VACCINATION AND PERSONAL HEALTH HISTORY (PHS FORM 731)

INTERNATIONAL CERTIFICATE OF VACCINATION OR REVACCINATION AGAINST SMALLPOX
CERTIFICAT INTERNATIONAL DE VACCINATION OU DE REVACCINATION CONTRE LA VARIOLE

This is to certify that   sex
Je soussigné(e) certifie que . . . . .sexe

whose signature follows   date of birth
dant la signature suit . . . . .né(e) le

has on the date indicated been vaccinated or revaccinated against smallpox with a freeze-dried liquid vaccine certified to fulfill the recommended requirements of the World Health Organization.
a été vacciné(e) ou revacciné(e) contre la variole á la date indiqueé ci-dessous avec un vaccin iyophilisé ou liquide certifié conforme aux normes recommandée par L´ Organisation rnondiale de Ia Santé.

INTERNATIONAL CERTIFICATE OF VACCINATION OR REVACCINATION AGAINST YELLOW FEVER
CERTIFICAT INTERNATIONAL DE VACCINATION OU DE REVACCINATION CONTRE LA FIEVRE JUANE

This is to certify that   sex
Je soussigné(e) certifie que . . . . .sexe

whose signature follows . . . . .date of birth
dant la signature suit . . . . .né(e) ie

has on the date indicated been vaccinated or revaccinated against yellow fever.
a été vacciné(e) ou revacciné (e) contre la fievre juane a la date indiquée.

INTERNATIONAL CERTIFICATE OF VACCINATION OR REVACCINATION AGAINST CHOLERA
CERTIFICATE INTERNATIONAL VACCINATION OU DE REVACCINATION CONTRE LE CHOLERA

This is to certify that   sex
Je soussigné(e) certifie que . . . . .sexe

whose signature follows . . . . .date of birth
dant la signature suit . . . . .né(e) le

has on the date indicated been vaccinated or revaccinated against cholera.
a été vacciné(e) ou revacciné(e) contre le choléra á date indiquée.

APPENDIX M: A BRIEF DESCRIPTION OF AIRCRAFT ON WHICH MOST SPACE-A TRAVEL OCCURS

The following transport, tanker and special mission aircraft are used by the military services (USPHS and NOOA do not have aircraft which are suitable for Space-A travel) for missions having Space-A air opportunities. **Only the major channel and support aircraft are listed.** We have not listed minor, some special mission or helicopter (rotary wing) aircraft due to space limitations. **We have provided for you a brief description of each aircraft with emphasis on performance and passenger accommodations.** The total number of each aircraft changes in the inventory due to acquisitions, conversions, reconfiguration and attrition. **Our best estimate of current specific aircraft inventories are listed below.**

C-5A/B/C GALAXY

The C-5A/B/C is a long-range, air-refuelable, heavy logistics transport capable of airlifting loads up to 291,000 pounds. This aircraft was developed, designed and configured to meet a wide range of military airlift missions. This is the "Western World's" largest aircraft.

PROGRAM/PROJECT CONTRACTOR: Lockheed Aeronautical Systems Company.
POWER SOURCE: Four General Electric TF39-GE-1C turbofan engines.
Each engine has 43,000 pounds of thrust.
DIMENSIONS: Wing span is 222 ft, 8.5 in. Length is 247 ft, 10 in. Height is 65 ft, 1.5 in.
WEIGHTS: Empty weight is 374,000 pounds. Maximum payload is 261,000 pounds. Gross weight is 837,000 pounds.
PERFORMANCE: Maximum speed at 25,000 ft is 571 mph. Service ceiling with 615,000 pounds gross weight is 35,750 ft. Range with maximum payload is 3,434 miles and range with maximum fuel is 6,469 miles. Between 1982-1987 the 77 C-5As were upgraded to C-5B capabilities. From 1985-1989, 50 C-5Bs were acquired.

APPENDIX M, continued

FACILITIES: Aircraft crew of six. Relief crew/rest area of 15. **Seating for 75 passengers, second deck airline type seats facing to the rear of the aircraft for safety purposes.** Cargo, first deck, 36 standard 463L pallets or mounted weapons and vehicles or a maximum of 340 passengers in a wide-body jet configuration. There is a program to repaint all USAF C-5A/Bs flat grey. AMC has control of all C-5A/B/Cs. Two C-5Cs have been modified to carry outsize space cargo by extending the cargo bay and modifying the aft doors.
INVENTORY: Total USAF 126.

C-009A/E NIGHTINGALE

This aircraft was designed as a commercial airliner. The DC-9 Series 30 commercial aircraft was reconfigured, modified and equipped to perform aeromedical (air ambulance) airlift transport missions. The C-009A/E performs aeromedical missions in the CONUS and in the European and Pacific Theaters.

PROGRAM/PROJECT CONTRACTOR: Douglas Aircraft Company. Division of McDonnell Douglas Corporation.
POWER SOURCE: Two Pratt & Whitney JT8D-9 turbofan engines. Each engine produces 14,500 pounds of thrust.
DIMENSIONS: Wing span is 93 ft, 3 in. Length is 119 ft, 3 in. Height is 27 ft, 6 in.
WEIGHT: Gross weight 108,000 pounds.
PERFORMANCE: The maximum cruising speed at 25,000 ft is 565 mph. Ceiling is 35,000 ft. Range is in excess of 2,000 miles.
FACILITIES: Aircraft crew of three (includes flight mechanic and spare parts) and five medical staff. There can be a combination of 40 litter (stretcher) or 40 ambulatory patients. Most MEDEVAC patients are ambulatory; they can walk but may be put in a litter for comfort. The ambulatory seats are spacious airline type seats. These are the seats used by Space-A passengers.

INVENTORY: Twenty-one in CONUS, four in Europe, three in Pacific, for a total inventory of 28 aircraft configured for aeromedical missions. Three are specifically configured C-9Cs which are assigned for Presidential and related missions. **The USN has 29 each C-9B SKYTRAIN II aircraft procured in FY 1985 to meet major Navy logistics requirements. This aircraft is configured for cargo and passenger (airline type seats, up to approximately 100). Total 60.**

C-17A GLOBEMASTER III

This is a new aircraft which is now undergoing initial operational testing. It is a heavy-lift, air-refuelable, cargo transport designed to meet inter-theater and intra-theater airlift for all types of cargo and passengers. This aircraft will be capable of using unimproved landing facilities (runways - 90 ft wide x 3,000 ft long). The initial operational capability (IOC) was 17 Jan 1995. A total of 48 aircraft have been approved through 1997. The planned total acquisition is 128 aircraft. **The passenger configurations for this aircraft have not been established.**

PROGRAM/PROJECT CONTRACTOR: McDonnell Douglas Aerospace Transport Aircraft Division of McDonnell Douglas Aerospace.
POWER SOURCE: Four Pratt & Whitney F117-PW 100 turbofans; 40,000 pounds of thrust on each aircraft.
DIMENSIONS: Wing span is 169 ft, 10 in. Length is 174 ft. Height is 55 ft, 1 in.
WEIGHT: Payload 172,000 pounds, Gross weight 585,000 pounds.
PERFORMANCE: Cruising speed (estimated) 518 mph, range with 160,000 pounds payload is 2,765 miles.
FACILITIES: Carries 102 troops/paratroops, 48 litter and 54 ambulatory patients and/or attendants. Airline type seating up to 154 passengers.
INVENTORY: Total USAF 29.

146 - Military Space-A Air Basic Training

APPENDIX M, continued

C-21A EXECUTIVE AIRCRAFT

There is a group of executive type aircraft in use in all of the Military Services. The C-21A is typical of these aircraft. **We will list the data for the C-21A and then list the inventory and passenger capacity of executive type aircraft in the Military Services.**

PROGRAM/PROJECT CONTRACTOR: Learjet Corporation.
POWER SOURCE: Two Garrett TFE731-2-turbojet engines. Each engine has 3,500 pounds thrust.
DIMENSIONS: Wing span is 39 ft, 6 in. Length is 48 ft, 8 in. Height is 12 ft, 3 in.
WEIGHT: Gross 18,300 pounds.
PERFORMANCE: Cruising speed is Mach 0.81. Service ceiling is 45,000 ft. Range with maximum passengers is 2,420 miles and with maximum cargo load is 1,653 miles.
FACILITIES: Aircraft crew of two. **Eight passengers in airline type seats** or cargo of 3,153 pounds. Also convertible to aeromedical (MEDEVAC) configuration.
INVENTORY: Total 470.

C-12A-J HURON (8 Passengers (PAXs)): USAF-77

C-20A/B GULFSTREAM III/IV (14-18 PAXs): USAF-10

C-21A EXECUTIVE AIRCRAFT (8 PAXs): USAF-88

C-22B BOEING 727 (approximately 100 PAXs): USAF-4

HU-25A GUARDIAN (approximately 12 PAXs): USCG-41

C-26-A FAIRCHILD METRO III (19-20 PAXs): USAF -13

C-27A STOL (53 PAXs): USAF-5

C-29A (125-800 BUSINESS JET, approximately 8 PAXs): USAF-6

APPENDIX M, continued

C-23A SHERPA (approximately 8 PAXs): USAF-13

VC-25A Presidential Transport, USAF-2, C-27A-11

The US Army operates a fleet of C-12, U-21 and older aircraft of approximately 200 in number. Each aircraft can seat approximately eight passengers.

C130A-J HERCULES

The C-130 Hercules is a very versatile aircraft which is used to perform a wide range of missions for all of the military services. The aircraft has been used mainly in a cargo and passenger role. It has also been used in specialized combat, electronic warfare, Arctic ice cap resupply, aerial spray, aeromedical MEDEVAC and aerial refueling among many similar missions. This aircraft is found in the inventory of all the military (Armed) services.

PROGRAM/PROJECT CONTRACTOR: Lockhead Aeronautical Systems Company.
POWER SOURCE: Four Allison T-56-A-15 turboprop engines. Each engine has 4,508 ehp.
DIMENSIONS: Wing span is 132 ft, 7 in. Length is 97 ft, 9 in. Height is 38 ft, 10 in.
PERFORMANCE: The maximum cruising speed 400 mph. The service ceiling for 130,000 pounds is 33,000 ft. The range with maximum payload is 2,356 miles.
FACILITIES: Aircraft crew of four, **54 passengers in commercial airline type seats,** on palletized seating 74 litter patients, five 463L standard pallets and assorted mounted weapons and vehicles. Seating ranges from side "bucket" seats along the sides of the aircraft to airline type seating with aisles and facing to the rear. The noise level is extremely high in this aircraft. Ear plugs are highly recommended for all passengers and crew.
INVENTORY: Total 983. C-130A-H and HC-130H/N/P: USAF-approximately 814, USN-117, USMC-42 (KC-130), USCG-30 (HC-130), USA-1 (EW MISSIONS).

148 - Military Space-A Air Basic Training

APPENDIX M, continued

KC-135E/R/T STRATOTANKER

This stratotanker was designed to military specifications. The aircraft is similar in size and design appearance to the commercial 707 aircraft but there the similarity ends. The KC-135 has different internal structural designs and materials which stress the ability to operate at high gross weights. The fuel carried in this tanker is located in the "wet wings" and in the fuel tanks below the floor in the fuselage. Passengers traveling on this aircraft are allowed, subject to mission restraints, to observe the Air to Air Refueling Operations which usually take place over the world's oceans.

PROGRAM/PROJECT CONTRACTOR: Boeing Military Airplanes.
POWER SOURCE: Four CFM international F108-CF-100 turbofan engines. Each engine has 22,224 pounds of thrust.
DIMENSIONS: Wing span is 130 ft, 10 in. Length is 136 ft, 3 in. Height is 38 ft, 4 in.
WEIGHT: Empty weight is 119,231 pounds. Gross 322,500 pounds.
PERFORMANCE: The maximum speed at 30,000 ft is 610 mph. Service ceiling 50,000 ft. Range with 12,000 pounds of transfer fuel is 11,192 miles.
FACILITIES: Aircraft crew of four or five. **Maximum of 80 passengers in airline type seats facing to the rear of the aircraft.**
INVENTORY: USAF 551.

C-135B STRATOLIFTER

This aircraft is similar to the KC-135 Stratotanker without the refueling equipment. These aircraft were initially purchased as an interim cargo/passenger aircraft placed in service before delivery of the C-141's. The appearance of this aircraft is similar to the KC-135.

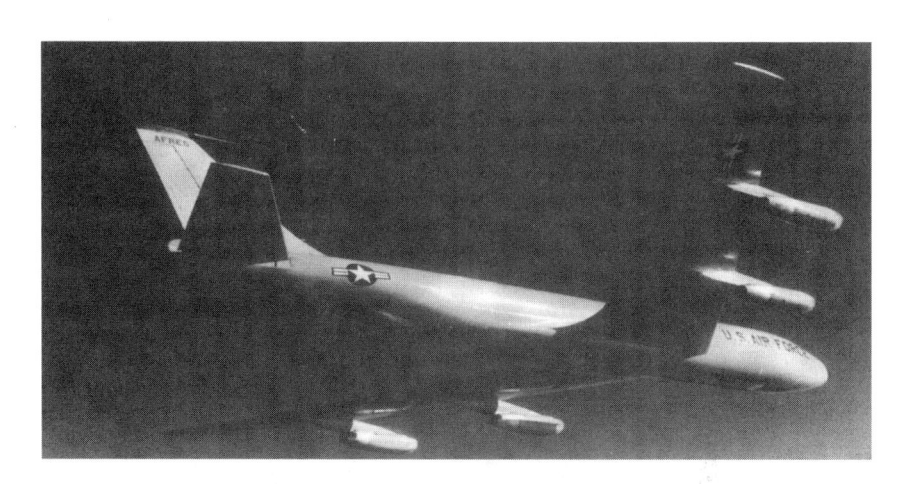

Military Space-A Air Basic Training - 149

APPENDIX M, continued

PROGRAM/PROJECT CONTRACTOR: Boeing Military Airplanes.
POWER SOURCE: Four CFM international F108-CF-100 turbofan engines. Each engine has 22,224 pounds of thrust.
DIMENSIONS: Wing span is 130 ft, 10 in. Length is 134 ft, 6 in. Height is 38 ft, 4 in.
WEIGHT: Empty 102,300 pounds. Gross 275,000 pounds.
FACILITIES: Maximum of 60 passengers in airline seats facing to the rear of the aircraft.
PERFORMANCE: Maximum speed 600 mph. Range with 54,000 pound payload is 4,625 miles.
INVENTORY: USAF 48.

C-137B/C STRATOLINER

APPENDIX M, continued

This is a special mission aircraft which has been modified from the commercial Boeing 707 transport. Two of these aircraft were the original "Air Force One" aircraft used by past United States Presidents.

PROGRAM/PROJECT CONTRACTOR: The Boeing Company.
POWER SOURCE: Four Pratt & Whitney JT3D-3 turbofan engines. Each engine has a 17,200 pound thrust.
DIMENSIONS: C-137B: Wing span is 130 ft, 10 in. Length 144 ft, 6 in. Height 42 ft, 10 in. C-137C: Wing span is 145 ft, 9 in. Length is 152 ft, 11 in. Height is 42 ft, 5 in.
WEIGHT: C-137B: Gross 258,000 pounds. C-137C: Gross 322,000 pounds.
PERFORMANCE: C-137C: Maximum speed 627 mph. Service ceiling 42,000 ft. Range 5,150 miles.
FACILITIES: This is a special mission aircraft with a variety of configurations. There are full-service galleys, dining, sleeping berths and airline type seating.
INVENTORY: USAF 9.

C-141A/B STARLIFTER

The C-141A/B STARLIFTER transport has undergone extensive modification to extend the airframe and modernization to all aspects of the aircraft. The result is a modern air transport which is fully capable of performing many missions from routine cargo and passengers to inter-theater MEDEVAC and humanitarian missions around the world. All of the C-141A/B fleet are scheduled for repainting to a flat grey.

PROGRAM/PROJECT CONTRACTOR: Lockheed-Georgia Company.
POWER SOURCE: Four Pratt & Whitney TF33-P-7 turbofan engines. Each engine has 21,000 pounds of thrust.
DIMENSIONS: Wing span is 159 ft, 11 in. Length is 168 ft, 3.5 in. Height is 39 ft, 3 in.
WEIGHT: Operating 149,000 pounds. Maximum payload 89,000 pounds. Gross 343,000 pounds.

PERFORMANCE: Maximum cruising speed is 566 mph. Range with maximum payload is 2,293 miles without air refueling.

FACILITIES: Air crew of five. **200 passengers in commercial airline seats facing to the rear of the aircraft.** 103 litter patients plus attendants. Cargo on 13 standard 463L pallets or alternate mounted weapons, vehicles or other cargo.
INVENTORY: USAF 202.

KC-10A EXTENDER

This advanced tanker/cargo aircraft is based on the commercial DC-10 Series, 30 CF. It has been modified to include fuselage fuel cells, aerial refueling operator station and boom. Military avionics have been added. The aircraft is fit to perform a role of extending and enhancing worldwide military mobility. The latest modifications to this aircraft are wing-mounted air-refueling pods designed to supplement the basic system and increase capability.

PROGRAM/PROJECT CONTRACTOR: Douglas Aircraft Company, Division of McDonnell Douglas Corporation.
POWER SOURCE: Three General Electric CF-6-50C2 turbofan engines. Each engine has 52,500 pounds of thrust.
DIMENSIONS: Wing span is 165 ft, 4.5 in. Length is 181 ft, 7 in. Height is 58 ft, 1 in.
WEIGHT: Gross 590,000 pounds.
PERFORMANCE: Cruising speed Mach 0.825. Service ceiling 42,000 ft. Range with maximum cargo 4,370 miles.
FACILITIES: Aircraft crew of four. **75 passengers in commercial airline seats facing to the rear of the aircraft.** 27 standard 463L pallets. Maximum cargo payload 169,409 pounds.
INVENTORY: USAF 59.

152 - Military Space-A Air Basic Training

APPENDIX M, *continued*

P-3C-ORION

This is a propeller-driven aircraft which has been used by the US Navy since 1958 in an Anti-Submarine Warfare (ASW) role. Many improvements have been incorporated in the basic airframe over the years. The latest improvements allow the aircraft to detect, track and attack quieter new generation submarines.

PROGRAM/PROJECT CONTRACTOR: Lockheed.
POWER SOURCE: Four Allison T-56-A-14 turboprop engines. Each engine has 4,900 ehp.
DIMENSIONS: Wing span is 100 ft. Length is 117 ft. Height is 34 ft.
WEIGHT: Gross weight is 139,760 pounds.
PERFORMANCE: Maximum speed 473 mph. Cruise speed 377 mph. Ceiling 28,300 ft.
FACILITIES: Aircraft crew of 10. **18 passengers in airline seats.**
INVENTORY: USN-133. Seventy-three older aircraft are to be retired in the very near future thus reducing the number of aircraft in regular and reserve P-3 squadrons. **Total 146.**

On behalf of all of our readers ─────────

Thank you AMC and other services offering Space-A air travel!

APPENDIX N: SPACE-A QUESTIONS AND ANSWERS

One of the biggest fringe benefits, dollar-wise, for uniformed services personnel and their family members is Space-A air travel on US military owned and operated aircraft. While there are some old pros who know all the ropes, having learned the hard way by flying Space-A, there are those who are a bit afraid to jump into the unknown. **This appendix is especially for those who want to know as much as they can about Space-A air travel.** Answers are based on information available to us at press time. Because policies can change or be interpreted differently, **these general answers must be regarded only as guides - not rules.** Specific questions, particularly those dealing with changes in policy, should be directed to military officials who are the final authority on the subject. We have divided the questions and answers into general functional categories. We hope that this appendix will aid readers in locating questions and answers in which they have a special interest in.

GENERAL INFORMATION

01. Is Space-A travel a reasonable substitute for travel on a commercial airline? The answer depends on you! If your travel schedule is flexible and your finances permit for a stay (sometimes in a "high-cost" area), while awaiting movement, space-available travel is a good travel choice. While some travelers sign up and travel may be the same day, many factors could come together to make buying a commercial ticket your best or only option. Remember, Space-A travel success depends on flexibility and good timing.

02. What facilities are available at AMC terminals (nursery, BX, snack bar)? Facilities at most military terminals are generally the same as commercial facilities. Facilities include exchanges, barber shops, snack bars, pay television (free television lounge in some military terminals), traveler assistance, baggage lockers or rooms, United Service Organization (USO) lounges, and nurseries (at major terminals). The type of facility available will vary according to the terminal size and location.

03. What documents are required for traveling Space-A? All travelers require a uniformed services ID card. Dependent family members and Retirees require a passport in most cases. Visas may be required for passport holders. In some cases immunization records are required. See Appendix B: Personnel Entrance Requirements in Military Living's *Military Space-A Air Opportunities Around the World* book for detailed requirements.

04. Will Space-A travel cost much? In general, no. Some terminals must collect a head tax or a federal inspection fee from Space-A passengers on commercial contract missions. Meals may be purchased at a nominal fee out of most air terminals while traveling on military aircraft. Meal service on AMC Category B full plane load charters is complimentary.

05. What fees will Space-A passengers be required to pay? All passengers departing CONUS, Alaska or Hawaii on a commercial aircraft from a commercial airport must pay

APPENDIX N, continued

a $6 federal departure tax that goes toward airport improvements. Also, all Space-A passengers departing on commercial contract mission **inbound to the United States** must pay a $5 immigration inspection fee, a $5 customs inspection fee and a $2 agriculture inspection fee. Some foreign departure terminals may also collect a departure tax, e.g., $27 AU when leaving Australia.

06. What are the trends in the availability of Space-A travel? Does it seem as if there will be more or less Space-A travel in the coming year? Although AMC has lead efforts to improve Space-A travel in the past few years, movement still remains a result of unused seats. Present DoD personnel and budget trends are effecting Space-A movement opportunity. AMC is dedicated to putting a passenger in every available seat.

07. How can I find where my name is on the Space-A register? Each terminal maintains a Space-A register (organized by priority and the date and time of registration for travel) that is updated daily. The register is conveniently located in the terminal and directly accessible to you. Travelers may call the terminal directly to find where they stand travel wise.

08. As a Reservist, where can I fly? Reserve members with DD Form 2 (Red) identification and DD Form 1853 may fly to, from, and between Alaska, Hawaii, Puerto Rico, the Virgin Islands, Guam, American Samoa, and CONUS. Additionally, when on active duty, members may fly anywhere overseas that AMC has flights operating.

09. As a Retiree, where can I fly? Retired members with DD Form 2 (Blue; the old one is gray) identification card may fly anywhere AMC has flights operating including CONUS, with the exception of occasional restricted areas such as Vietnam and Diego Garcia which has been restricted for may years. Some areas require special permission to enter, such as Kenya and Egypt.

10. Can I have family members travel with another military member if given power of attorney, other releases, or authority? No, with the exception of Category V, command-sponsored dependents may only travel when accompanied by their sponsor.

11. Who determines eligibility to fly Space-A? The four services jointly establish Space-A eligibility. AMC's first responsibility is air lifting official DoD traffic. Space-A passengers are accommodated only after official duty passengers and cargo.

12. How long does my name stay on the Space-A list? All travelers remain on the register for 60 days after registration, for the duration of their travel orders authorization, or until they are selected for travel, whichever occurs first. Revalidation has been eliminated.

13. What is country sign-up and how does it affect me? Under this program, you may sign up for five different countries rather than five different destinations. You are also eligible for the "ALL" sign-up which makes you eligible for all other destinations served. This gives you a greater selection of destinations from which to choose.

Military Space-A Air Basic Training - 155

APPENDIX N, continued

14. What is remote sign-up? Remote sign-up allows passengers to enter the backlog by telefaxing copies of proper service documentation along with desired country destinations and family members' first names to the aerial port of departure. The telefax data header will establish date/time of sign-up; therefore, active duty personnel must ensure the telefax is sent no earlier than the effective date of leave. Mail entries will also be permitted. The original date and time of sign-up shall be documented and stay with the passenger until his or her destination is reached. On reaching destination, the passenger may again sign up for space available travel to return to home station. **NOTE:** If applicable, statement that all required border clearance documents are current, is required.

15. What is self sign-up? Self sign-up is a program that allows passengers to sign up at a terminal without waiting in line. Most locations now provide self sign-up counters with easy to follow instructions for registration.

BAGGAGE

16. How much baggage can Space-A passengers check? Each Space-A passenger (regardless of age) can check two pieces of baggage totaling 140 pounds. Air Mobility Command (AMC) limits the size of each item to 62 linear inches. This measurement is obtained by adding together the item's length, width and height. The rules permit some exceptions to the 62 linear inches size limitation. For active duty personnel, all duffel bags, sea bags, Air Force issue B-4 bags and civilian-origin versions that have the same approximate dimensions can be checked. Similarly, the size restrictions do not apply to golf bags with golf clubs, snow skis, folding bicycles, fishing equipment, musical instruments and rucksacks. Any one of these oversized items listed above may be checked if it is the only piece checked and meets weight requirements of 140 pounds total.

17. We have heard that families and other groups can "pool" their baggage authorization. What's the story? Space-A passengers traveling together as a group (that is, listed on a single Military Transportation Authorization or AMC Form 140 (Space Available Travel Request)) may pool their baggage authorization so long as the total number of checked pieces does not exceed the number of travelers times 140 pounds, i.e., a five person family travel group could not exceed 700 pounds (5 x 140 pounds = 700 pounds) and 10 pieces (5x2=10).

18. How much baggage can I carry with me into the passenger cabins? All passengers boarding the aircraft can carry on one or more pieces so long as they fit under the passenger's seat, in the overhead compartment or other approved storage area, e.g., closets for hang-up garment bags. If available storage space is important to your baggage carrying needs, inquire at the terminal regarding storage areas for carry-on baggage before checking your baggage for a particular flight. As a guideline carry-on bags should not exceed 45 linear inches (length + width + height = 45 inches). **Passengers traveling with infants can also carry on any Federal Aviation Administration (FAA) approved infant car seat regardless of any other baggage.** Each AMC facility has a list of the FAA approved car seats. Passengers can call the FAA at tel: (202) 426-3800 to determine if new seats have been added to the list of approved seats.

156 - Military Space-A Air Basic Training

APPENDIX N, continued

19. Is the baggage limit the same for all aircraft? No. The baggage limit for smaller executive aircraft and the C-009A/E Nightingale is considerably less. On small two-engine executive and operational support aircraft, **the baggage limit for Space-A passengers is 30 pounds.** Also, on the C-009A/E aircraft the size limit for carry-on baggage is 18" long, 5" wide and 19" high or 42" overall.

20. As a Space-A passenger, may I pay for excess checked baggage over 140 pound or two pieces? No. Only duty status passengers may pay for excess baggage.

NOTE: See Appendix O: SPACE-A TRAVEL TIPS for more information on baggage.

ELIGIBILITY

21. May all Active Duty and Retired members of all the Uniformed Services fly Space-A? Yes. All Active Duty and Retired members (as well as their eligible family members) of all seven uniformed services (US Army, US Navy, US Marine Corps, US Coast Guard, US Public Health Service Officer Corps, National Oceanic and Atmospheric Administration Officer Corps and US Air Force) may fly Space-A as provided for in DoDD 4515.13-R as revised. Dependent family members may only accompany their sponsor on flights going overseas and in overseas areas. Dependents may not fly point to point in CONUS unless the same mission/flight continues overseas. As the result of a recent change in the regulation, one adult active duty dependent may accompany the sponsor on CONUS point-to-point flights when the sponsor is on "emergency leave" and when the sponsor is on an approved house hunting trip prior to a PCS.

22. May National Guard and Reservists fly Space-A? National Guard members and Reservists in an Active paid status may fly anywhere in CONUS, Alaska, Hawaii, Puerto Rico, Guam, American Samoa and the US Virgin Islands. **Guard and Reserve members cannot fly Space-A to a foreign country. There is a Congressional House of Representatives voice vote on the 1998 Defense Authorization Bill to allow National Guard and Reserve members and their families to fly to foreign countries beginning 1 October 1997. Caution: This is not law at press time.** Guard and Reserve members must have the ID Card, DD Form 2 (Red), and DD Form 1853, Authentication of Reserve Status for Travel Eligibility (authenticated by the Unit Commander within the last six months). The same is true of Guard and Reserve personnel who have received official notification of retirement eligibility but have not reached retirement age (60). This "gray area" retirement eligible group must present their ID cards (Red) and retirement eligibility notices (letters) or possess a red DD Form 2 which has been generated from the DEERS data base.

23. When may National Guard and Reservist eligible family members fly Space-A? When the sponsor retires and receives retired pay and full benefits at age 60, eligible family members may then fly Space-A. Family members must be accompanied by their sponsor when flying Space-A and may only fly on flights going overseas and in the overseas area, except CONUS legs of overseas flights.

Military Space-A Air Basic Training - 157

APPENDIX N, continued

24. Is there any difference in Space-A rules regarding eligibility for Active Duty versus Retired service members? Yes. First of all, Active Duty sponsors personnel have priority (Categories I Emergency Leave (retirees may be added to this category when approved under special circumstances), II EML, III Ordinary Leave, IV Unaccompanied Dependents on EML and V Permissive TDY) on Space-A flights at all times. Other differences include the fact that Active Duty personnel may take their "dependent" mothers and fathers (who have ID Cards DD Form 1173), with them on Space-A trips. **Dependent in-laws are NOT included in this privilege.** Retired members do not have this privilege, and Retired members and their families travel in Category VI.

25. I am a 100% disabled American veteran (DAV). I've heard that some of us can fly Space-A and some can't. Could you give me more information on 100% DAVs and Space-A? Disabled American veterans must be RETIRED from a uniformed service to qualify for Space-A travel. Those members who were separated in lieu of being retired are not eligible. Here's an easy way to check your eligibility. If your monthly retired check is paid by a uniformed services finance center, e.g., Defense Finance and Accounting Service, Cleveland Center, and your ID card is DD Form 2 (old cards are gray in color; new cards are blue), you can fly Space-A. If you are paid by the Veterans Administration and your ID card is a DD Form 1173 (butterscotch in color), you cannot fly Space-A. The color of ID cards and their form numbers are the key to being allowed to sign up for a Space-A flight. The DD Form 1173 is the same ID form used by dependents. In any case, dependents are not generally allowed to fly Space-A without their sponsors, so this butterscotch color card is a red flag alerting the officials at the Space-A desk that the carrier of the DD Form 1173 is not eligible to fly Space-A unaccompanied.

26. I am retired military and disabled and carry a blue ID card. Can I have a brother, sister, or friend accompany me to help me? The only persons permitted to accompany you are your dependents (not in the CONUS) or other persons eligible for Space-A travel. Every effort shall be made to transport passengers with disabilities who are otherwise eligible to travel. Passenger service personnel and crew members shall provide assistance in boarding, seating, and deplaning passengers with special needs.

27. May a retired service member, who relies on a guide dog because of vision deficiency, travel with the animal aboard military aircraft Space-A? Yes. This is allowed when the dog is properly harnessed and muzzled and the animal does not obstruct the aisle. Also, the dog may not occupy a seat in the aircraft, it must sit at the feet of the service member.

28. Who may fly on National Guard and Reserve flights of the Military Services? All uniformed services personnel and their eligible dependents may fly on most National Guard and Reserve flights depending upon the mission. The National Guard and Reserve have some of the best flights available. The catch is that they are not generally scheduled flights. Many different types of flight missions are given to National Guard and Reserve units; therefore, one can often find some very special flights to places not normally seen on flight schedules. Most National Guard and Reserve departure locations are listed in Military Living's *Military Space-A Air Opportunities Around The World* book.

158 - Military Space-A Air Basic Training

APPENDIX N, continued

29. Are active duty personnel in a leave or pass status traveling Space-A, always required to wear the service uniform? No. All active duty members (except USMC flying on USMC Marine aircraft) in a leave or pass status traveling Space-A on military department owned and operated aircraft are not required to wear the class A or B uniform of their service.

30. May an Active Duty service member use Space-A to take dependents to his/her unaccompanied duty station overseas or back from overseas to CONUS after the unaccompanied duty tour is completed? No. Family members may use Space-A only when they are with the sponsor on an accompanied tour (on service orders) overseas. The Space-A privilege is intended only for a visit to an overseas or CONUS area on a round-trip basis with the sponsor. **Space-A cannot be used to establish a home for dependents overseas or in CONUS.**

"You may think it's absolutely ingenious. I think it detracts from the uniform."

PAX LOUNGE
NO SLEEPING IN
CHAIRS OR ON FLOOR

31. May an active duty service member sign out on leave, sign up (register) for Space-A and if there is a wait for the flight, go back to work to avoid loss of leave time? When registering for Space-A travel, either by fax, mail/courier or in person, the member must have an approved leave or pass authorization effective on or before the date of registration for Space-A travel. You must show your approved leave with an effective date on or before your sign-up date. If a member registers for Space-A travel but voluntarily returns to work during the intervening days before the actual flight departure, leave will be charged for those days. **You must be on leave throughout your entire Space-A leave travel period.**

32. What does it mean to be "bumped"? The mission needs of space required passengers or cargo may require the removal of Space-A passengers at any point. If removed after being manifested (approved for this particular flight) on a flight or en route, you may re-register with the date and time adjusted to reflect the date and time of registration at the point of origin. The Space-A passengers will be placed no higher than the bottom of their category on the Space-A register. **Space-A passengers cannot be bumped by other Space-A passengers.**

33. What can service families do if they become extremely ill while overseas and need to return to the United States? Air medical evacuation (MEDEVAC) through AMC is available to Active Duty, Retired and their eligible family members. Space-A travelers should get in touch with a US military medical facility, preferably a hospital, or the American Embassy or Consulate to be considered for this service. In a change of military regulations, the remains of a retiree who died overseas may be returned on AMC aircraft to the US for burial. Watch our R&R Space-A Report® for more info.

34. What is "show time"? "Show time" is the time when a roll call of prospective Space-required and Space-A passengers, who are waiting for a specific flight, is made. The total available seats are allocated to travelers based on priority category and date/time of sign-up. See Section I for details. Failure to make "show time" will result in not making the flight and "show times" can be changed without notice depending on flight arrivals and departures.

35. Why can't passengers arriving at the terminal after "show time" for a flight be processed for that flight? Passengers should realize that many tasks are performed before a flight departs. Every possible effort will be made to process passengers arriving after "show time" if it doesn't jeopardize the aircraft's departure time or mission safety.

"Hey Dad, there's one of those new Korean fighters with a red star on it."

36. Are there special eligibility requirements for pregnant women and infants? Yes. Children must be older than six weeks to fly on military aircraft. If the infant is younger than six weeks old, there must be written permission from a physician to fly for mother and child. Pregnant women may fly without approval until their 34th week of pregnancy. In a medical emergency, a pregnant woman of more than 34 weeks or a child younger than six weeks and the mother will be flown on a medical evacuation (MEDEVAC) flight as patients.

37. What is the scope of the DoD student travel program? Dependent students who attend school in the United States are authorized one round-trip travel per fiscal year from the school location to the parents' duty station overseas, including US Possessions. The student travel program began in 1984 as a quality of life initiative for service members stationed overseas who had children attending secondary or undergraduate school in the United States. The plan has fluctuated over the years. The rule for the travel program applies to service members permanently assigned outside CONUS authorized to have family members reside with them. The student dependent must be unmarried, under age 23, pursuing a secondary or undergraduate education and possess a valid DD Form 1173 ID card.

APPENDIX N, continued

"Oh yeah? Well, my dad's got the Space-A ribbon with six oak leaf clusters!"

38. What is the Environmental and Morale Leave (EML) Program? This program is designed to provide environmental relief from a duty station which has some "drawbacks" and to offer a source of affordable recreation otherwise not available. In simple terms, it boils down to allowing Active Duty military personnel and their dependents to fly Space-A on military aircraft. There are, however, a couple of big differences in EML leave and regular Space-A leave. **First, dependents are permitted to travel accompanied or UNACCOMPANIED by their sponsor.** They may utilize "suitably equipped DoD logistic-type aircraft" as well as AMC channel and contract aircraft. **Secondly, EML has a Category II classification which is higher than regular Active Duty, Category III and Retired Space-A classification (Category VI).** Military sponsors and/or dependents on EML revert to ordinary leave status when they arrive in CONUS. They regain their EML status only when they depart CONUS for their EML program area. A good bit of EML travel is utilized in the Middle and Far East areas. This means that fewer flights may be available from this area for lower category personnel. The EML program is a tremendous morale booster to those assigned in far-off places and is very popular in these areas.

39. My husband was killed in Vietnam and is buried in the Punch Bowl (National Memorial Cemetery of the Pacific) in Hawaii. The children and I would like to take a trip to Hawaii to visit his grave. Can we fly in a Space-A status? No. Sorry, but widow/ers are not afforded the privilege of Space-A air travel. The rules state that family members must be accompanied by their military sponsor, so naturally this is impossible. **There have been proposals advanced, namely by the National Association of Uniformed Services/Society of Military Widows (NAUS/SMW) and others, to support a change to the DoD Space-A Directive which does not provide for widow/ers of uniformed personnel from using overseas (and any other) Space-A travel.**

40. May I register (sign-up) by fax, E-mail, letter/courier or in person at the same departure terminal more than one time for five different foreign countries in order to improve my chances for selection to a particular country? Space-A passengers may have only one registration (sign-up) record at a passenger terminal specifying a maximum

APPENDIX N, continued

of five countries (the fifth country may be "All" in order to allow the widest opportunity for Space-A air travel). This record may be changed at any time to include adding or deleting countries to which a passenger wants to travel, but the Julian date and time will be adjusted to the date of the change. No passenger may have two or more records with separate information; however, you may sign-up at several departure terminals in order to improve your chances for selection for air travel. This may change in the near future if "round-trip sign-up or one-time sign up" is approved. For example, in the Washington, DC/Philadelphia area you can sign up at McGuire AFB, Philadelphia IAP, Andrews AFB and Dover AFB for air travel to Central Europe.

41. What happens to your sign-up records at a departure location when you fly from that station? Note carefully that once passengers are selected for a flight, their name **will be removed from the station standby register for all destinations.**

42. May pets be transported Space-A? Not by Space-A passengers. Active Duty personnel may move pets Space-A on military contract flights when the sponsor is traveling on a permanent change of station.

43. I am retired. When I was on Active Duty, my personnel officer issued me travel and leave orders which specified travel documents and other requirements for visiting foreign countries. Where can I now get that information? Appendix B: Personnel Entrance Requirements in Military Living's *Military Space-A Air Opportunities Around The World* book. You may also check the latest changes to the DoD Foreign Clearance Guides at local personnel offices, AMC Space-A counter or most other air departure locations.

44. As a Space-A passenger, will I be subjected to security screening prior to boarding a flight? Yes. In most cases you and your baggage will receive electronic and/or personal security screening prior to boarding the flight or entering a secure area for aircraft boarding.

45. May adult family members who are dependent children because of a handicap or a permanent disability, and who have a valid DD Form 1173 military ID card, travel with their sponsor regardless of age? Yes. They may travel on the same basis as any other dependent on flights going overseas and in the overseas theater. Documentation of the dependent's permanent disability may be required.

FOOD AND BEVERAGE SERVICE

46. Is food served to Space-A passengers on the flight? Food and soft drinks are free on AMC contract flights. There is a charge if Space-A passengers want to eat on other flights. You can purchase healthy heart menus from the in-flight kitchen. The snack menu, at $1.75, includes sandwich, salad or vegetables, fruit and milk or soft drink. The breakfast menu, at $1.75, includes cereal or bagel, fruit, danish and milk or juice. The sandwich meal, at $2.75, includes sandwich, fruit, vegetable or salad, snack or dessert, milk, juice or soft drink. These meals are served at the appropriate time in the flight.

APPENDIX N, continued

Reservations are made at the time of seat assignment or other times in the flight processing. You may bring your own snacks (food) aboard. **New prices are established on 1 October each year.**

47. Are specialized meals available to Space-A passengers? Specialized meals are made available for duty passengers only for medical or religious reasons. If you need special food, we suggest you bring your own to maintain flexibility. Check with the Air Passenger Terminals regarding any restrictions on carrying food aboard as this can differ from place to place. While you can make your requirements known to passenger processing personnel at the time of flight processing, the chance of having additional specialized meals available at the last minute for passengers might be slim.

"Sorry sir. You should have revalidated this free refill receipt by seventeen hundred hours."

48. How are alcoholic beverages handled? Alcoholic beverages are not served on military aircraft. All open (seals broken) containers of alcoholic beverages will be confiscated if on your person or in your carry-on baggage. In many cases, sealed alcoholic containers may be checked. Check with the Air Passenger Terminal for more information. You may not consume alcoholic beverages from your own supply on a military aircraft. AMC commercial contract flights, which frequently carry Space-A passengers, offer beer and wine to everyone of legal age for a fee.

49. How is food service handled on USN, USMC, USCG, USAF (USAFR, USAG) and other non-AMC flights? Most departure terminals have food service for crews and passengers. If the

"Looks like everything's changed except SOS, Willie."

flight duration is more than approximately four hours, you will be notified in time to obtain your own box of food and drinks. Most flights have coffee and tea and all flights have drinking water on board.

CHANCES OF FLYING SPACE-A

50. How about Space-A availability? Space-A air opportunities change daily and, in fact, even hourly. There are more than 300 very active locations at which uniformed personnel, their eligible family members, and others may fly Space-A. There are also many other less active locations which offer some Space-A air opportunities. We estimate that more than 800,000 Space-A flights (all services) are taken every year. Availability is subject to time of the year, air mission, needs of the military services, quantity of flights, frequency of flights and the number of people attempting to fly Space-A.

51. What is the best time of the year to travel Space-A? The best time is a function of departure locations, arrival locations, space-required needs and the number of people waiting for Space-A transportation. Generally the best times to travel Space-A are autumn, late winter, early spring and after 15 July. It is best to avoid travel between 1-5 January, 15 May-15 July, 15-30 November and 15-25 December when traffic is heaviest.

52. Who flies Space-A the most - enlisted personnel, officers, retired members or dependents? Enlisted members travel Space-A more than all other groups.

53. Which uniformed service uses Space-A more than the others? Air Force members travel Space-A more than members from any other service followed by the US Army, US Navy and US Marine Corps.

PRIORITY FOR SPACE -A TRAVEL

54. Who has priority on Space-A flights? The DoD has established a priority system for allocating Space-A air travel. **This system is described in detail in Appendix A, which is taken from Chapter 6, Space Available Travel, DoDD 4515.13-R.** The general categories and their travel priorities are as follows:

Category I: Emergency leave, unfunded travel.

Category II: Environmental and Morale Leave (EML).

Category III: Ordinary leave, close blood or affinitive relatives,

"I'd like to toast the military air transport that started us on this trip."

164 - Military Space-A Air Basic Training

APPENDIX N, continued

house hunting permissive TDY, Medal of Honor holders, cadets of the service academies and others.

Category IV: Unaccompanied dependents on EML and DoDDS teachers on EML during summer vacation.

Category V: Permissive TDY (Non-house Hunting), Foreign military, students, dependents and others.

Category VI: Retired, dependents, reserve, ROTC, NUPOC and CEC.

55. May any eligible passenger make reservations for Space-A travel? No. Space-A passengers may not make reservations and are not guaranteed seats. The application for Space-A travel is not a reservation. The DoD is not obligated to continue Space-A passengers' travel or to return them to their point of origin.

56. Does rank/grade have anything to do with who gets a Space-A flight? No. Travel opportunities are available on a first-in first-out basis within DoD established categories. Travel is afforded on an equitable basis to officers, enlisted personnel, DoD/other civilian employees and their dependents without regard to rank or grade, military or civilian or branch of service.

57. Are there any circumstances under which a Retired service member in Category VI may be upgraded to a higher category? You bet there are. If you are traveling Space-A overseas and an emergency occurs at home, you may be upgraded to Category I, Emergency Leave, Unfunded Travel, by the installation commander or his representative under par 7-C, Chapter 6, DoDD 4515.13-R. However, you should have the emergency verified, in writing, by the Red Cross before attempting to obtain an upgrade.

TEMPORARY DUTY AND SPACE-A TRAVEL

58. May uniformed services personnel on official temporary duty orders (TDY) elect to travel Space-A to the TDY point (station)? No. Uniformed services personnel on official TDY orders must travel in a duty status to the TDY point and return.

59. Is there any way family members can travel Space-A to their sponsor's TDY point? No. Family members are not authorized Space-A to and from a sponsor's TDY point. TDY personnel may not travel Space-A between their duty station and TDY point as a means to have their dependents travel with them.

60. Can the service member take leave and travel Space-A from the TDY point? Upon arrival at the TDY point, personnel must conduct their business in a TDY status. They may then take ordinary leave while at the TDY point and travel Space-A from the TDY point to another location, but leave must be terminated prior to return travel from the TDY point of origin to the service member's duty station or next TDY location.

Military Space-A Air Basic Training - 165

APPENDIX N, continued

61. May family members travel Space-A when the sponsor takes leave at the TDY point? Family members may join the sponsor at the TDY point (at their own expense) in order to travel Space-A with the sponsor while the sponsor is on leave.

62. May the service member and dependents travel Space-A between CONUS and overseas? When the service member's permanent duty station and TDY location are within CONUS, Space-A travel to an overseas area and return is authorized. Also, when the service member's duty station and TDY location are overseas, Space-A travel to CONUS and return is authorized. (NOTE: Dependents may not travel point to point Space-A within CONUS except on the CONUS legs of overseas flights, emergency leave and PCS house hunting.)

63. When the service member's duty station and TDY location are in different countries overseas, and the service member travels Space-A to CONUS, may they return Space-A to their duty station? No. The service member must return Space-A from CONUS to the overseas TDY point or to a location other than the permanent duty station. He must return to the TDY point (at personal expense, if necessary, if Space-A travel is not possible to the TDY point) in order to complete travel to the permanent duty station in TDY status.

64. What is a simple summary of the above complex guidelines? The bottom line is that service members must always travel between their permanent duty station and a TDY point or between two TDY points in a TDY status.

OTHER

65. May Space-A eligible passengers take Space-A air transportation around the world? No. There are insufficient Space-A flights to circumnavigate the earth north to south or south to north. There are adequate flights to travel around the earth east to west or west to east. However, there is one choke point, Diego Garcia, Chagos Archipelago (NKW/FJDG), IO (UK), through which you are not authorized to travel Space-A. The Secretary of Defense (SECDEF) has limited access to Diego Garcia to mission-essential personnel. Space-A travel through Diego Garcia, including circuitous travel for personnel on official orders, is not authorized. This prohibition is found in SECDEF message 250439Z JAN 1986 and

"The regulation states that you must be requested to come to Guantanamo by someone you know there."

APPENDIX N, continued

the DoD Foreign Clearance Guides. Commercial facilities at this UK territory in the Indian Ocean are extremely limited to nonexistent. The Diego Garcia Naval Base does not have lodging, messing and other support facilities essential for non-mission essential travelers.

66. Should I expect to find more than one Space-A roster on base? No. Only one Space-A roster shall be maintained on a base, installation or post. The maintenance of such a roster is the responsibility of the AMC passenger or terminal service activity. If there is no AMC transportation activity, then the base, installation or post commander designates the agency responsible for maintaining the Space-A roster. You may find an exception at locations where a second service has a separate facility such as Andrews AFB and the Washington NAF.

67. Can people travel Space-A to Alaska or South America? Yes. Travelers may obtain Space-A travel to Alaska, South America, and other interesting locations; i.e., Australia, New Zealand, etc. Travel to Alaska is relatively easy when departing from the West Coast (Travis AFB, California, and McChord AFB, Washington). Travel to South America and other remote areas is much more difficult. Infrequent flights to remote areas are primarily cargo missions and have few seats available for passenger movement. Expect long waiting periods for movement.

68. I am retired and am traveling on a passport and my flight originated overseas. Where in the CONUS can I fly into? When traveling on a passport, (family members, retired Uniform Service, Reserve, etc.,) you may return to CONUS only through authorized ports of entry where customs and immigration clearance is available. While you may depart CONUS literally from any military airfield, reentry locations for passport holders are limited. Active duty passengers who do not require immigration clearance have more reentry options open.

69. Is it easier to go to some destinations? Space available travel occurs year round. However, travelers will find it is much more difficult to travel during the summer months (June-August) and the November-December holiday periods. It is particularly important that passengers be prepared to make alternate arrangements if they are not able to travel during these times.

Please visit Military Living's Home Page on the World Wide Web

★ ★ ★ ★ ★ ★ ★ ★ ★

http://www.militaryliving.com

APPENDIX O: SPACE-A TRAVEL TIPS

DOCUMENTS

Carry passports, military IDs and travelers checks with you and not in your luggage. Make photo copies of your ID cards, credit/debit cards, title page of passports, immunization records, title page of international driver's permit, list of travelers' checks, list of baggage contents and other important documents. Take one copy with you (not in your luggage) and leave one copy at home or at the office where it is accessible from overseas.

MEDICATIONS

Take all medications (prescriptions and over-the-counter) in their original (labeled) containers, and take any essential medications with you on the plane/train, not in your baggage. If you require prescription refills overseas, take an original physician's prescription for each drug.

If possible, and when necessary, it is recommended by physicians and travelers that you do not take Dramamine until the plane has been in the air for a while.

CLOTHING

If you are planning to launder clothes, pack a well wrapped (plastic bag) liquid laundry soap as opposed to a powder soap. Woolite works well for hand as well as machine washing and comes in both liquid and powder form. Note that laundromats overseas may not have a "permanent-press" cycle on the washer/dryer. They also have a much smaller capacity than US laundry machines.

Know the climate at your destination. Travel light. In most cases you will be carrying your own bags. Wear wash-and-wear type clothes. Travel in casual clothes that are loose-fitting and comfortable. Plan your wardrobe such that you can take off or add clothes in layers. Always wear a jacket, light-weight or heavy depending on the weather at your destination. Include a light raincoat or all-purpose coat in lieu of the jacket. Always wear comfortable shoes with low heels or no heels. Pack socks, underwear, etc., in plastic bags.

BAGGAGE

Folding luggage carriers do not count as weight against your checked baggage.

Because of security problems and other reasons, many US bases may no longer have lockers available for storing your luggage. If lockers are available, they will most likely be located outside the terminal, e.g., Rhein-Main AB, GE.

APPENDIX O, continued

Consider using soft-sided luggage to get more into each suitcase. Allow space for items you purchase overseas, or take a collapsible suitcase to bring gifts home.

There are very few porters at European and Far Eastern airports and train stations, and there are limited to no porters at Space-A terminals. Pack only what you can carry or roll comfortably. Can you carry your bags for one mile (15-20 minutes) without setting them down? If not, your bags are too heavy. Get a shoulder bag with small outer compartments. The bag must fit under your seat in the aircraft, and it should be stain resistant and waterproof. Never carry one large bag but split travel articles into two bags for ease in carrying. Bring less clothes and more money. As a general rule, pack a first time, and then cut your original amount of clothes in half and repack.

Always put your name and address in the inside of your bags as well as on the outside tag of each bag. If the outside tag is lost, your bag can still be returned to you. Put identifying marks (e.g., 1" wide masking tape) in bright colored tape on the outside of your bags for easy identification. (We have a large "C" on each side of our bags.) Lock your bags to protect against partial loss or to at least slow down the would be thief. Officials (Hotel Bell stand and porters) have keys for different types of bags to be used in an emergency.

As said earlier, always lock and strap, if available, every bag (place straps from luggage inside before locking). Never pack cash, jewelry, medicine or other valuables or hard to get items in your bags. After you have packed your bags, **never leave them unattended, anywhere, for any reason, at any time, until they are checked for travel.**

CUSTOMS

Keep receipts for Value Added Tax refunds and for proof of purchase at US Customs.

AMC PLANES AND FLIGHTS

In a C-005A/B/C, your seats are above the cargo area, and the seats are airline seats. **In a C-141B, your seats are in lieu of cargo.** There may be regular seats or red fabric/canvas fold down seats. Avoid seats 1A and 1B in a C-005A/B/C. They are against the bulkhead and do not recline, as well as being opposite the restroom(s).

Boarding may be quite different from commercial airlines. There may be ladders to climb, or passengers might be boarded from the open flight line rather than through an enclosed passenger gate. For these reasons slacks are better than skirts for women.

Climate in the plane may not be standard. In each type of plane there are hot spots and cold spots. Try to dress in layers for comfort and convenience. The flight crew will supply a small pillow, a blanket and earplugs (on some flights).

APPENDIX O, continued

Planes are usually boarded and deplaned with DV/VIPs or families first. (May not be followed at all stations/locations.)

Bring something to eat, to read or games to play on the plane. You can also buy a meal on the flight. The food is good, and it also gives you something to do during the 7-9 hour flight to Europe.

Usually there is a DV/VIP lounge in the AMC airport terminal available to O-6 and above of the Uniformed Services and to E-9s of the Armed Services.

MONEY

Exchange some US currency for the currency of at least your first destination country before you go overseas. Exchange at least $25 for local transportation and tips.

Distribute travelers' checks among those traveling in your group. Consider travelers' checks in various US denominations ($20, $50 or $100) as well as in foreign currency denominations (French francs, Italian lire, German marks, British pounds sterling, Japanese yen and other Asian currencies).

If possible, bring foreign coins with you for telephones, tips, etc. Bring along US change to use in the vending machines on US bases/installations. Bring a personal check or two to cash at an Officers' Club/NCO Club overseas. (You will need a US military club card to cash a check in overseas clubs.) When dealing with foreign coinage, watch for non-money coins, e.g., telephone tokens in Italy and UK.

Bring a pocket calculator to convert local prices into US dollars.

Border towns will usually accept either country's money.

Bring along US dollars for the flight home ($12 per person for federal inspection when departing on a contract mission; $2.75 per person for a small meal). Be prepared to take a commercial flight home, and have enough money or Credit/Debit card for that type of flight.

Be aware that foreign banks may close early on some days; usually the exchanges at major airports and train stations are open 24 hours a day. Exchange your travelers' checks at banks or exchanges rather than in stores or restaurants. Hotels and stores tend to charge expensive exchange commissions.

MasterCard and Visa are widely accepted in Europe as is American Express. Internationally accepted credit cards can be used for cash advances (execute/use with care for security reasons). Also, carry one or two airline credit cards in case of an emergency. Arrange to have funds sent to you via wire to a local bank. For tips and payment for services, carry some foreign currency and coins if available, or **carry new US one dollar**

APPENDIX O, continued

bills which are readily accepted by service personnel in foreign countries (strongly recommended). You know how much the tip is worth and the dollar is readily accepted by service personnel in foreign countries.

BILLETING

Check for hotel/motel accommodations at post offices (AU, NZ and UK), the tourist offices at main train stations and airports. There are also computer matching services at these locations that will provide a list of accommodations, base or location, price range, length of stay and your needed accommodation.

Your room rate will most often include a continental breakfast.

The room rate will vary according to the following:
 Class of hotel (Deluxe, First Class, Second Class, etc.);
 Type of accommodations (Double bed, King-size bed);
 With or without toilet (W/C) in room;
 With or without bath/shower in room;
 Whether or not the hotel has a restaurant;
 Whether or not the hotel has a parking lot;
 Whether or not the hotel has an elevator (lift).

In Great Britain, area libraries and post offices usually have a list of local Bed and Breakfast ("B&B") establishments.

Consider traveling before or after the tourist season in a country; when "in season" rates are no longer in effect. Watch out for trade or other seasonal fares/events Book Fair in Frankfurt and Oktoberfest in Munich) that will tie up a large number of hotel rooms.

Address and telephone numbers (800) can be obtained from the research section of your local library.

Write the foreign country's tourist office; in the US, most are located in New York City and other gateway cities. Addresses and telephone numbers are available in base and public libraries. They will send various kinds of tourist information as well as hotel/motel price lists.

Look for different types of accommodations such as a "Bed and Breakfast" or a "Pension."

APPENDIX O, continued

TRANSPORTATION

European and most Asian transportation runs on time!

Use the local public transportation system whenever and wherever possible. Note that there is usually a "smoking" and "non-smoking" section on public transportation.

Public transportation (buses/subways) usually accepts exact change only. You may have to buy a ticket before boarding, but frequently no one collects bus or tram tickets from you (i.e., the Frankfurt, GE light rail system). NOTE: Do not fail to buy and retain your ticket. The fine for not buying a ticket is extremely high.

Look for special tourist rates or tourist passes offered by your hotel or the local tourist office. Ask about special transportation rates for round-trip travel or time-limited travel, i.e., weekend, five, seven, or fifteen-day passes.

Most European train stations and airports are open 24 hours a day.

Note the difference between First Class and Second Class on trains. Trains in Europe and Asia are heavily utilized, and Second Class may be jammed with students and vacationers during holiday times (Easter, Christmas, New Year's, school breaks, etc.).

Note that in most cases you can reserve a seat on a train, etc., especially if you want a window seat or a seat facing in the same direction in which the train is traveling (many seats are reversible).

As in the US, food and drink aboard a train or boat is expensive. You may want to bring your own snack, drink or lunch on board.

Be aware of the different fare structures, e.g., a special rate for children (may not be based on age but height), **military** and animals.

A few points on rental cars: (1) Check the base MWR office for rentals, (2) rent away from the airport to save money and use low rental agencies, (3) return the car full of gas, (4) your insurance may cover the rental car, (5) consider drive-aways, (6) you pay a refundable deposit, (7) they put in the first tank of gas and you put in the rest, (8) rental car reservations are essential in most foreign countries, (9) you can make reservations from the US for major car rental companies, (10) check any car damage very carefully before renting, **and make sure that damages are documented on the rental agreement.**

LOCAL CUSTOMS

Know if a visa is necessary for your entry into or exit from the country. See Military Living's ***Military Space-A Air Opportunities Around the World*** book or the DoD Foreign Clearance Guide(s) at AMC Space-A counters or military personnel offices which issue worldwide travel orders.

APPENDIX O, continued

Know what language is spoken in the part of the country you are visiting, e.g., Switzerland has no official language of its own; rather, the Swiss speak a Swiss-German in the north, French near Geneva, Italian in the south and English everywhere.

Bring an English (Foreign Language) dictionary with you. Try to learn the basics in the appropriate foreign language, e.g., "Hello," "Goodbye," "Please," "Thank You," "Good Morning," "Good Evening," "Yes," "No," "One," "Two," "Toilet," "train station," "restaurant," etc.

Study the local customs and manners in the country you plan to visit. For example, know when to shake hands, how to greet a guest and when to ask for the menu.

Restaurant menus are often available in English; ask the waiter or hostess for an English-language menu.

Know when the local and national holidays are in the country you are visiting. Know the stores that are open late. **Get a local map and mark the location of your hotel on it, and memorize or write down the address where you are staying.**

Look for an English-speaking tour. You'll get more out of it if the guide does not have to translate into multiple languages.

Plan to visit the countryside not just the big cities.

Note the time differences between where you are and the East Coast of the US, especially in late April and October when our time changes. Typically, there are a telephone, telegraph and post office located in one central and several other locations.

Be sure to send postcards and other mail to the US via air mail.

OTHER TIPS

Travel Preparation Time Schedule - Ninety (90) days before departure: documents: health, language training, guide books and maps, money requirements, travelers' checks. Sixty (60) days before departure: documents: ID, passport, visas, international driver's permit, immunizations. Thirty (30) days before departure: health insurance, money. Seven (7) days before departure: clothes, insurance, luggage, medicines, glasses, film, audio/video tape.

The successful Space-A traveler has time, patience, funds and is flexible in all aspects of travel.

Have a map of your destination area for orientation purposes and to avoid becoming lost. It is also useful for measuring local travel distances and paying fares.

APPENDIX O, continued

Be flexible in selecting your Space-A route. A direct line to your desired destination may not be the only route to your destination. If possible, select a place with frequently scheduled departures to your planned destination.

When leaving your car at a departure location, be aware that you may not be able to return via Space-A to your car's location.

Some bases are more fun than others; try to pick a fun and inexpensive base if you expect to wait for a few days before obtaining a flight.

Get information from libraries, book and map stores, tourist offices (state, regional and national), travel agents, uniformed services personnel and their families and friends about your destination. See Military Living's *US Forces Travel Guide to Overseas US Military Installation*s, ISBN 0-914862-43-X, an excellent guide to US installations in 28 foreign countries and much, much more. See the appendices which are indispensible to overseas travel. See coupon in the back of this book.

The New United States Military Installation Road Map is Here!

MILITARY PUBLICATIONS *Living*™

P.O. Box 2347, Falls Church, VA 22042-0347
Phone: **703-237-0203** or 1-800-448-5731
Fax: 703-237-2233   E-mail: milliving@aol.com
Please visit our homepage at:
http://www.militaryliving.com

Military Living's
MILITARY INSTALLATION ROAD MAP

- Over 600 Major & Minor Installations of Uniformed Services and NASA
- Latest Base Closure Information (To include facilities remaining open at "closed" bases)
- Main Commercial/DSN Telephone Numbers
- Location Cross Reference & 10 Major Support Facilities Symbols
- Detailed Insets of 16 Concentrated Military Areas
- Interstates, U.S. and State Highways, Other Routes and Roads

Copyright © 1997

174 - Military Space-A Air Basic Training

APPENDIX P: BEFORE YOU GO --- TRAVEL AIDS AND TRAVEL PUBLICATIONS

The Government Printing Office (GPO) prints many pamphlets which are helpful to travelers. A selection published by the **United States Department of State, Bureau of Consular Affairs; Department of the Treasury, U. S. Customs Service; United States Department of Transportation, Federal Trade Commission and other government agencies and private travel organizations** follows. The publishing office, pamphlet number and ordering information are listed below. You may order any U. S. Government publication from the U. S. Government Printing Office, Superintendent of Documents, Mail stop: SSOP, Washington, DC 20402-9328 or via telephone using VISA or MasterCard, **Tel: 202-512-1800.** Most of the pamphlets cost $1.00; exceptions are noted.

UNITED STATES DEPARTMENT OF STATE PUBLICATIONS

---**A SAFE TRIP ABROAD,** #9493, $1.25.

---**CONSULAR INFORMATION SHEETS,** (Specify Foreign Country), Bureau of Consular Affairs, Washington, DC 20520, Free with a #10 self-addressed stamped envelope. For recorded travel information, Tel: 202-647-5225.

---**KEY OFFICERS of FOREIGN SERVICE POSTS,** #10287, $3.75.

---Tips for **AMERICANS RESIDING ABROAD,** #9745.

---Tips for Travelers to the **CARIBBEAN,** #10111, ISBN 0-16-042068-7.

---Tips for Travelers to **CUBA,** #9232, GPO 193-779.

---Tips for Travelers to **CENTRAL and SOUTH AMERICA,** #9682.

---Tips for Travelers to **EASTERN EUROPE,** #6329.

---Tips for Travelers to **MEXICO,** #10270.

---Tips for Travelers to the **MIDDLE EAST and NORTH AFRICA,** #10167, ISBN 0-16-045317-8, $1.50.

---Tips for Travelers to the **PEOPLE'S REPUBLIC of CHINA,** #9199, GPO: 1995-387-471: 89.

---Tips for Travelers to **RUSSIA,** #9971, ISBN 0-16-038092-8.

---Tips for Travelers to **RUSSIA and THE NEWLY INDEPENDENT STATES,** #10269, ISBN 0-16-048235-6.

Military Space-A Air Basic Training - 175

APPENDIX P, continued

---Tips for Travelers to **SAUDI ARABIA,** #9369, GPO 0-487-678.

---Tips for Travelers to **SOUTH ASIA,** #10266, ISBN 0-16-048142-2.

---Tips for Travelers to **SUB-SAHARAN AFRICA,** #9628, $1.50.

---**TRAVEL TIPS** for **OLDER AMERICANS,** #9309.

---**TRAVEL WARNING on DRUGS ABROAD,** #9558.

---**YOUR TRIP ABROAD,** #9926, ISBN 0-16-036113-3, $1.25.

The following two publications may be ordered for 50 cents each from the Consumer Information Center, Pueblo, CO 81009.

---**FOREIGN ENTRY REQUIREMENTS,** #371B.

---**PASSPORTS: APPLYING for THEM the EASY WAY.**

DEPARTMENT of the TREASURY PUBLICATIONS

---**IMPORTING A CAR,** #520, GPO 312-762/65301.

---**KNOW BEFORE YOU GO, Customs Hints for Returning Residents,** #512, GPO 294-052: QL 3.

---**PETS, WILDLIFE,** U. S. Customs, GPO 259-187: QL 3.

---**TRADEMARK INFORMATION for TRAVELERS,** #508.

---**UNITED STATES CUSTOMS HIGHLIGHTS for GOVERNMENT PERSONNEL, CIVILIAN & MILITARY,** #518, GPO 229-152: 90415.

OTHER GOVERNMENT AGENCIES

---**BUYER BEWARE!,** Division of Law Enforcement, U. S. Fish and Wildlife Service, PO Box 3247, Arlington, VA 22203-3247.

---**CAR RENTAL GUIDE,** Federal Trade Commission, #F025913, Free.

---**FLY-RIGHTS,** #133B, DOT, $1.75.

---**FLY SMART,** #575B, DOT, Free.

176 - Military Space-A Air Basic Training

APPENDIX P, continued

---HEALTH INFORMATION FOR INTERNATIONAL TRAVELERS, HHS pub #(CDC) 89-8280, $7.00.

---HOW TO DO IT!, Vote Absentee, FS-13, DOD, Free.

---NEW HORIZONS for the AIR TRAVELER with a DISABILITY, Department of Transportation, Office of Consumer Affairs, 400 Seventh Street SW., Washington, DC 20590, Free.

---TAX HIGHLIGHTS for U. S. CITIZENS and RESIDENTS GOING ABROAD, #593, IRS.

---TIPS FOR TAXPAYERS LIVING ABROAD, #1423, Catalogue #10359A.

---TRAVEL TIPS On Bringing Food, Plant, and Animal Products into the United States, #1083, United States Department of Agriculture.

---VOICE OF AMERICA (VOA) ENGLISH BROADCAST GUIDE, Voice of America, Audience Mail Unit, 330 Independence Avenue SW, Room G-759, Washington, DC 20547 USA, fax: 1-202-619-3919. Please include your postal address when writing via fax. Free. Tours of Washington Hq VOA offered Tue, Wed, and Thu at 1040, 1340 and 1440 hours and can be arranged by Tel: 202-619-3919.

PRIVATE TRAVEL ORGANIZATIONS

---AMERICAN SOCIETY OF TRAVEL AGENTS (ASTA), Public Relations Department, 1101 King Street, Alexandria, VA 22314, Tel: 703-739-2782, fax: 703-684-8319. To receive the following pamphlets; AVOIDING TRAVEL PROBLEMS, CAR RENTAL TIPS, DESTINATION GOOD HEALTH, HOLIDAY TRAVEL, HOTEL TIPS, OVERSEAS TRAVEL, PACKING TIPS, TRAVEL SAFETY, TIP ON TIPPING and WHY USE AN ASTA TRAVEL AGENT, send a #10 self-addressed stamped ($1.01 postage) envelope to ASTA at the above address, Free.

---INTERNATIONAL ASSOCIATION FOR MEDICAL ASSISTANCE TO TRAVELERS (IAMAT), 417 Center Street, Lewiston, NY 14092-3633, Tel: 716-754-4883. This is a no-membership-fee organization that publishes a directory of English-speaking physicians at IAMAT Centers in hundreds of cities all over the world (including some very remote places). You may join this organization for a tax deductible (we believe) contribution of your choice. They will provide you with the directory, a passport-sized medical record to be completed by your physician before departure, world immunization charts, and world climate charts. The centers will have daily lists of approved physicians available on a 24-hour basis. The scheduled fees (as of January 1996) agreed to be charged are: Office call $45; house/hotel call $55; night, Sunday and local holiday call $65. These fees do not apply to consultations, hospital or laboratory fees. Free (Donation requested).

APPENDIX P, continued

---THE INTERNATIONAL DIRECTORY OF ACCESS GUIDES, Rehabilitation International USA Inc., 20 West 40th Street, New York, NY 10018, Free.

---DIRECTORY OF USOs WORLDWIDE, United Service Organization (USO) World Headquarters, Washington Navy Yard, 901 "M" Street S.E. Bldg 198, Washington, DC 20374, Tel: 202-610-5700, Free.

---WASHINGTON POST TRAVEL INFORMATION, by fax (24 hours a day) 1-800-945-5190 with major credit/debit cards. See the Sunday Travel Section for a list and code numbers of available articles. Variable cost $2-4.

MILITARY TRAVEL CLUB R&R SPACE-A REPORT®
six issues per year

Military Living's R&R Space-A Report®
❏ 1 year-$15   ❏ 2 years-$24   ❏ 3 years-$33   ❏ 5 years-$49

Guaranteed subscription - if you are unhappy for any reason, we will return the cost of your unused issues. Subscribers renew year after year.

- **Learn how to $AVE by using military travel**
- **Get the latest breaking military travel news**
- **28th year serving the military**

To subscribe, call, fax, E-mail or write us at:

Military Living Publications
P.O. Box 2347, Falls Church, VA 22042-0347
Phone: **703-237-0203**, FAX: 703-237-2233
E-mail: milliving@aol.com

Please visit our homepage at:
http://www.militaryliving.com

APPENDIX Q: PASSPORTS

The required personnel entry documents vary from country to country, but you probably will require one or more of the following: passport or other proof of citizenship, visa, or tourist card. A few countries also require evidence that you have enough money for your trip and/or your ongoing transportation tickets. To find out what you need, consult: (1) This Appendix; (2) Appendix S: Visa Information; (3) Appendix B: Personnel Entrance Requirements, found in Military Living's ***Military Space-A Air Opportunities Around the World***; and (4) Embassies or nearest consulates of the countries you plan to visit. These official institutions representing foreign governments in the U.S. are located in Washington, DC and major U.S. cities and have the most up-to-date information. They are, therefore, your best source. Consult your local library or Foreign Entry Requirements, Pub M-264 for addresses and telephone numbers.

Who Needs A Passport?: U.S. citizens need passports to depart or enter the U.S. and to enter most foreign countries. Exceptions include short-term travel between the U.S., Mexico and Canada. For many Caribbean countries, a birth certificate or voter registration card is acceptable proof of U.S. citizenship; however, a valid U.S. passport is the best travel documentation available and, with appropriate visas, is acceptable in all countries. With the number of international child custody cases on the rise, several countries have instituted a passport requirement to prevent potential international child abductions. For example, Mexico has a law regarding children traveling alone or with only one parent. If the child travels with one parent, a written notarized consent must be obtained by the other parent. No authorization is needed if the child travels alone and is in possession of a U.S. passport. Children traveling alone with a birth certificate require authorization from both parents.

When To Apply: Demand for passports becomes heavy in January and begins to decline in August each year. You can help reduce U.S. Government expenses and avoid delays by applying between September and December; however, even in those months, periods of high demand for passports can occur. Apply several months in advance of your planned departure whenever possible. If you need a visa, allow additional time. (Passport agencies will expedite issuance in cases of genuine, documented emergencies with confirmed travel tickets in hand.)

How To Apply: For your first passport, you must present, in person, a completed form SDP-11, Passport Application, at one of the passport agencies listed in Appendix R Passport Agencies, or at one of several thousand Federal or State courts or U.S. Post Offices authorized to accept passport applications. Contact the nearest passport agency for the addresses of the passport acceptance facilities in your area. If you have had a previous passport and wish to obtain another, you may be eligible to apply by mail. If you do not qualify, you must apply in person at an authorized office.

APPENDIX Q, continued

What You Need To Obtain A Passport:

(1) A properly completed Passport Application (Form DSP-11).

(2) Proof of U.S. Citizenship.
A) Use your previously issued passport or one in which you were included. If you are applying for your first passport or cannot submit a previous passport, you must submit other evidence of citizenship.
B) If you were born in the U.S. you should produce a birth certificate. This must show that the birth record was filed shortly after birth and must be certified with the registrar's signature and raised, impressed, embossed, or multi-colored seal. You can obtain a certified copy from the bureau of Vital Statistics in the state or territory where you were born. (Notifications of Birth Registration or Birth Announcements are not normally accepted for passport purposes.) A delayed birth certificate (one filed more than one year after the date of birth) is acceptable provided it shows a plausible basis for creating this record.

If you cannot obtain a birth certificate submit a notice from a state registrar stating that no birth record exists, accompanied by the best secondary evidence possible. This may include a baptismal certificate, a hospital birth record, affidavits of persons having personal knowledge of the facts of your birth, or other documentary evidence such as early U.S. census, school, family Bible records, newspaper files, and insurance papers. A personal knowledge affidavit should be supported by at least one public record reflecting birth in the U.S.

C) If you were born abroad you can use: 1) A Certificate of Naturalization; 2) A Certificate of Citizenship; 3) A Report of Birth Abroad of a Citizen of the U.S.A. (FS-240); or 4) A Certification of Birth (FS-545 or DS-1350). If you did not have any of these documents and are a U.S. citizen, you should take all available proof of citizenship to the nearest U.S. passport agency and request assistance in proving your citizenship.

(3) Proof of Identity: You must also establish your identity to the satisfaction of the person accepting your application. The following items generally are acceptable documents of identity if they contain your signature and if they readily identify you by physical description or photograph: 1) A previous U.S. passport; 2) A Certificate of Naturalization or Citizenship; 3) A valid driver's license; and 4) A government (federal, state, municipal) ID card. The following documents are not acceptable: 1) Social Security Card; 2) Learner's or temporary driver's license; 3) Credit card of any type; 4) Any temporary or expired ID card or document; 5) Any document which has been altered or changed in any manner. If you are unable to present one of the first four documents to establish your identity, you must be accompanied by a person who has known you for at least two years and who is a U.S. citizen or permanent resident alien of the U.S. That person must sign an affidavit in the presence of the same person who executes the passport application. The witness will be required to establish his or her own identity.

(4) Photographs - Present two identical photographs of yourself which must be sufficiently recent (normally taken within the past six months) to be a good likeness. The photographs must not exceed 2" x 2" in size. The image size measure from the bottom of

APPENDIX Q, continued

your chin to the top of your head (including hair) must not be less than 1" or more than 1-3/8", with your head taking up most of the photograph. Passport photographs are acceptable in either black and white or color. Photographs must be clear, front view, full faced, and printed on thin white paper with a plain white or off-white background. Photographs should be portrait type prints taken in normal street attire without a hat and must include no more than the head and shoulders or upper torso. Dark glasses are not acceptable except when worn for medical reasons. Only applicants who are on Active Duty in the U.S. Uniformed Services and are proceeding abroad in the discharge of their duties may submit photographs in service uniform. (Passport Services encourages photographs in which the applicant is relaxed and smiling.) Newspaper and magazine prints and most vending machine prints are not acceptable for use in passports. No inclusion of family members in your passport. Since January 1981, all persons have been required to obtain individual passports in their own name. You may not include your spouse or children in your passport.

When To Apply In Person: You must apply in person for your passport if: (1) This is your first passport; (2) You are under 18 years of age (applicants between the ages of 13 and 18 must appear in person before the clerk or agent executing the application; for children under the age of 13, parents or legal guardians may apply on their behalf); and (3) Your most recent previous passport was issued more than 12 years ago or you were under age 16 when you received it. Applicants who are required to appear in person may do so at a U.S. passport agency or at one of the post offices or clerks of court authorized to accept passport applications. If you are over 18 and must apply in person, the total charge will be $65 for a 10 year passport; if you are under 18 years of age, you will pay $40 for a 5-year passport. Form DSP-11 is the appropriate form to use.

When To Apply By Mail: You may apply by mail if: (1) You have been issued a passport within 12 years prior to the date of a new application; (2) You are able to submit your most recent U.S. passport with your new application; and (3) Your previous passport was not issued before your 16th birthday.

How To Apply By Mail: If you are eligible to apply by mail, obtain Form DSP-82, "Application for Passport by Mail," from one of the offices accepting applications or from your travel agent, and complete the information requested on the reverse side of the form: (1) Sign and date the application; (2) Attach your previous passport (two identical 2" x 2" photographs which are sufficiently recent, normally taken within the past six months, to be a good likeness, and the $55 passport renewal fee; (3) Mail the completed application and attachments to one of the passport agencies listed in Appendix R. An incomplete or improperly prepared application will delay issuance of your passport.

Payment Of Passport Fees: The following forms of payment are acceptable: (1) Bank draft or cashier's check; (2) Check: certified, personal, travelers (for exact amount); and (3) Money order: U.S. postal, international, currency exchange bank. Cash should not be sent through the mail and is not always accepted by post offices and clerks of court.

APPENDIX Q, continued

Diplomatic & Official Passports: If you are being assigned abroad on U.S. Government business and wish to apply by mail for a no-fee type passport (no-fee regular, official, diplomatic), you must submit the mail-in application form, your authorization to apply for a no-fee passport, your previous passport, and two photographs to the Passport Agency in Washington, DC for processing.

After You Receive Your Passport: Be sure to sign it and fill in the personal notification data page. Your previous passport will be returned to you with your new passport.

Additional Visa Pages: If you require additional visa pages before your passport expires, you can obtain them by submitting your passport to one of the passport agencies listed in Appendix R. You may also request a 48-page passport at the time of application if you are planning to travel abroad frequently.

Validity Of An Altered Or Mutilated Passport: If you mutilate or alter your U.S. passport in any way (other than changing the address and personal notification data) you may render it invalid, cause yourself much inconvenience, and expose yourself to possible prosecution under the law (Section 1543 of Title 22 of the U.S. Code). Mutilated or altered passports should be turned in to passport agents, authorized postal employees, or U.S. consular offices abroad.

Loss Or Theft Of U.S. Passport: Your passport is a valuable document of citizenship and identity which should be carefully safeguarded. Its loss may cause you unnecessary travel complications as well as significant expense. If your passport is lost or stolen in the U.S., report the loss or theft immediately to Passport Services, Washington Passport Agency, 1111 19th Street NW, Department of State, Washington, DC 20524-0002, or to the nearest passport agency. Should your passport be lost or stolen abroad, report the loss immediately to the nearest U.S. embassy or consulate and to the local police authorities. If you can provide the consular officer with the information contained in the passport, it will facilitate the issuance of a new passport. Therefore, we suggest you photocopy the data page of your passport and keep it in a separate place, or leave the passport number, date, and place of issuance with a relative or friend in the U.S.

Other Passport Information: Sometimes travelers will depart for their intended trip with a passport that is about to expire. Travelers should be aware that there are a number of countries which will not permit visitors to enter and will not place visas in passports which have a remaining validity of less than six months. If you return to the U.S. with an expired passport, you are subject to a passport waiver fee of $80. This fee is payable to the Immigration and Naturalization Service at the port of entry. Additional passport information may be obtained from any of the passport agencies listed in this appendix.

APPENDIX R: PASSPORT AGENCIES

Boston Passport Agency, Room 247, Thomas P. O'Neill Federal Bldg, 10 Causeway Street, Boston, MA 02222-1094. *Recording: (617) 565-6998, **Public Inquiries: (617) 565-6990.

Chicago Passport Agency, Suite 380, Kluczynski Federal Bldg, 230 South Dearborn Street, Chicago, IL 60604-1564. *Recording (312) 353-5426, **Public Inquiries: (312) 353-7155.

Honolulu Passport Agency, Room C-106, New Federal Bldg, 300 Ala Moana Blvd, PO Box 50185, Honolulu, HI 96850. *Recording: (808) 541-1919, **Public Inquiries: (808) 541-1918.

Houston Passport Agency, Suite 1100, Concord Towers, 1919 Smith Street, Houston, TX 77002-4874. *Recording: (713) 653-3159, **Public Inquiries: (713) 229-3600.

Los Angeles Passport Agency, Room 13100, 11000 Wilshire Blvd, Los Angeles, CA 90024-3615. *Recording (213) 209-7070, **Public Inquiries: (213) 209-7075.

Miami Passport Agency, 16th Floor, Federal Office Bldg, 51 Southwest First Avenue, Miami, FL 33130-1680. *Recording: (305) 536-5395 (English), (305) 536-4448 (Spanish), **Public Inquiries: (305) 536-4681/83.

New Orleans Passport Agency, Postal Services Bldg, Room T-12005, 701 Loyola Avenue, New Orleans, LA 70113-1931. *Recording: (504) 589-6728, **Public Inquiries: (504) 589-6161/63.

New York Passport Agency, Room 270, Rockefeller Center, 630 Fifth Avenue, New York, NY 10111-0031. *Recording: (212) 541-7700, **Public Inquiries: (212) 541-7710.

Philadelphia Passport Agency, Room 4426, Federal Bldg, 600 Arch Street, Philadelphia, PA 19106-1684. *Recording: (215) 597-7482, **Public Inquiries: (215) 597-7480/81.

San Francisco Passport Agency, Suite 200, 525 Market Street, San Francisco, CA 94105-2773. *Recording: (415) 974-7972, **Public Inquiries: (415) 974-9941/48.

Seattle Passport Agency, Room 992, Federal Office Bldg, 915 Second Avenue, Seattle, WA 98174-1091. *Recording: (206) 442-7941/43, **Public Inquiries: (206) 442-7788.

Stamford Passport Agency, One Landmark Square, Street Level, Stamford, CT 06901-2767. *Recording: (203) 325-4401, **Public Inquiries: (203) 325-3538/39/30.

Washington Passport Agency, 1111 19th St NW, Washington, DC 20524-0002. *Recording: (202) 647-0518, **Public Inquiries: (202) 647-0518.

***The 24-hour recording includes general passport info, passport agency location and hours of operation. **For other questions, call the Public Inquiries number.**

DO YOU NEED... IMMEDIATE PASSPORT ASSISTANCE, PASSPORT INFORMATION OR JUST THE STATUS ON YOUR PENDING PASSPORT APPLICATION? IF SO, YOU MAY CALL..........

THE NATIONAL PASSPORT INFORMATION CENTER

Passport Services committed itself to responding to the needs of its customers and established the **National Passport Information Center (NPIC)**.

The National Passport Information Center opened in November 1996. You may reach the center by calling 1-900-225-5674 (1-900-CAL-LNPI) or TDD: 1-900-225-7778 (For the hearing impaired).

Live operators are available 8 a.m. - 8 p.m. Eastern Time, Monday-Friday, excluding Federal holidays. Automated Voice Response Unit (VRU) service is available 24-hours a day, seven days a week.

Automated service is $.35 per minute and is available 24-hours-a-day. Live operator service is $1.05 per minute and is available from 8 a.m. - 8 p.m. Eastern Time, Monday - Friday, excluding Federal holidays. If your 900 service is blocked, you may use a credit card to call 1-888-362-8668 or TDD: 1-888-498-3648 at $4.95 per call. Callers must be over 18 years old to use this service.

U.S. Department of State, Washington, D.C.

APPENDIX S: VISA INFORMATION

OBTAINING A FOREIGN VISA

A visa is a permit to enter and leave the country to be visited. It is a stamp of endorsement placed in a passport by a consular official of the country to which entry is requested. Many countries require visitors from other nations to have in their possession a valid visa obtained before departing from their home country. A visa may be obtained from foreign embassies or consulates located in the US. (Visas are not always obtainable at the airport of entry of the foreign location and verification of visa issuance must be made in advance of departure.) Various types of visas are issued depending upon the nature of the visit and the intended length of stay. **Passport services of the Department of State cannot help you obtain visas.**

A valid passport must be submitted when applying for a visa of any type. Because the visa is usually stamped directly onto one of the blank pages in your passport, you will need to fill out a form and give your passport to an official of each foreign embassy or consulate. The process may take several weeks for each visa, so apply well in advance. The visa requirements of each country will differ.

Some visas require a fee. You may need one or more photographs when submitting your visa applications. They should be full-faced, on white background and should not be larger than 3" x 3" nor smaller than 2.5" x 2.5."

Several countries do not require US citizens to obtain passports and visas for certain types of travel, mostly tourist. Instead, they issue a simple tourist card which can be obtained from the nearest consulate of the country in question (presentation of a birth certificate or similar documentary proof of citizenship may be required). In some countries, the transportation company is authorized to grant tourist cards. A fee is required for some tourist cards.

Some Arab or African countries will not issue visas or allow entry if your passport indicates travel to Israel or South Africa. Consult the nearest US Passport Agency for guidance if this applies to you.

The official institutions (embassies or consulates) representing foreign governments in the US are located in Washington, DC (see below) and major US cities and have the most up-to-date information. They are, therefore, your best source. Double check visa requirements before you leave. (*The Congressional Directory*, **available at most public libraries, lists their addresses and phone numbers.**)

For your convenience we have listed below the names, addresses and phone numbers of embassies in the countries where stations are frequently used by DoD-owned or controlled aircraft. US Trust Territories and possessions overseas have the same requirements as the US has for US citizens upon return from a foreign country. If you wish to travel to a country not listed below, visa and other personnel entry requirements can be obtained from the "*DoD Foreign Clearance Guides*" **available at**

Military Space-A Air Basic Training - 185

APPENDIX S, continued

most AMC (USAF) and other passenger service counters or at many military personnel offices. For complete personnel entrance requirements to foreign countries, see Appendix B in *Military Space-A Air Opportunities Around the World.*

NOTE: Embassies may close on their respective national holidays. Call before going to be sure they are open. We have listed only the Washington, DC based foreign embassies. There may be consulates of these embassies in other major cities which have visa issuing authority.

ANTIGUA-BARBUDA (AN-BD)
Embassy of Antigua and Barbuda
3216 New Mexico Ave NW
Washington, DC 20016
Tel: (202) 362-5122/5166/5211

ARGENTINA (AG)
Consular Section of the Argentine Embassy
1718 Connecticut Ave NW
Washington, DC 20009
Tel: (202) 797-8826

AUSTRALIA (AU)
Embassy of Australia
1601 Massachusetts Ave NW
Washington, DC 20036
Tel: 1-800-242-2878/(202) 797-3145

AZORES
See Portugal
Tel: (202) 332-3007

BAHRAIN (BA)
Embassy of the State Of Bahrain
3502 International Dr NW
Washington, DC 20008
Tel: (202) 342-0741

BARBUDA (BD)
See Antigua
Tel: (202) 362-5122/5166/5211

BELGIUM (BE)
Embassy of Belgium
3330 Garfield Street NW
Washington, DC 20008
Tel: (202) 333-6900

BELIZE (BZ)
Embassy of Belize
2535 Massachusetts Ave NW
Washington, DC 20008
Tel: (202) 332-9636

BOLIVIA (BO)
Embassy of Bolivia (Consulate Section)
3014 Massachusetts Ave NW
Washington, DC 20008
Tel: (202)232-4828 or (202) 483-4410

BRAZIL (BR)
Brazilian Embassy (Consular Section)
3009 Whitehaven Street NW
Washington, DC 20008
Tel: (202) 745-2820/2831

CANADA (CN)
Canadian Embassy
501 Pennsylvania Ave NW
Washington, DC 20001
Tel: (202) 682-1740

CHAD (CD)
Embassy of the Republic of Chad
2002 R Street NW
Washington, DC 20009
Tel: (202) 462-4009

CHILE (CH)
Embassy of Chile
1732 Massachusetts Ave NW
Washington DC 20036
Tel: (202) 785-3159

COLOMBIA (CL)
Embassy of Colombia (Consulate)
1825 Connecticut Ave NW, Suite 218
Washington, DC 20009
Tel: (202) 332-7476

APPENDIX S, continued

COSTA RICA (CS)
Embassy of Costa Rica
(Consular Section)
2112 S Street NW
Washington, DC 20008
Tel: (202) 328-6628

CUBA (CU)
Entry to Cuba is permitted only through Guantanamo Bay (US property), and a visa is not required.

CYPRUS (CY)
Embassy of the Republic of Cyprus
2211 R Street NW
Washington, DC 20008
Tel: (202) 462-5772

DENMARK (DN) (including GREENLAND)
Royal Danish Embassy
3200 Whitehaven Street NW
Washington, DC 20008
Tel: (202) 234-4300

DIEGO GARCIA (INDIAN OCEAN)
See United Kingdom
Tel: (202) 588-7800

DOMINICAN REPUBLIC (DR)
Embassy of the Dominican Republic
1715 22nd Street NW
Washington, DC 20008
Tel: (202) 332-6280

ECUADOR (EC)
(including the Galapagos Islands)
Embassy of Ecuador
2535 15th Street NW
Washington DC 20009
Tel: (202) 234-7166

EGYPT (EG)
Embassy of the Arab Republic of Egypt
3521 International Court NW
Washington, DC 20008
Tel: (202) 966-6342/48

EL SALVADOR (ES)
Embassy of El Salvador
Consulate General of El Salvador
1010 16th Street NW, 3rd Floor
Washington, DC 20036
Tel: (202) 331-4032

ENGLAND
See United Kingdom
Tel: (202) 588-7800

GERMANY (GE)
Embassy of the Federal Republic of Germany
4645 Reservoir Road NW
Washington, DC 20007
Tel: (202) 298-4000

GREAT BRITAIN AND NORTHERN IRELAND
See United Kingdom
Tel: (202) 588-7800

GREECE (GR)
Embassy of Greece (Consular Section)
2211 Massachusetts Ave NW
Washington, DC 20008
Tel: (202) 939-5818

GREENLAND (GL)
See Denmark
Tel: (202) 234-4300

GUATEMALA (GT)
Embassy of Guatemala
2220 R Street NW
Washington, DC 20008-4081
Tel: (202) 745-4952

HAITI (HA)
Embassy of Haiti
2311 Massachusetts Ave NW
Washington, DC 20008
Tel: (202) 332-4090

HONDURAS (HO)
Embassy of Honduras (Consular Section)
1612 K Street NW, Suite 310
Washington, DC 20006
Tel: (202) 223-0185

APPENDIX S, continued

HONG KONG
Chinese Embassy
2300 Connecticut Ave NW
Washington, DC 20008
Tel: (202) 265-9809

ICELAND (IC)
Embassy of Iceland
1156 15th Street NW, Suite 1200
Washington DC, 20005
Tel: (202) 265-6653/55

INDONESIA (IE)
Embassy of the Republic of Indonesia
2020 Massachusetts Ave NW
Washington, DC 20036
Tel: (202) 775-5200

ISRAEL (IS)
Embassy of Israel
3514 International Dr NW
Washington, DC 20008
Tel: (202) 364-5500

ITALY (IT)
Embassy of Italy
1601 Fuller Street NW
Washington, DC 20009
Tel: (202) 328-5500

JAMAICA (JM)
Embassy of Jamaica
1520 New Hampshire Ave NW
Washington, DC 20036
Tel: (202) 452-0660

JAPAN (JA)
Embassy of Japan
2520 Massachusetts Ave NW
Washington, DC 20008
Tel: (202) 939-6800

JORDAN (JR)
Embassy of the Hashemite Kingdom of Jordan
3504 International Dr NW
Washington, DC 20008
Tel: (202) 966-2664

KENYA (KE)
Embassy of Kenya
2249 R Street NW
Washington, DC 20008
Tel: (202) 387-6101

KOREA (RK)
Embassy of the Republic of Korea
(Consular Division)
2320 Massachusetts Ave NW
Washington, DC 20008
Tel: (202) 939-5663

KUWAIT (KW)
Embassy of the State of Kuwait
2940 Tilden Street NW
Washington, DC 20008
Tel: (202) 966-0702

LIBERIA (LI)
Embassy of the Republic of Liberia
5303 Colorado Ave NW
Washington, DC 20011
Tel: (202) 723-0437

MALAYSIA (MA)
Embassy of Malaysia
2401 Massachusetts Ave NW
Washington, DC 20008
Tel: (202) 328-2700.

MARSHALL ISLANDS, REPUBLIC OF (MI)
Embassy of Marshall Islands
2433 Massachusetts Ave NW
Washington, DC 20008
Tel: (202) 234-5414

MICRONESIA, FEDERATED STATES OF (FM) (Kosrae, Yap, Ponape and Truk)
Embassy of the Federated States of Micronesia
1725 N Street NW
Washington, DC 20036
Tel: (202) 223-4383

APPENDIX S, continued

NETHERLANDS (NT)
Embassy of the Netherlands
4200 Wisconsin Ave NW
Washington, DC 20016
Tel: (202) 244-5300

NEW ZEALAND (NZ)
Embassy of New Zealand
37 Observatory Circle NW
Washington, DC 20008
Tel: (202) 328-4800

NICARAGUA (NI)
Consulate of Nicaragua
1627 New Hampshire Ave NW
Washington, DC 20009
Tel: (202) 939-6531/32

NIGER (NG)
Embassy of the Republic of Niger
2204 R Street NW
Washington, DC 20008
Tel: (202) 483-4224

NORWAY (NO)
Royal Norwegian Embassy
2720 34th Street NW
Washington, DC 20008
Tel: (202) 333-6000

OMAN (OM)
Embassy of the Sultanate of Oman
2535 Belmont Road NW
Washington, DC 20008
Tel: (202) 387-1980/81/82

PALAU, REPUBLIC OF (PL)
Representative Office
444 North Capitol Street, Suite 619
Washington, DC 20001
Tel: (202) 452-6814

PANAMA (PN)
Embassy of Panama
2862 McGill Terrace NW
Washington, DC 20008
Tel: (202) 483-1407

PARAGUAY (PG)
Embassy of Paraguay
2400 Massachusetts Ave NW
Washington, DC 20008
Tel: (202) 483-6960

PERU (PE)
Embassy of Peru
1700 Massachusetts Ave NW
Washington, DC 20036
Tel: (202) 833-9860/69

PHILIPPINES (RP)
Embassy of the Philippines
1600 Massachusetts Ave NW
Washington, DC 20036
Tel: (202) 467-9300

PORTUGAL (PO)
(includes the Azores and Madeira Islands)
Consulate
Tel: (202) 322-3007

SAUDI ARABIA (SA)
The Royal Embassy of Saudi Arabia
601 New Hampshire Ave NW
Washington, DC 20037
Tel: (202) 944-3126

SCOTLAND
See United Kingdom
Tel: (202) 588-7800

SENEGAL (SE)
Embassy of the Republic of Senegal
2112 Wyoming Ave NW
Washington, DC 20008
Tel: (202) 234-0540

SINGAPORE (SG)
Embassy of Singapore
3501 International Place NW
Washington, DC 20008
Tel: (202) 537-3100

SOLOMON ISLANDS (SI)
See United Kingdom
Tel: (202) 588-7800

APPENDIX S, continued

SOMALIA (SM)
Consulate of the Somali Democratic Republic in New York
Tel: (212) 688-9410

SPAIN (SP)
Embassy of Spain
2375 Pennsylvania Ave NW
Washington, DC 20037
Tel: (202) 425-0100 or (202) 728-2330

SUDAN (SU)
Embassy of the Republic of the Sudan
2210 Massachusetts Ave NW
Washington, DC 20008
Tel: (202) 338-8565/70

SURINAME (SR)
Embassy of the Republic of Suriname
4301 Connecticut Ave NW, Suite 108
Washington, DC 20008
Tel: (202) 244-7488/7490

THAILAND (TH)
Embassy of Thailand
1024 Wisconsin Ave NW
Washington, DC 20007
Tel: (202) 944-3608

TURKEY, (TU)
Embassy of the Republic of Turkey
1714 Massachusetts Ave NW
Washington, DC 20036
Tel: (202) 659-0742

UNITED ARAB EMIRATES (UA)
Embassy of United Arab Emirates
3000 K Street, NW
Washington, DC 20007
Tel: (202) 338-6500

UNITED KINGDOM (UK) (England, Northern Ireland, Scotland and Wales)
British Embassy (Consular Section)
19 Observatory Circle NW
Washington, DC 20008
Tel: (202) 588-7800

URUGUAY (UG)
Embassy of Uruguay
1918 F Street NW
Washington, DC 20008
Tel: (202) 331-4219

VENEZUELA (VE)
Embassy of Venezuela (Consulate)
1099 30th Street NW
Washington, DC 20007
Tel: (202) 342-2214

VIETNAM
Embassy of Vietnam
1233 20th Street NW, Suite 501
Washington, DC 20036
Tel: (202) 861-2293/0694

ZAIRE (ZA)
Embassy of the Republic of Zaire
1800 New Hampshire Ave NW
Washington, DC 20009
Tel: (202) 234-7690/91

APPENDIX T: CUSTOMS AND DUTY

DECLARATIONS: You must declare all articles acquired abroad and in your possession at the time of your return. This includes: 1) Articles that you purchased; 2) Gifts presented to you while abroad, such as wedding or birthday presents; 3) Articles purchased in the duty-free shops; 4) Repairs or alterations made to any articles taken abroad and returned, whether or not repairs or alterations were free of charge; 5) Items you have been requested to bring home for another person; and 6) Any articles you intend to sell or use in your business. In addition, you must declare any articles acquired in the U.S. Virgin Islands, American Samoa, or Guam and not accompanying you at the time of your return. The price actually paid for each article must be stated on your declaration in U.S. currency or its equivalent in the country of acquisition. If the article was not purchased, obtain an estimate of its fair retail value in the country in which it was acquired. Note: The wearing or use of any article acquired abroad does not exempt it from duty. It must be declared at the price you paid for it. The customs officer will make an appropriate reduction in its value for significant wear and use.

Oral Declarations: Customs declarations forms are distributed on vessels and planes and should be prepared in advance of arrival for presentation to the immigration and customs inspectors. Fill out the ID portion of the declaration form. You may declare orally to the customs inspector the articles you acquired abroad if the articles are accompanying you, and you have not exceeded the duty-free exemption allowed. A customs officer may, however, ask you to prepare a written list if it is necessary.

Written Declaration: A written declaration will be necessary when: 1) The total fair retail value of articles acquired abroad exceeds your personal exemption; 2) More than 1 liter (33.8 fl oz) of alcoholic beverages, 200 cigarettes (one carton), or 100 cigars are included; 3) Some of the items are not intended for your personal or household use, such as commercial samples, items for sale or use in your business, or articles you are bringing home for another person; 4) Articles acquired in the U.S. Virgin Islands, American Samoa, or Guam are being sent to the U.S.; 5) A customs duty or internal revenue tax is collectible on any article in your possession; 6) A customs officer requests a written list; and 7) If you have used your exemption in the last 30 days.

Family Declaration: The head of a family may make a joint declaration for all members residing in the same household and returning together to the U.S. Family members making a joint declaration may combine their personal exemptions, even if the articles acquired by one member of the family exceed the personal exemption allowed. Infants and children returning to the U.S. are entitled to the same exemptions as adults (except for alcoholic beverages). Children born abroad, who have never resided in the U.S., are entitled to the customs exemptions granted nonresidents.

WARNING! If you understate the value of an article you declare, or if you otherwise misrepresent an article in your declaration, you may have to pay a penalty in addition to payment of duty. Under certain circumstances, the article could be seized and forfeited if the penalty is not paid. It is well known that some merchants abroad offer travelers invoices or bills of sale showing false or understated values. This practice not only delays your customs examination, but can prove very costly. If you fail to declare an article acquired abroad, not only is the article subject to seizure and forfeiture, but you will be liable for a personal penalty in an amount equal to the value of the article in the U.S. In addition, you may also be liable to criminal prosecution. Don't rely on advice given by persons outside the Customs Service. It may be bad advice which could lead you to violate the customs laws and incur costly penalties. If in doubt about whether an article should be declared, always declare it first and then direct your question to the customs inspector. If in doubt about the value of an article, declare the article at the actual price paid (transaction value). Customs inspectors handle tourist items day after day and become acquainted with the normal foreign values. Moreover, current commercial prices of foreign items are available at all times and on-the-spot comparisons of these values can be made. Play it safe - avoid customs penalties.

YOUR EXEMPTIONS: In clearing U.S. Customs, a traveler is considered either a "returning resident of the U.S." or a "nonresident." Generally speaking, if you leave the U.S. for purposes of traveling, working or studying abroad and return to resume residency in the U.S., you are considered a returning resident by Customs. However, U.S. residents living abroad temporarily are entitled to be classified as nonresidents, and thus receive more liberal Customs exemptions on short visits to the U.S., provided they export any foreign-acquired items at the completion of their visit. Residents of American Samoa, Guam or the U.S. Virgin Islands, who are American citizens, are also considered as returning U.S. residents. Articles acquired abroad and brought into the U.S. are subject to applicable duty and internal revenue tax, but as a returning resident you are allowed certain exemptions from paying duty on items acquired while abroad.

$400 Exemption: Articles totaling $400 (based on the fair value of each item in the country where acquired) may be entered free of duty, subject to limitations for liquors, cigarettes & cigars, if: 1) Articles were acquired as an incident of your trip for personal or household use; 2) You bring the articles with you at the time of your return to the U.S. and they are properly declared to Customs. Articles purchased and left for alterations or other reasons cannot be applied to your $400 exemption when shipped to follow at a later date. The 10% flat rate of duty does not apply to mailed articles. Duty is assessed when received; 3) You are returning from a stay abroad of at least 48 hours. Example: A resident who leaves U.S. territory at 1:30 PM on June 1st would complete the required 48-hour period at 1:30 PM on June 3rd. This time limitation does not apply if you are returning from Mexico or the U.S. Virgin Islands; 4) You have not used this $400 exemption, or any part of it, within the preceding 30-day period. Also, your exemption is not cumulative. If you use a portion of your exemption on entering the U.S., then you must wait for 30 days before you are entitled to another exemption other than a $25 exemption; and 5) Articles are not prohibited or restricted.

Cigars & Cigarettes: Not more than 100 cigars and 200 cigarettes (one carton) may be included in your exemption. Products of Cuban tobacco may be included if purchased in Cuba. This exemption is available to each person regardless of age. Your cigarettes, however, may be subject to a tax imposed by state and local authorities.

APPENDIX T, continued

Liquor: One liter (33.8 fl oz) of alcoholic beverages may be included in this exemption if: 1) You are 21 years of age or older; 2) it is for your own use or for use as a gift; and 3) it is not in violation of the laws of the state in which you arrive. Note: Most states restrict the quantity of alcoholic beverages which you may import. Information about state restrictions and taxes should be obtained from the state government, as laws vary from state to state. Alcoholic beverages in excess of the one liter limitation are subject to duty and internal revenue tax. Shipping of alcoholic beverages by mail is prohibited by U.S. Postal laws. Alcoholic beverages include wine and beer as well as distilled spirits.

$800 Exemption: If you return directly or indirectly from the U.S. Virgin Islands, American Samoa or Guam, you may receive a customs exemption of $800 (based on the transaction value of the articles in the country where acquired). Not more than $400 of this exemption may be applied to merchandise obtained elsewhere than in these islands. If you are 21 or older, you may bring in free of duty and tax five liters of alcoholic beverages. That's 169 fluid ounces or about 6 & 1/2 fifths. However, at least four liters must be purchased in the islands and at least one liter must have been produced there. Articles acquired in and sent from these islands to the U.S. may be claimed under your duty-free personal exemption if properly declared. Other provisions under the $400 exemption apply.

$25 Exemption: If you cannot claim the $400 or $800 exemption because of the 30-day or 48-hour minimum limitations, you may bring in free of duty and tax articles acquired abroad for your personal or household use if the total fair retail value does not exceed $25. This is an individual exemption and may not be grouped with other members of a family on one customs declaration. You may include any of the following: 50 cigarettes, 10 cigars, 150 ml (4 fl oz) of alcoholic beverages, or 150 ml of alcoholic perfume. Cuban tobacco products brought directly from Cuba may be included. Alcoholic beverages cannot be mailed into the U.S. Customs enforces the liquor laws of the state in which you arrive. Because state laws vary greatly as to the quantity of alcoholic beverages which can be brought in, we suggest you consult the appropriate state authorities. If any article brought with you is subject to duty or tax, or if the total value of all dutiable articles exceeds $25, no article may be exempted from duty or tax.

GIFTS: Bona fide gifts of not more than $50 in fair retail value where shipped can be received by friends and relations in the U.S. free of duty and tax if the same person does not receive more than $50 in gift shipments in one day. The "day" in reference is the day in which the parcel(s) are received for customs processing. This amount is increased to $100 if shipped from the U.S. Virgin Islands, American Samoa or Guam. These gifts are not declared by you upon your return to the U.S. Gifts accompanying you are considered to be for your personal use and may be included within your exemption. This includes gifts given to you by others while abroad and those you intend to give to others after you return. Gifts intended for business, promotional, or other commercial purposes may not be included. Perfume containing alcohol valued at more than $5 retail, tobacco products, and alcoholic beverages are excluded from the gift provision. Gifts intended for more than one person may be consolidated in the same package provided they are individually wrapped and labeled with the name of the recipient. Be sure the outer wrapping of the package is marked: (1) Unsolicited gift; (2) Nature of the gift; and (3) Its fair retail value. In addition, a consolidated gift parcel should be marked as such on the outside with the names of the recipients listed and the value of each gift. This will facilitate customs clearance of your package. If any article imported in the gift parcel is subject to duty and tax, or if the total value of all articles exceeds the bona fide gift allowance, no article may be exempt from duty or tax. If a parcel is subject to duty, the U.S. Postal Service will collect the duty plus a handling charge in the form of "Postage Due" stamps. Duty cannot be prepaid. You, as a traveler, cannot send a "gift" parcel to yourself nor can persons traveling together send "gifts" to each other. Gifts ordered by mail from the U.S. do not qualify under this duty-free gift provision and are subject to duty.

OTHER ARTICLES (FREE OF DUTY OR DUTIABLE): Duty preferences are granted to certain developing countries under the Generalized System of Preferences (GSP). Some products from these countries have been exempted from duty which would otherwise be collected if imported from any other country. For details, obtain the leaflet GSP & The Traveler from your nearest Customs Office. Many products of certain Caribbean countries are also exempt from duty under the Caribbean Basin Initiative (CBI). Most products of Israel may enter the U.S. either free of duty or at a reduced duty rate. Check with Customs. The U.S.-Canada Free Trade Agreement was implemented on January 1, 1989. U.S. returning residents arriving directly or indirectly from Canada are eligible for free or reduced duty rates as applicable on goods originating in Canada as defined in the Agreement.

Personal belongings of U.S. origin are entitled to entry free of duty. Personal belongings taken abroad, such as worn clothing, etc., may be sent home by mail before you return and receive free entry provided they have not been altered or repaired while abroad. These packages should be marked "American Goods Returned." When a claim of U.S. origin is made, this marking facilitates customs processing.

Foreign-made personal articles taken abroad are dutiable each time they are brought into our country unless you have acceptable proof of prior possession. Documents which fully describe the article, such as a bill of sale, insurance policy, jewelers appraisal, or receipt for purchase, may be considered reasonable proof of prior possession. Items, such as watches, cameras, tape recorders, or other articles which may be readily identified by serial number or permanently affixed markings, may be taken to the Customs office nearest you and registered before your departure. The Certificate of Registration provided will expedite free entry of these items when you return. Keep the certificate as it is valid for any future trips as long as the information on it remains legible. Registration cannot be accomplished by phone nor can blank registration forms be given or mailed to you to be filled out at a later time.

Payment of Duty, required at the time of your arrival on articles accompanying you, may be made by any of the following ways: 1) U.S. currency (foreign currency is not acceptable); 2) Personal check in the exact amount of duty, drawn on a national or state bank or trust company of the U.S., made payable to the "U.S. Customs Service";

APPENDIX T, continued

3) Government check, money order or travelers' checks are acceptable if they do not exceed the amount of the duty by more than $50. Second endorsements are not acceptable. ID must be presented, e.g., traveler's passport or driver's license; and 4) In some locations you may pay duty with credit cards from Discover, MasterCard or Visa.

A complete booklet of customs hints for returning U.S. citizens, "Know Before You Go," is free by writing the Department of the Treasury, U.S. Customs Service, Washington, DC 20229. Ask for Customs Publication No. 512.

Also be aware that certain souvenirs commonly available abroad may not be legally imported into the U.S. Several U.S. laws and an international treaty, designed to combat excessive exploitation of endangered species, make it a crime to bring many wildlife souvenirs back to the U.S. Be alert for certain reptile skins and leathers, depending on their country of origin, live birds and bird feathers; ivory from Asian and African elephants; certain plants, and fur from spotted cats, marine mammals, and polar bears. There are many others.

For more information and a pamphlet called Buyer Beware!, write the Division of Law Enforcement, U.S. Fish and Wildlife Service, P.O. Box 3247, Arlington, VA 22203-3247.

Many food products are restricted or prohibited from entry into the U.S.; food items can harbor foreign pests and diseases that can damage American crops and livestock. Be sure of the restrictions before attempting to carry any food or meat products into the U.S. Check your local phone book for the nearest office of the U.S. Department of Agriculture, Animal and Plant Health Inspection Service.

If you plan to buy trademarked items while abroad, be aware of trademark restrictions on certain manufactured products. Although many trademark owners do not place restrictions on the number of goods a traveler may import, it is an owner's right to do so even if goods are for the traveler's own personal use. Some commonly purchased trademarked items are: cameras and other optical goods, audio and video equipment, jewelry and precious metalware, perfume and like products. Trademark Information for Travelers (Customs Publication No. 508) provides the most recent list of potential trademark restricted items. Write to the Department of the Treasury, U.S. Customs Service, Washington, DC 20229.

SPECIAL CUSTOMS HIGHLIGHTS FOR CIVILIAN AND MILITARY GOVERNMENT PERSONNEL

The U.S. Customs Service is responsible for clearing all merchandise entering the United States. All imported goods are subject to a customs duty unless specifically exempted from this duty by law. Persons arriving in the U.S. from foreign countries are classified for customs purposes as either residents of the United States or nonresidents. Certain exemptions from payment of duty on the articles brought with them are provided.

Military Space-A Air Basic Training - 195

APPENDIX T, continued

A special provision allows U.S. Government personnel (military and civilian) to enter their personal and household effects without payment of tax when returning from an extended duty assignment overseas. Should they return to the U.S. for purposes of leave or TDY before their overseas assignment is concluded, they may claim the customs status of either a returning resident or a nonresident. Members of their family residing with them also may claim either status when returning for a short visit. The classification and rates of duty, or exemptions there from, on imported goods are governed by the Tariff Schedules of the United States (TSUS). Under item 817.00 of the Tariff Schedules, personal and household effects of any person (military or civilian) employed by the U.S. Government, and members of his family residing with him at his post or station, may be entered free of duty unless items are restricted, prohibited, or limited as in the case of liquor and tobacco.

To claim this exemption, the person in the service of the United States must be returning to the states under Government order upon termination of an assignment to extended duty outside the Customs territory of the U.S.

An assignment to extended duty abroad must be of at least 140 days duration, except as noted for Navy personnel. Military and civilian personnel are entitled to free entry privileges, if: 1) They are returning, at any time, upon termination of an assignment of extended duty; or 2) They are under permanent change of station orders to another post or station abroad, necessitating return of their personal and household effects to the United States.

Navy personnel serving aboard a United States naval vessel or supporting a naval vessel when it departs from the U.S. on an intended deployment of 120 days or more outside the country and who continue to serve on the vessel until it returns to the U.S. are entitled to the extended duty exemption.

Free entry of accompanied and unaccompanied effects of family members who have resided with the employee cannot be claimed under item 817.00 when imported before the employee's receipt of orders when terminating his extended duty assignment. Persons not entitled to this exemption: 1) Employees of private businesses and commercial organizations working under contract for the U.S. Government; 2) Persons under research fellowships granted by the United States Government; 3) Peace Corps volunteers or employees of UNICEF; 4) Persons going abroad under the Fulbright-Hayes Act of 1961 or under the Mutual Educational and Cultural Exchange Act of 1961. Item 817.00 applies, however, to any person evacuated to the United States under U.S. Government orders or instructions.

CUSTOMS DECLARATIONS

Accompanied Baggage: Articles which accompany you upon your return to the United States on PCS orders should be declared on Customs Form CF 6059B "Customs Declaration," if you travel on a commercial carrier. If you travel on a carrier owned or operated by the U.S. Government, including charter aircraft, you will execute Department

APPENDIX T, continued

of Defense form DD 1854, "Customs Accompanied Baggage Declaration." Be prepared to show the customs officer a copy of your travel orders.

Unaccompanied Baggage: If you are a DoD civilian or military member returning to the U.S. from extended duty overseas, you should execute DD form 1252, "U.S. Customs Declaration for Personal Property Shipments," to facilitate the entry of your unaccompanied baggage and/or household goods into the U.S. A copy of your PCS orders, terminating your assignment to extended duty abroad, should accompany DD form 1252. This form is also used by a DoD sponsored or directed individual or employee of a nonappropriated fund agency which is an integral part of the military services.

All other Government employees should complete "Declaration for Free Entry of Unaccompanied Articles," Customs form 3299, and attach a copy of their orders.

By these declarations you certify that the shipment consists of personal and household effects which were in your direct personal possession while abroad and the articles are not imported for the account of another person or intended for sale. Employees completing CF 3299 must list restricted articles (e.g., trademarked items, firearms), and goods not subject to their exemption (e.g., excess liquor, articles carried for other persons) on the declaration and show the actual prices paid. DoD employees and military members whose shipment of personal and household effects are cleared by a military customs inspector (MCI) will indicate to the MCI any articles which are restricted or subject to customs duty. A notation will be made by the MCI on DD form 1252 and the shipment will be examined by U.S. Customs upon its arrival in the U.S. Shipments from other areas where MCIs are not assigned will be cleared upon arrival in the U.S.

"Hide the jewelry in the blue suitcase, Muriel. Hide the jewelry in the blue suitcase, Muriel."

Effects sent by mail are eligible for duty-free entry if the articles were in the returnee's possession prior to leaving the duty station. A copy of the government orders terminating the assignment must accompany the articles in a sealed envelope securely affixed to the outer wrapper of the parcel. The parcel should also be marked clearly on the outside "Returned Personal Effects - Orders Enclosed."

Articles taken with you from the United States need not be listed on your declaration. If such articles were repaired in a foreign country, list the cost of repairs. If the repaired or altered article is changed sufficiently to become a different article, it must be declared at its full value.

APPENDIX T, continued

Effects sent home before your orders are issued, or purchased overseas and not delivered to you abroad but sent to your address in the states, do not qualify for free entry.

Merchandise of foreign origin purchased in overseas Post or Base Exchanges is subject to customs treatment and other import requirements and regulations including trademark restrictions.

LIMITATIONS

Tobacco: Not more than 100 cigars may be imported free of duty as personal effects. There is no limitation on the numbers of cigarettes. Products of Cuban tobacco are prohibited to arriving U.S. citizens and residents unless acquired in Cuba.

Liquor: Not more than four liters (135.2 fluid ounces) of alcoholic beverages, of which three liters must be bottled in the United States and of U.S. manufacture, may be imported free of duty as personal effects, if: 1) It accompanies the employee or the member of his family making claim for entry at the time that person arrives in the U.S.; 2) The member of the employee's family claiming the exemption is 21 years age or older (U.S. civilian or military personnel are exempt from the age requirement); 3) The person requesting free entry does not claim the customs exemption for alcoholic beverages as a returning U.S. resident or nonresident.

No alcoholic beverages may be imported into the U.S. by mail nor can Customs release liquor in violation of the laws of the state where it is entered. As laws vary from state to state, this information may be obtained from state liquor authorities.

MILITARY PUBLICATIONS *Living*™

"Where the Fun Begins!"

198 - Military Space-A Air Basic Training

APPENDIX U: AIR MOBILITY COMMAND (AMC) IN-FLIGHT FOOD SERVICE

No matter where you travel throughout the Air Mobility Command (AMC), you will find totally different, greatly improved flight meals. Flight menus have traditionally lacked variety, quality and overall customer appeal. An exciting new in-flight food service program has been developed by the AMC Food Service Branch. The program was established to improve the quality, nutritional content, packaging and presentation of flight meals within AMC.

Improvements to the food service program include the addition of "Healthy Heart" and breakfast menus, the exclusive use of deli meats, fresh fruits and vegetables, pasta salads, fruit cups, two-percent milk, cholesterol-free snacks, and whole wheat bread. "Junk food" items high in fats and sodium, such as candies and cream-filled pastries, are no longer served.

This food service and the in-flight kitchens that produce it are positioned throughout the world. All passengers ordering in-flight meals, even from Space-A terminals in exotic locales, will experience the same high-quality and nutritious food AMC now provides.

Following are some sample menus available on AMC flights. In-flight menu prices are established at the beginning of each fiscal year (1 October) and may vary at different locations.

SANDWICH MEALS $2.75

When selecting your sandwich, please indicate the supplement packages you would like to compliment your meal. Diet soft drinks may be substituted upon request. Menus subject to change due to non-availability.

SANDWICH MENUS

1. Turkey and American Cheese Hoagie
2. Turkey, Ham and Swiss Cheese Hoagie
3. Ham, Roast Beef Hoagie
4. Ham, American Cheese Hoagie
5. Roast Beef, Swiss on Whole Wheat
6. Ham, Corned Beef and American Cheese on Whole Wheat
7. Ham and Swiss Cheese on Rye
8. Turkey, Ham and American Cheese on Whole Wheat
9. Ham and Provolone Cheese on Whole Wheat
10. Corned Beef and Swiss Cheese on Rye
*11. Turkey on Whole Wheat
*12. Peanut Butter and Jelly on Whole Wheat
13. Ham, Roast Beef and American Cheese Kaiser
14. Turkey and Swiss Cheese on Whole Wheat
15. Fried Chicken with Dinner Roll
*16. Baked Chicken with Dinner Roll

*HEALTHY HEART MENUS

Military Space-A Air Basic Training - 199

APPENDIX U, continued

STANDARD SUPPLEMENT PACKAGE

A. Fruit Cup
Vegetable Tray
Assorted Veg Bread
Assorted Snack Item
Soft Drink and Juice
Condiments, Flight Pack

B. Fresh Fruit
Italian Veg Pasta Salad
Raisins
Snack Pack Pudding
Lowfat White Milk & Juice
Condiments, Flight Pack

C. Fresh Fruit
Vegetable Tray
Snack Pack Pudding
Raisins
Soft Drink and Juice
Condiments, Flight Pack

D. Fruit Cup
Italian Veg Pasta Salad
Assorted Snack Item
Assorted Veg Bread
Lowfat White Milk & Juice
Condiments, Flight Pack

SNACK MEALS $1.75

SNACK MENUS

A. Fried or Baked Chicken
Vegetable Tray
Fresh Fruit
Dinner Roll with Margarine
Lowfat Milk
Condiments, Flight Pack

B. Ham and Cheese on Wheat
Fresh Fruit
Vegetable Tray
Danish
Lowfat Milk
Condiments, Flight Pack

C. Turkey, Ham and Swiss
Cheese on Whole Wheat
Fresh Fruit
Vegetable Tray
Soft Drink
Condiments, Flight Pack

D. Corned Beef, Swiss on Rye
Italian Veg Pasta Salad
Fresh Fruit
Lowfat Milk
Condiments, Flight Pack

E. Roast Beef and Provolone Hoagie
Italian Veg Pasta Salad
Fresh Fruit
Fruit Juice
Condiments, Flight Pack

HEALTHY HEART MENUS

F. Chef Salad
Diet Dressing, Crackers
Fresh Fruit
Skim Milk
Flight Pack

G. Baked Chicken
Fresh Fruit
Vegetable Tray
Raisins
Vegetable Juice
Flight Pack

H. Turkey and Swiss Cheese on
Whole Wheat
Vegetable Tray
Fresh Fruit
Skim Milk
Condiments, Flight Pack

I. Tuna (unprepared)
Salad Dressing
Wheat Bread
Vegetable Tray
Fresh Fruit
Vegetable Juice
Flight Pack

200 - Military Space-A Air Basic Training

APPENDIX U, continued

BREAKFAST MENU $1.75

J. Breakfast Cereal
Fresh Fruit
Danish
Lowfat Milk, Fruit Juice
Yogurt
Flight Pack

K. Ham and Swiss Cheese on Bagel
Fresh Fruit Danish
Fruit Juice
Condiments, Flight Pack

NOTE: If Healthy Heart Menus are not available, a hot TV-Dinner with soft drink, juice or milk and snacks is $2.75.

You See the Military Installations First!

Features each state and possession plus 36 city maps with large military populations. Includes almost 635 military installations to include military RV/Camping areas, both on and off the installations. Look for it at your Exchange and $ave!

APPENDIX V: MAJOR WORLDWIDE SPACE-A ROUTES

Most of the major worldwide passenger and cargo routes were established during and immediately after World War II. The routes have remained in full-time operation utilizing Uniformed Services organic and contractor aircraft since that time. Major air routes are changed or reoriented when the need to support an area with intra-theater airlift changes, i.e., the US Forces withdrew from South Vietnam. Also the number and frequency of missions flown on these major routes change as the requirements for inter-theater airlift change.

The missions that are flown on these major worldwide routes are on a scheduled and a non-scheduled basis to meet the operational needs of the Uniformed Services and the Unified and Specified commands overseas. These missions are performed by organic units of the Active USAF, USAFRES, USANG and Contractors assigned to the Air Force, Air Mobility Command (AMC).

Missions on these major worldwide routes are manned by crews and aircraft that are assigned in the CONUS and fly overseas to one or more countries or U. S. Possessions and then return to their home station. There are some theater airlift assets which are stationed overseas and fly local theater missions.

We will enumerate the major routing on which Space-A air opportunities are available each month of the year. We have divided these routes into regions of the world where these routes exist. Complete details regarding routing/stations, schedules, days en route and equipment are contained in Military Living's **Military Space-A Air Opportunities Around The World**. Also, you may find a graphic presentation of these data and much more in Military Living's **Military Space-A Air Opportunities Air Route Map**.

NORTH ATLANTIC ROUTE

Missions on this route originate at McGuire AFB, NJ (WRI), Andrews AFB, MD (ADW), Wright-Patterson AFB, OH (FFO), Norfolk NAS, VA (NGU), Allen C. Thompson Field, MS (JAN) and are routed direct or in a few cases through Philadelphia IAP, PA (PHL) to Keflavik Airport/Naval Base, IC (KEF). These flights continue on to the European mainland at Ramstein AB, GE (RMS) and Lajes Field AB (Azores), PO (LGS). Most of these flights return to their CONUS bases via Keflavik Airport or Lajes Field AB. There are also missions from Andrews AFB and McGuire AFB to Thule AB (Greenland), DN (THU) and return. Most of these routes require 2 to 3 days of flying and en route time using heavy lift (C-005A/B/C, KC-10A, C-17A, KC-135A-R, C-141A/B) Air Force and contractor (DC010, B757, L1011, etc) aircraft.

MIDDLE ATLANTIC ROUTE

This is the most densely traveled route in the Air Mobility Command System (AMC). Missions on this route originate at Bangor ANGB, ME (BGR), Westover ARB, MA (CEF), Pease ANGB, NH (PSM), Stewart IAP/ANGB, NY (SWF), McGuire AFB, NJ (WRI), Philadelphia IAP, PA (PHL), Wright-Patterson AFB, OH (FFO), Rickenbacker

Field/ANGB, OH (LCK), Andrews AFB, MD (ADW), Dulles IAP, VA (IAD), Dover AFB, DE (DOV), Norfolk NAS, VA (NGU), Charleston AFB/IAP, SC (CHS), The Wm B Hartsfield Atlanta IAP, GA (ATL), Fairchild AFB, WA (SKA) and Travis AFB, CA (SUU). Most of the originating stations stage through the primary east coast stations of McGuire AFB, Andrews AFB, Dover AFB, Norfolk NAS and Charleston AFB/IAP. Staging means that flights which originate at inland and west coast stations stop for crew rest, cargo and passengers at these primary east coast stations for approximately 3 to 15 hours depending upon the mission requirements. These flights continue on to the Primary Middle Atlantic Stations in Europe: Lajes Field AB, PO (LGS), RAF Mildenhall, UK (MHZ), Rota NAS, SP (RTA), Ramstein AB, GE (RMS), and Rhein-Main AB, GE (FRF). Many of these flights continue into the Mediterranean area and the middle east before they turn around and return to CONUS through the Primary European Middle Atlantic Stations and to their assigned (home) stations. These complete missions require 2 to 7 or more days of flying and en route time, using Air Force and commercial heavy lift aircraft.

SOUTH ATLANTIC ROUTE

Missions on this route originate at many of the same stations as the Middle Atlantic Route. The primary originating stations on the east coast of CONUS are: Andrews AFB, MD (ADW), Dover AFB, DE (DOV), McGuire AFB, NJ (WRI), Philadelphia IAP, PA (PHL), Wright-Patterson AFB, OH (FFO), Charleston AFB/IAP, SC (CHS), and Norfolk NAS, VA (NGU). Several flights originate at the following west coast stations: McChord AFB, WA (TCM) and Travis AFB, CA (SUU). Many of these missions fly through the Primary Middle Atlantic Stations in Europe (as listed above in the Middle Atlantic Route) before continuing on to their mission stations in the Mediterranean and Middle East. These stations west to east are: Lajes Field AB (Azores), PO, (LGS), Aviano AB, IT (AVB), Capodichino Airport (Naples), IT (NAP), Olbia/Costa Smeralda Airport, IT (OLB), Sigonella Airport (Sicily), IT (SIZ), Akrotiri RAFB, CY (AKT), Cairo IAP, EG, (CAI), Araxos Greek AB, GR (GRX), Souda Bay NSA (Crete), GR (SOC), Bahrain IAP/NSA, BA (BAH) (turnaround point), Ataturk/Yesilkoy Airport (Istanbul), TU (YES), Incirlik Airport (Adana), TU (ADA) (turnaround point), Ben Gurion IAP (Tel Aviv), IS, (TLV), Dhahran IAP, SA (DHA) (turnaround point), Riyadh IAP, SA (RUH) (limited entry to SA), Thumrait Oman AFB, OM (TTH), Ad Dafrah Airfield, AE (MAM), Al Fujayrah IAP, AR (FUJ), Kuwait IAP, KW (KWI) (turnaround point) and Diego Garcia Atoll, IO/UK (NKW) (turnaround point). Most of these flights turn around and return through the Primary Middle Atlantic Stations in Europe and then continue on to CONUS and their home stations. These complete missions require 2-9 days or more of flying and en route time, using Air Force and commercial heavy lift aircraft.

ATLANTIC THEATER ROUTE

The missions in the Atlantic Theater originate at Ramstein AB, GE (RMS) and RAF Mildenhall, UK (MHZ). These missions are largely accomplished by theater assigned aircraft and crews. Most of the missions from RAF Mildenhall fly to Dover AFB, DE (DOV) and return. The missions from Ramstein AB fly to the following destinations and return to Ramstein AB: Incirlik Airport (Adana), TU (ADA), Akrotiri RAFB, CY (AKT), Cigli AB, TU (IGL), Ataturk/Yesilkoy Airport (Istanbul), TU (YES), Esenboga Airport (Ankara), TU (ESB), Dahran IAP, SA (DHA), RAF Mildenhall, UK (MHZ), Aviano AB, IT (AVB), Shaheed MWAFFAQ, OM (J2X), Sigonella NAS/Airport (Sicily), IT (SIZ), Capodichino Airport (Naples), IT (NAP), Souda Bay NSA (Crete), GR (SOC), Olbia/Costa Smeralda Airport, IT (OLB), Araxos Greek AFB, GR (GRX), Rota NAS, SP (RTA), There are numerous missions flown on the routes each month.

ATLANTIC/AFRICA ROUTE

Missions on this route originate at Charleston AFB/IAP, SC (CHS) and McGuire AFB, NJ (WRI). Most of the flights travel through Lajes Field AB (Azores), PO (LGS) before continuing on to the African continent. Stations visited from west to east are: Dakar Yoff Airport, SE (DKR), Niamey IAP, NG (NIM), N'Djamena IAP, CD (NDJ), Kinshassa N'Djili Airport, ZA (FIH), Jomo Kenyatta IAP, KE (NBO). These flights turn around in West Africa and return to CONUS and their home stations. As a footnote to African travel, most stations on this route require the permission of the Office of Defense Attache (ODA) to visit the country via Space-A travel.

CARIBBEAN, CENTRAL AND SOUTH AMERICA ROUTES

There are missions which cover the Caribbean area, Central America area and South America area. However; similar to the European area these three areas are interconnected in terms of missions. Please note that the destinations in South America are south of the equator and thus have reverse seasons from North America.

CARIBBEAN ROUTE

Missions on the Caribbean route originate at the following stations: McGuire AFB, NJ (WRI), Andrews AFB, MD (ADW), Wright-Patterson AFB, OH (FFO), Norfolk NAS, VA (NGU), Pope AFB, NC (POB), Charleston AFB/IAP, SC (CHS), Memphis IAP, TN (MEM), Moody AFB, GA (VAD) and Dyess AFB, TX (DYS). From these originating stations there are missions to: Roosevelt Roads NAS, PR (NRR), Alexander Hamilton Airport, VI (STX), Port-au-Prince IAP, HA (PAP), San Isidro AB, DR (SDQ), Guantanamo Bay NAS, CU (NBW), Norman Manley IAP, JM (KIN), VC Bird IAP, AN (SJH), Ascension Auxiliary AF, UK (ASI). Most of the above flights stage through Norfolk NAS, VA and return through Norfolk NAS en route to their originating (home) stations.

CENTRAL AMERICA ROUTE

Missions on the Central America route originate at the following stations: Dover AFB, DE (DOV), Charleston AFB/IAP, SC (CHS), The Wm B Hartsfield/Atlanta IAP, GA (ATL), Allen C. Thompson Field, MS (JAN) and Kelley AFB, TX (SKF). From these originating stations there are missions to: Howard AFB, PN (HOW) and Soto Cano AB,

APPENDIX V, continued

HO (PLA). Most flights stage through Charleston AFB/IAP, SC (CHS). Missions return from Panama and Honduras to their home stations.

SOUTH AMERICA ROUTE

Missions on the South America route originate at the following stations: McGuire AFB, NJ (WRI) and Charleston AFB/IAP, SC (CHS). From these originating stations missions fly to: Jorge Chevez IAP (Lima), PE (LIM), Arturo Merino Benitez IAP (Santiago), CH (SCL), JF Kennedy IAP (La Paz), BO (LPB), Brasilia Airport, BR (BSB), Rio De Janeiro IAP, BR (RIO), Pres. Stroessner Airport (Asuncion), PG (ASU), Ezeiza IAP (Buenos Aires), AR (BUE), Carrasco IAP (Montevideo), UR (MVD). These missions are known as the "Capitol Run" because of the capital cities in South America which they serve. Approximately every two weeks these missions fly south on the east coast of South America visiting stations and then north on the west coast of South America. The next two weeks' missions operates in reverse, first south on the West Coast of South America and then north on the east coast of South America. After the Capitol Run, these flights return to their home stations.

NORTH PACIFIC ROUTE

Missions on the North Pacific route originate at the following stations: Sky Harbor IAP, AZ (PHX), Los Angeles IAP, CA (LAX), Travis AFB, CA (SUU) and McChord AFB, WA (TCM). From these originating stations missions fly to: Elmendorf AFB, AK (EDF), Eielson AFB, AK (EIL), Yokota AB, JA (OKO), Anchorage IAP/Kulis ANGB, AK (ANC), Misawa AB, JA (MSJ), Iwakuni MCAB, JA (IWA), Osan AB, RK (OSN), Kadena AB, JA (DNA), Andersen AFB, GU (UAM). These missions turn around at Osan AB, Yokota AB and Kadena AB and return through Alaska to their home stations.

CENTRAL PACIFIC ROUTE

Missions on the Central Pacific route originate at the following stations: March ARB, CA (RIV), Travis AFB, CA (SUU), McGuire AFB, NJ (WRI), Grand Forks AFB, ND (RDR), Rickenbacker ANGB, OH (LCK), Altus AFB, OK (LTS), Tinker AFB, OK (TIK), Charleston AFB/IAP, SC (CHS), Fairchild AFB, WA (SKA) and McChord AFB, WA (TCM). From these originating stations missions fly to: Hickam AFB, HI (HIK), Kwajalein Atoll, KA (KWA), Johnson Atoll, JO (JON), Andersen AFB, GU (UAM), Yokota AB, JA (OKO), Osan AB, RK (OSN), Most of these missions transient through Hickam AFB and Andersen AFB, turn around at Yokota AB and Osan AB and return through Hickam AFB and Travis AFB en route their home stations. This route is very rich in flights each month of the year. Yokoto AB is the business station in the AMC system.

PACIFIC THEATER ROUTE

These missions like the European Theater Route originate outside the CONUS in the overseas theater. Missions on the Pacific Theater Route originate at the following stations: Kadena AB (Okinawa), JA (DNA) and Yokota AB, JA (OKO). From these originating

Military Space-A Air Basic Training - 205

APPENDIX V, continued

stations missions fly to: Jakarta Airport, IE (DJK), Fukuoka Airport, JA (FUK), Misawa AB, JA (MSJ), Kunsan AB, RK (KUZ), RSAF Paya Lebar (Singapore), SG (SGP), Diego Garcia Atoll, UK (NKW), Al Fujayrah IAP, AE (FUJ), Iwakuni MCAS, JA (IWA), Don Muang Airport (Bangkok) TH, (BKK), U-Tapao RTN, TH (VBU), Andersen AFB, GU (UAM), Hickam AFB, HI (HIK), Travis AFB, CA (SUU), Osan AB, RK (OSN), Kimhae AB, RK (KHE), Babelthuap IAP, PL (ROR), Kosrae IAP, FM (KSA), Truk IAP, FM (TKK),

SOUTH PACIFIC ROUTE

These missions originate at: McChord AFB, WA (TCM) and Travis AFB, CA (SUU). The missions from McChord AFB fly the following route once per week, over a 7 day period including en route stops: Travis AFB, CA (SUU), Hickam AFB, HI (HIK), Pago Pago IAP, AS (PPG), Christchurch, NZ (CHC), Richmond RAAFB, AU (RDM), Woomera AS, AU (UMR), Richmond RAAF, Christchurch IAP, Pago Pago IAP, Hickam AFB, McChord AFB. The missions from Travis AFB fly the following route once per week over a 6 day period including en route stops: Hickam AFB, HI (HIK), Pago Pago IAP, AS (PPG), Richmond RAAF, AU (RCM), Alice Springs Airport, AU (ASP), Richmond RAAF, Pago Pago IAP, Hickam AFB, Travis AFB.

APPENDIX W: PASSENGER BILL OF RIGHTS

The US Air Force, Air Mobility Command (AMC) has recently (1996-97) developed the "Passenger Bill of Rights" listed below. This notice is posted in passenger lounges at AMC installations.

- Courteous Service

- Accurate Information

- Maximmum Opportunity to Travel, Compatible With Mission Requirements

- Safe Flight

- Clean Comfortable Facilities

- Transportation to and from Aircraft

- Your Baggage - Right Place, On Time, Undamaged

206 - Military Space-A Air Basic Training

APPENDIX X: STATE, POSSESSION, AND COUNTRY ABBREVIATIONS

STATE ABBREVIATIONS

AL-Alabama
AK-Alaska
AR-Arkansas
AZ-Arizona
CA-California
CO-Colorado
CT-Connecticut
DC-District of Columbia
DE-Delaware
FL-Florida
GA-Georgia
HI-Hawaii
IA-Iowa
ID-Idaho
IL-Illinois
IN-Indiana
KS-Kansas
KY-Kentucky
LA-Louisiana
MA-Massachusetts
MD-Maryland
ME-Maine
MI-Michigan
MN-Minnesota
MO-Missouri
MS-Mississippi

MT-Montana
NE-Nebraska
NC-North Carolina
ND-North Dakota
NV-Nevada
NH-New Hampshire
NJ-New Jersey
NM-New Mexico
NY-New York
OH-Ohio
OK-Oklahoma
OR-Oregon
PA-Pennsylvania
RI-Rhode island
SC-South Carolina
SD-South Dakota
TN-Tennessee
TX-Texas
UT-Utah
VA-Virginia
VT-Vermont
WA-Washington
WI-Wisconsin
WV-West Virginia
WY-Wyoming

POSSESSION ABBREVIATIONS

AS-American Samoa
GU-Guam
JO-Johnston Atoll
KA-Kwajalein Atoll

MW-Midway Island
PR-Puerto Rico
VI-US Virgin Islands
WK-Wake Island

*COUNTRY ABBREVIATIONS

AG-Argentina
AI-Ascension Island (UK)
AN-Antigua/Barbuda
AU-Australia

BA-Bahrain
BB-Barbados
BE-Belgium
BH-Bahamas

APPENDIX X, continued

BM-Bermuda
BO-Bolivia
BR-Brazil
BZ-Belize
CD-Chad
CH-Chile
CL-Columbia
CN-Canada
CR-Crete (GR)
CS-Costa Rica
CU-Cuba
CY-Cyprus
DN-Denmark
DR-Dominican Republic
EC-Ecuador
EG-Egypt
ES-El Salvador
FM-Federated States of Micronesia
GE-Germany
GL-Greenland (DN)
GR-Greece
GT-Guatemala
GY-Guyana
HA-Haiti
HO-Honduras
HK-Hong Kong (China)
IC-Iceland
IE-Indonesia
IO-Indian Ocean Diego Garcia (UK)
IR-Ireland
IS-Israel
IT-Italy
JA-Japan
JM-Jamaica
JR-Jordan
KE-Kenya

KW-Kuwait
LI-Liberia
MA-Malaysia
MI-Marshall Islands
NG-Niger
NI-Nicaragua
NO-Norway
NT-Netherlands
NZ-New Zealand
OM-Oman
PE-Peru
PG-Paraguay
PN-Republic of Panama
PO-Portugal (Azores)
PW-Palau (RP)
RK-Republic of Korea
RP-Republic of the Philippines
SA-Saudi Arabia
SE-Senegal
SG-Singapore
SI-Solomon Islands
SM-Somalia
SP-Spain
SR-Suriname
SU-Sudan
TH-Thailand
TU-Turkey
UA-United Arab Emirates
UG-Uruguay
UK-United Kingdom
US-United States
VE-Venezuela
ZA-Zaire

*Countries for which abbreviations are provided have been limited to those countries where Space-A travel is generally scheduled. Prime governing nations are noted within parentheses.

APPENDIX Y: GENERAL ABBREVIATIONS USED IN THIS BOOK

The general abbreviations used in this book are listed below. Commonly understood abbreviations (e.g. Mon-Fri for Monday through Friday) and standard abbreviations used in addresses have not been included in order to save space.

A
AAA-American Automobile Association
AB-Air Base
AFB-Air Force Base
AMC-Air Mobility Command
APOD-Aerial Port of Debarkation
APOE-Aerial Port of Embarkation
APT-Airport
AS-Air Station

B
BEQ-Bachelor Enlisted Quarters
BOQ-Bachelor Officers' Quarters
BX-Base Exchange

C
Cat-Category
CONUS-Continental United States

D
DoD-Department of Defense
DoDD-Department of Defense Directive
DoDDS-Department of Defense Dependent Schools
DoT-Department of Transportation
DV-Distinguished Visitor

E
EML-Environmental Morale Leave

F
FAA-Federal Aviation Administration
FEDEX-Federal Express
FEML-Funded Environmental Morale Leave

I
IAP-International Airport
ICAO-International Civil Aviation Organization
ID-Identification

L
LI-Location Identifier
LST-Local Standard Time

M
MAC-Military Airlift Command
MEDEVAC-Medical Evacuation

MWR-Morale, Welfare and Recreation
MCI-Military Customs Inspector

N
NAF-Naval Air Facility
NAS-Naval Air Station
NB-Naval Base
NCO-Noncommissioned Officer
NOAA- National Oceanic and Atmospheric Administration

O
OCONUS-Outside Continental United States

P
PCS-Permanent Change of Station
PHS-Public Health Service
PX-Post Exchange

R
RAF-Royal Air Force
RAAF-Royal Australian Air Force
ROTC-Reserve Officers' Training Corps
RSAF-Royal Singapore Air Force

S
SAC-Strategic Air Command
SATO-Scheduled Airline Ticket Offices
SOFA-Status of Forces Agreement

T
TAD-Temporary Attached Duty
TDY-Temporary Duty
TML-Temporary Military Lodging

U
USA-United States Army
USAF-United States Air Force
USCG-United States Coast Guard
USMC-United States Marine Corps
USN-United States Navy
USPHS-United States Public Health Service
USPS-United States Postal Service

V
VIP-Very Important Person

AFTERWORD

CONGRATULATIONS

You have just graduated from Space-A Air Basic Training!!

What was "Greek" to many of us is now old hat. You can travel by Space-A with confidence as far as understanding how the system works. Now, it is time to move on to our more advanced Space-A air travel publications.

Military Living has another publication, *Military Space-A Air Opportunities Around the World*, which will show where the flights are going. It has more valuable information to help you be successful in your journey. This publication will help you plan your upcoming trips. Get ready to enjoy one of the military's biggest morale boosters, Space-A travel.

MILITARY PUBLICATIONS *Living*™

"Where the Fun Begins!"

Please visit Military Living's Home Page on the World Wide Web

★ ★ ★ ★ ★ ★ ★ ★ ★

http://www.militaryliving.com

210 - Military Space-A Air Basic Training

MILITARY Living's™
MILITARY TRAVEL CLUB
R&R SPACE-A REPORT®

One Year for only $15.00

- **$AVE** - pay no airfare by traveling Space Available on military flights. Military Living is the leading authority on Space-A air travel.

- **$AVE** - with military lodging. Stay around the world at military lodging locations. Learn about the new locations first. Enjoy increased safety.

- **$AVE** - with military RV camping and rec areas. Did you know the military has over 225 campgrounds and rec areas? Learn about all the latest news FIRST.

- **$AVE** - by shopping at military commissaries, exchanges, and gas stations en route. Learn where the new ones are located.

- **$AVE** - by learning from other military readers like yourselves. We bring you the best in Reader Trip Reports in *Military Living's R&R Space-A Report®*.

Military Space-A Air Basic Training - 211

SPACE AVAILABLE TRAVEL REQUEST PULLOUT
(AMC FORM 140, Feb 95)

SPACE AVAILABLE TRAVEL REQUEST *This form is affected by the Privacy Act of 1974 - See below.*	INSERT HERE

This information is required for space available travel registration. Upon completion, place the upper right corner of this form and the back of your leave form into the Date/Time validator. Be sure to deposit one copy of this request into the box; retain carbon copy for the Space Available roll call. Space-A sign-up is good for a 60-day period, or when your leave expires, whichever comes first. For facsimile (fax) requests, telefax header will establish date and time of sign-up.

PLEASE PRINT CLEARLY

1. NAME (*Last, First, MI*)

2. RANK, GRADE	3. SSN	4. SEATS REQUIRED

5. TRAVEL STATUS (*Type of leave*) — FOR OVERSEAS TRAVEL:

CATEGORY I - Civ or Mil Dependent on Emergency Leave	Border Clearance Document Current?
CATEGORY II - Environmental Morale Leave (EML)	
CATEGORY III - Active Duty on Ordinary Leave / House Hunting	☐ YES ☐ NO
CATEGORY IV - (EML) Unaccompanied Dependents	
CATEGORY V - Permissive TDY or TAD / Student Travel	(See note on reverse)
CATEGORY VI - Retired Military / Reserves	

6. SERVICE:	ARMY	NAVY	AF	MARINES	OTHER

7. DATE LEAVE BEGINS (*Active Duty Only*)	8. DATE LEAVE ENDS (*If extended, you must notify us before this date*)

9. COUNTRY CHOICES (*List up to 5, one choice may be all*)

10. LIST NAMES OF DEPENDENTS TRAVELING AND TYPE OF PASSPORT (*US or Foreign*)

11. I CERTIFY THAT I AM ON LEAVE OR PASS STATUS AT THE TIME I REGISTER FOR SPACE AVAILABLE TRAVEL AND WILL REMAIN IN SUCH STATUS WHEN AWAITING AND/OR HAVE BEEN ACCEPTED FOR SPACE AVAILABLE TRAVEL. IF ACCOMPANIED BY DEPENDENTS, I FURTHER CERTIFY THAT MY TRAVEL IS NOT IN CONJUNCTION WITH TDY/TAD AND THAT I AM NOT USING SPACE AVAILABLE TRAVEL TO TRANSPORT MY DEPENDENTS TO OR FROM MY RESTRICTED DUTY STATION OR ALL OTHER (UNACCOMPANIED) TOUR LOCATION STATIONS. I CERTIFY THAT MY REQUEST FOR AND ACCEPTANCE OF TRANSPORTATION VIA DOD OWNED OR CONTROLLED AIRCRAFT IS NOT FOR PERSONAL GAIN NOR FOR, OR IN CONNECTION WITH BUSINESS OF ANY NATURE AND THAT THIS TRIP WILL NOT RESULT IN ANY FORM OF RENUMERATION TO MYSELF OR TO MY FAMILY. I UNDERSTAND VIOLATION OF ANY OF THE ABOVE COULD RESULT IN BILLING AND OR PUNITIVE ACTION.

12. DATE	13. SIGNATURE

PRIVACY ACT STATEMENT

AUTHORITY 10 USC. 8013; EO 9397, 22 November 1943.
PRINCIPAL PURPOSE: To apply for air travel. SSN is needed for positive ID.
ROUTINE USE(S): Records from this system of records may be disclosed for any of the blanket routine uses published by the Air Force.
DISCLOSURE IS VOLUNTARY: Failure to provide the information may result in member not being accepted for travel on military aircraft.
Disclosure of SSN is voluntary.

AMC FORM 140, FEB 95 (*EF*) (*PerFORM PRO*)	AMC COPY

212 - Military Space-A Air Basic Training

CENTRAL ORDER COUPON
Military Living Publications
P.O. Box 2347, Falls Church, VA 22042-0347
TEL: (703) 237-0203 FAX: (703) 237-2233
E-mail: milliving@aol.com Home Page: http://www.militaryliving.com

Publications (Prices as of 1 September 1997)		QTY
R&R Space-A Report®: *The worldwide travel newsletter. 6 issues per year.* 1 yr/$15.00 - 2 yrs/$24.00 - 3 yrs/$33.00 - 5 yrs/$49.00		
Military Space-A Air Basic Training.	$14.95	
Military Space-A Opportunities Air Route Map. (Folded)	$13.95	
Military Space-A Air Opportunities Around the World.	$18.95	
Temporary Military Lodging Around the World.	$16.95	
Military RV, Camping & Rec Areas Around the World.	$14.95	
U.S. Forces Travel Guide to U.S. Military Installations.	$14.95	
U.S. Forces Travel Guide to Overseas U.S. Military Installations.	$17.95	
U.S. Military Museums, Historic Sites & Exhibits. (Soft Cover)	$17.95	
United States Military Road Atlas.	$18.95	
U.S. Military Installation Road Map. (Folded)	$7.95	
COLLECTOR'S ITEM! Desert Shield Commemorative Maps. (Folded) (2 flat wall maps in a hard tube)	$8.00 $18.00	
Assignment Washington Military Road Atlas.	$11.95	
California State Military Road Map. (Folded) Florida State Military Road Map. (Folded) Mid-Atlantic States Military Road Map (Folded) Texas State Military Road Map. (Folded)	$5.95 $5.95 $5.95 $5.95	
Military Living Magazine, Camaraderie Washington. *Local Area magazine. 1 year (4 seasonal issues)*	$8.00	
Virginia Addresses add 4.5% sales tax (Books, Maps & Atlases only)		
ALL ORDERS SHIPPED FIRST CLASS MAIL	TOTAL $	

*If you are an R&R Space-A Report subscriber, you may deduct $1.00 per book. (No discount on the R&R Report itself or on the maps or atlas.) Mail Order Prices are for U.S. APO & FPO addresses. Please consult publisher for International Mail Price. Sorry, no billing.
We're as close as your telephone...by using our Telephone Ordering Service. We honor American Express, MasterCard, Visa and Discover. Call us at **703-237-0203** (Voice Mail after hours) or Fax 703-237-2233 and order today! Sorry, no collect calls. Or fill out and mail the order coupon on the next page.

NAME:_____
STREET:_____
CITY/STATE/ZIP:_____
PHONE:_____ SIGNATURE:_____
RANK (or rank of sponsor):_____Branch of Service:_____
Active Duty:___Retired:___Widow/er:___100% Disabled Veteran:___Guard:___Reservist:___Other:___
Card #_____ Card Expiration Date:_____

Mail check/money order to Military Living Publications, P.O. Box 2347 Falls Church, VA 22042-0347.
Tel: 703-237-0203, Fax: 703-237-2233.
Save $$$ by purchasing any of our books, Maps, and Atlases at your Military Exchange.
Prices subject to change. Please check here if we may ship and bill the difference................ ☐